invasion *of* light

HOW JESUS CAN USE YOU AND ME TO
WIN THE BATTLE FOR SOULS AND SOCIETIES

invasion *of* light

BRIAN MARK WELLER
and J.J. WELLER

INVASION OF LIGHT: HOW JESUS CAN USE YOU AND ME TO WIN THE BATTLE FOR SOULS AND SOCIETIES

CONTENTS

PREFACE

Is the harvest really great, or has Jesus's promise expired? Can we expect to successfully disciple nations today, or must the church fail its God-given mission? These questions serve as the crux of the book you hold in your hands; the fulcrum upon which every page turns. If the church must fail its mission, then there's no use seeking biblical and historical keys to missionary success. If, however, "the harvest is plentiful but the workers are few" (Matthew 9:37), then it's our solemn responsibility to scour the Bible and history for the most powerful strategies for harvest, and, more importantly, to thrust ourselves as laborers into God's great harvest, applying those strategies by the strength God works in us. In this book, we take that positive view of Christian ministry, and seek to convey some of the Bible's clearest strategies for victory.

Before you mine out these principles for yourself, we want to give a few notes about how to read this book. First, we recommend you read with one eye ever toward the Word of God. In these pages, we've sought to convey some of the most compelling ministry lessons we've learned through years of prayer, Bible study, reading, and experience in ministry and mission work. We've done our best to remain faithful to God's Word; yet, we recognize we are fallible men with potential for error. Therefore, we plead with every reader to study with the mind of the Bereans, who "searched the Scriptures daily to find out whether these things were so" (Acts 17:11 NKJV). We don't see our book as the last work on ministry you should ever read; rather, we hope it serves a useful role in the vast conversation about Christian life and witness today. For you, the reader, we pray that that this book might convey even a handful of truths which will bring fresh and radical fruit into your life and ministry.

Second, we suggest you read with full intention of application. We learned these practical ministry principles in the Word, but have tried and proven most of them by experience (sometimes more faithfully, and other times less so). We must always remember that lived-out wisdom is all that counts for a theme as practical as missional living. Never be an armchair theologian; take what you learn and try to apply it as soon as possible. In that way, God will grant you practical wisdom far beyond what we've had space to convey in this book.

Third, we urge you to read the endnotes, where we often add important details, caveats, and qualifications that wouldn't have fit the main text of the book. If you find yourself questioning an idea, we may very well have foreseen the confusion and written an endnote to resolve it.

Finally, we suggest you read most of the book in a corporate voice. In much of the book, our words flow together like two strands of a rope. Even many sentences end with an interjection from the other author. Therefore, think little of who is writing where, except where explicitly stated. As father and son, we've happily shared a 'pulpit' worldwide, and here we happily share the page.

May God use this book to enlighten your eyes, ignite your faith, strengthen your resolve, and stamp your heart with His eternal purposes. Onward—into the world's darkest corners! It's time to invade with light!

Brian and JJ Weller, January 2022

Part 1.

An Invasion of Darkness;
An Invasion of Light

CHAPTER ONE

TWO KINGDOMS CLASH

You are living in one of the greatest spiritual collisions in history. As we speak, Hell's hordes are fighting tooth and nail to shipwreck the church, sabotage the lost, isolate the unreached, and destroy society as we know it. And you know what? Only we, Christ's ambassadors, can stem the tide.

That sentence may shock you. You may see it as hyper-spiritual, self-important, or man-centered—but both scripture and history confirm it with undeniable clarity. Whenever society has sunk to new lows, only Jesus's disciples have been able to turn the tide for righteousness. We *alone* have received Christ's special anointing "to proclaim liberty to the captives," "trample on snakes and scorpions," and "overcome all the power of the enemy" (Luke 4:18 NKJV, Luke 10:19 NIV). As Paul declared, "We are . . . Christ's ambassadors, as though God were making His appeal through us" (2 Corinthians 5:20). And today, the world needs our influence more than ever because Satan has invaded culture with worse darkness than we've known in centuries.

Have you considered the decay of our society lately? Take a moment to think about it. How would you feel if you had fallen into a coma in the early 1950s and awoke to today's morning news?[1] Wouldn't you feel terrified by the ways culture has fallen? Might you wonder if you had entered a dystopian movie? You might have fallen asleep in a fairly stable world (though unstable enough)—but this era you woke up in is the most sexualized, depressed, violent, polarized, and confused time in modern history. It seems impossible the world could have changed this much in a single generation. To be honest, it even seems impossible the world could have changed this much in a decade. But it has—and legions of demons lurk behind the decline.

In the shadow of such awful darkness, many modern believers have lifted their arms and accepted defeat. Look at the average American Christian, and what do you see? Most are discouraged. Many lazily await the Rapture, hoping it will save them from the madness. Plenty hide behind the protective bubble of Christian company, rarely stretching out a helping hand to the victims of the dark invasion. Most of us live shackled by fear and timidity. We'd never say it aloud, but our spiritual inaction shouts our true conviction: "The Kingdom of Darkness has won—retreat!" Yes, more than ever, the church of Jesus Christ desperately needs to hear the call to victory in spiritual battle. In this book, we want to announce that call.

Fellow disciple, it's no time to retreat—it's time to go to spiritual war for God's kingdom. It may seem to you that God's cause has lost in the world, but that's mere satanic sleight of hand. We may feel like underdogs, but Satan has already been defeated! We must stop groveling, remember Jesus's victory, and enlist in God's mission with joy! Have we forgotten that Jesus has already won?

HOW JESUS DEFEATED THE DARKNESS

Colossians 2:15 declares Jesus's blowout win over Satan and his soldiers of evil: "Having disarmed the powers and authorities, [Jesus] made a public spectacle of them, triumphing over them by the cross." As soon as Jesus died on the cross, the temple veil tore from top to bottom (Matthew 27:51). In one sacrificial act, God removed the separation between Himself and mankind. A mediator had now come between God and man—Jesus Christ (1 Timothy 2:5). Jesus declared His victory as king: "It is finished!" (John 19:30). At that moment, Satan was already vanquished, God's spiritual kingdom established, and our salvation secured.

The work of redemption completed, Jesus descended into Hell and took the "keys of Hell and of death" (Revelation 1:18 KJV). Then He rose from the dead and sat at the right hand of God the Father where He reigns as the Lord of Lords and King of Kings. Now, as Charles Spurgeon declared, "Nothing in Heaven, or Earth, or in places under the Earth, is left to itself to engender anarchy. Everywhere, serene above the floods, the Lord sitteth King for ever and ever."[2]

And while it may seem hard to believe, Jesus's ultimate, final victory is on its way, too. At the end of this age, Jesus will return in power and glory—not as a baby in a manger, nor as a gentle carpenter, but as a king on a white horse to execute judgment and set everything right again. At that moment, King Jesus will at last utterly destroy the Kingdom of Darkness, casting Satan and every agent of evil "into the lake of burning sulfur [where] they will be tormented day and night for ever and ever" (Revelation 20:10). In a moment, all their plans will fall to the ground, God's plans will win the day, and Jesus will establish a new Heaven and new Earth without any sin, separation, or sadness. Bottom line, Jesus wins. If you're on His team, you're going to win with Him.

These truths may leave you a bit bewildered. If Jesus has already won, why does it look like Satan is winning? In a word: Satan is the sorest loser in the Universe. Simply put, Satan is like a prisoner in his cell furiously awaiting execution day. His sentence has been given. He knows his time is short. He knows execution day is coming. He knows Jesus will soon undo all he has worked for—and he's hot with rage. He's absolutely blistered about the coming kingdom, and he doesn't want us to carry Jesus's message of liberation and salvation to the rest of the world—so he's working overtime to steal, kill, and destroy everything in his path with the little time he has left. It's time to ask ourselves: "Am I just going to let him kill without a fight?"

Listen. It's time for us to stop fearing that deranged prisoner. Jesus is the victorious king, and we're on *His* team. Now, until He returns, we need to believe His ultimate victory and work to see His kingdom transform our world. No smaller goal is appropriate to our glorious Savior, for Jesus taught us to pray, "Your kingdom come, your will be done, on Earth as it is in Heaven" (Matthew 6:10). Let us live to spread the influence of His reign, knowing His "light shines in the darkness, and the darkness has not overcome it!" (John 1:5).

ADVANCING UNTIL HE RETURNS

Now, don't get us wrong—we understand Jesus *could* come back in our generation. If He does, much darker times lie ahead—still, we anticipate His return just like you. We don't believe we can change the day of His appearing, and we *never* want to hamper your eager expectation for it (see 2 Peter 3:12). Instead, we want to call you to *hope and prepare* as if Jesus will return in this generation, but to *pray, minister, and strategize* as if He'll give us centuries more to advance His kingdom. No longer can we use Jesus's return as an excuse for our powerless Christianity! No longer can we afford to assume God is done moving in the world! The fact is, no one truly knows when the Lord will come back (Matthew 25:13)—so we have no biblical right to abandon the harvest, crying, "It's all downhill from here!"

Besides, Jesus explicitly commanded us to disciple entire nations until *the very end of the age* (Matthew 28:19-20). He likens the last days to a harvest (Matthew 13:39)—and reveals that heavenly fruit and satanic apostasy will "grow together until" He returns (Matthew 13:30; see also 13:24-29, 36-43). In simpler words: no matter what age we're in—and no matter how dark it gets—we can trust Jesus for a great harvest of souls (Matthew 9:37)! He desires that His spiritual kingdom would begin breaking in *now*, radically impacting societies—person by person, soul by soul.[3] Yes, Jesus commands us to trim our lamps and advance His restoration project, bearing exponential fruit until His glorious appearing (see Matthew 25:1-30)! "Blessed is that servant whom his master will find so doing when He comes!" (Matthew 24:46 ESV).

HOW GOD HEALS THE WORLD

That leads to the vital question this book sets out to answer—one of utmost importance to every follower of Jesus. How can Jesus bring healing in our broken world? What method has He chosen to put the broken pieces of humanity back together? How can He redeem your mission field, your home country, your family, your friends, your workplace, and your school? The answer is simple but startling: God wants to transform the world through you and me, Christ's ambassadors. God's kingdom restores lives when we stand up, step out, and invade our world with Jesus's light through godly words, actions, and prayers. As Paul declared: "We are therefore Christ's ambassadors, as though God were making His appeal through us. We implore you on Christ's behalf: Be reconciled to God!" (2 Corinthians 5:20).

This ambassadorial call is a high one; perhaps much higher than you ever dreamed for yourself. But if you submit to this lofty call, God can change you from an idle bystander into a weapon of mass salvation. With time, you won't even believe the miracles He'll perform through you (we say this from surprised experience). The most amazing things come to pass wherever God's kingdom visits Earth through Heaven's ambassadors.

WHEN GOD'S KINGDOM VISITS EARTH

Yes, when God's kingdom visits Earth, sinners see the light of the gospel, repent, and receive forgiveness. The weight of guilt is removed. Addictions are broken. Evil is conquered. The sick are healed. The demonized are delivered. Fears are vanquished. God's heavenly love comes to live in our hearts. The fruit of the Spirit flourish. Nominal Christians experience the King's glory, becoming radical disciples. Churches are revived. Zeal for God's mission is ignited. God is glorified!

And there's no reason that transformation can't happen on a massive scale today. After all, Jesus appointed us as "a light for the [nations], that [we] may bring salvation to the ends of the earth" (Acts 13:47). God could very well still reshape whole societies if we live out our calling![4] But much of that good invasion must take place through everyday ambassadors in everyday situations.

Think about it: if every Bible-believing Christian won one person to the Lord, countless millions would surge into the Kingdom. *That alone* would turn the tide in a society (and, let us add, that alone *can* turn the tide). And with darkness lurking in the open, it may be more apt to happen now than before. As the darkness gets uglier, the light will seem more wonderful when the Holy Spirit draws hearts. If we speak up, God's Word can have a genuine effect in countless souls to convict of sin, reveal Jesus, and draw to repentance.

You see, to live as Heaven's ambassador, you don't need a famous ministry. Nor do you need a mass evangelism plan. You just need to ask, "God, where do I begin? Who can I reach? How can I engage in Your mission?" To invade with light, the only ability you need is *availability*.

AN INVASION OF LIGHT: A FLOOD OF KINGDOM LIFE

The message of this book is simple. When Jesus died on the cross, the prison doors opened wide. His resurrection declared the captives can now run free. Now, we must go into all the world and proclaim the gospel of liberation. We must lift our voices and say: "The enemy has been defeated. The good King is enthroned. Step out of dark captivity into God's marvelous light of salvation!"

The invasion of light will never succeed until we do. If we refuse to stand up for Jesus, the lost masses can only continue racing toward the fiery judgment of God. But if we humble ourselves, call on His name, and faithfully live and preach the gospel, God will unleash the Kingdom's restoring power upon many in our world. The Kingdom will come—not only to revive Christians, but to flow like a river of light into dark societies. His river of light will flood the darkest parts of the world, giving hope through Jesus Christ—the King who remains the same yesterday, today, and forever. As Ezekiel 47:9 promises, "Wherever the river flows, everything will flourish" (BSB). The only question is—will you join the counter-invasion?

If you answer "yes" to that question, we want to help prepare you to "fight the good fight of faith" (1 Timothy 6:12). In the following chapters, you'll rediscover

- the kingdom you serve,

- the enemy you face,

- the character you'll need,

- the message you must preach,

- the spiritual weapons at your disposal,

- the example you must follow (Jesus Himself),

- how to find your place in God's kingdom,

- and much, much more.

Are you up for the challenge? If so, read on, ambassador of Heaven. Together, let's start the invasion of light.

CHAPTER TWO

THE CASE FOR HOLY REVOLUTION
IN THE LAST DAYS

If you're like most Christians, you're probably asking one crucial question right now. "Is an invasion of light even possible in such dark times?"

We get it. Our world is in such dire condition. In many ways, it's morally unrecognizable even compared to the 1950s—and honestly, culture didn't look so pretty back then either (if you don't believe us, read *Why Revival Tarries*, Leonard Ravenhill's famous repentance manifesto from 1959). Sure, Western society has advanced in some ways. But apart from those scarce gleams of hope, our world looks severely bleak.[1] In fact, many Christians see our entire modern world as *beyond redemption*.

In this chapter, we want to challenge that view and inspire you to fight for the advancement of God's spiritual kingdom in the world.[2] Unknown to many Christians, the world has passed through even worse days than these. Only when Heaven's ambassadors stood up and fulfilled their heavenly calling did society improve. Therefore, our world's only hope for positive change lies in *our willingness to invade with God's light*—person by person, soul by soul.

EXCUSING OURSELVES IN THE LAST DAYS?

Jesus's message was revolutionary. The apostles' message was revolutionary too. Everywhere they went, they called the world to glorify God by living utterly counter-cultural lives. Then why do we in the modern church often seem so tepid—even timid? Why do today's Christians so rarely fight for the world's redemption? One famous scriptural excuse lies behind much of our last days laziness. When faced with the calling to invade with light, many professing Christians retort with the Apostle Paul's warning to Timothy:

> But mark this: There will be terrible times in the last days. People will be lovers of themselves, lovers of money, boastful, proud, abusive, disobedient to their parents, ungrateful, unholy, without love, unforgiving, slanderous, without self-control, brutal, not lovers of the good, treacherous, rash, conceited, lovers of pleasure rather than lovers of God—having a form of godliness but denying its power. (2 Timothy 3:1-5)

Well, I guess you can put this book down then, right? Here, Paul promises terrible times will come in the last days, and you can't do anything about it. When those last days come, people will act like . . . well, like they do now. When this sign is fulfilled, we'll know for sure that Jesus will rapture the church out at any moment, and all attempts for positive change will prove utterly futile. Therefore, drop your long-term mission plan, pack your bags, and get rapture ready—flight 777 is on the way any moment . . . right?

Well, not quite. That interpretation assumes Paul meant only to predict a terrible hour of future turmoil—particularly one that wouldn't occur for two thousand years. But if you read the whole passage, you'll see Paul didn't necessarily mean to talk about the distant future at all. Instead, he intended to warn Timothy about a darkness that had *already begun to spread* in his own lifetime (though it has certainly continued spreading today).[3] That's why he immediately warned Timothy: "Have nothing to do with such people. . . . But they will not get very far because, as in the case of those men, their folly will be clear to everyone" (2 Timothy 3:5, 9). (Even if Paul did mean only to speak of today, shouldn't we work overtime to win as many to Jesus as possible?)

You may feel even more surprised by Paul's evangelistic boldness despite the growing apostasy around him. Many modern Christians have used "the last days" as an excuse for retreat—but did Paul encourage the same? No way. Instead, Paul saw the reality of the last days as a motivation for holy revolution. In the same letter, he boldly commanded Timothy:

> In the presence of God and of Christ Jesus, who will judge the living and the dead, and in view of His appearing and His kingdom, I give you this charge: Preach the word; be prepared in season and out of season; correct, rebuke and encourage—with great patience and careful instruction. For the time will come when people will not put up with sound doctrine. . . .

But you, keep your head in all situations, endure hardship, do the work of
an evangelist, discharge all the duties of your ministry. (2 Timothy 4:1-3, 5)

The biblical truth is crystal clear. Paul and Timothy lived in the last days like
us—but that didn't weaken their will to preach the gospel and invade the world
with Jesus's light. Instead, they ran full force into the public square to declare
Jesus's truth to all who would hear.

Paul and Timothy's radical boldness leads us to a profoundly different concept
of *last days ministry* than many hold today. Many twenty-first century Christians
believe the last-days church has little or no hope for victory in the world, and
therefore they work little for the invasion of light. But Paul and Timothy saw
themselves as part of the last days church, and they didn't share our defeatist
attitude, nor did they face defeat in the gospel battle. Let's admit it—together
with the early church, they "turned the world upside down" (Acts 17:6 NKJV).
And the invasion of light didn't stop with the earliest church—as we'll see in the
next chapter, Christ's ambassadors continued turning the world upside down for
almost two millennia. How did this advancement occur in *the last days*? Very few
know the secret. According to the Bible, the last days are not *purely* times of evil.

THE LAST DAYS: A CLASH OF EVIL AND OUTPOURING

Almost every evangelical Christian rightly sees "the last days" as a season of great
turmoil. Unfortunately, most of us have missed another crucial part of the story. You
see, God didn't only warn that the last days would bring tribulation, persecution,
and apostasy. He also promised the last days would bring tremendous spiritual
outpouring and awakening. In Acts 2, Peter reminded the crowd of God's end-
time promise through the prophet Joel: "In the last days, God says, I will pour
out My Spirit on all people" (Acts 2:17). The promise continues:

Your sons and daughters will prophesy, your young men will see visions, your
old men will dream dreams. Even on My servants, both men and women,
I will pour out My Spirit in those days, and they will prophesy. I will show
wonders in the heavens above and signs on the Earth below, blood and fire and
billows of smoke. The sun will be turned to darkness and the moon to blood
before the coming of the great and glorious day of the Lord. And everyone
who calls on the name of the Lord will be saved. (Acts 2:17-21)

Perhaps these verses make you scratch your head. "Wait a second, Peter—
you're saying we'll see *spiritual outpouring in the last days*? Did you flunk out of
seminary? Everyone knows the last days will be times of apostasy and sin!" Yes,
Jesus promised lawlessness would abound in the last days—but He also promised
other last days realities that many modern Christians have forgotten. Remember,
Jesus also promised the Holy Spirit would move in supernatural power in the last
days, turning Christians into powerful witnesses (Acts 1:8), convicting the world
of sin (John 16:8), revealing the beauty of the gospel (John 15:26), healing the sick

(Mark 16:18), raising the dead (Matthew 10:8), casting out demons (Mark 16:17), drawing masses of lost souls to Jesus (John 12:32), gathering a church from every tribe and tongue (Revelation 7:9), and training those newborn converts into obedient disciples (Titus 2:14). If you ask us, that's called *awakening*.

And this great last days outpouring isn't coming at some later date—it's available to every Christian *now*! When Peter declared this promise of last days awakening, he boldly announced God had begun to pour it out that very day (see Acts 2:16, 33). By citing Joel's prophecy, Peter declared: "The last days are here—the New Covenant revival has begun! Soon Jesus will return to judge every rebel—but meanwhile, God will powerfully pour out His Spirit on every hungry heart! Run to King Jesus and receive His mercy while you can—the long-awaited times of refreshing have begun breaking in!"

Whether Peter knew it or not, God was using him to forge an unstoppable invasion of light that momentous Pentecost Sunday. The drastic spiritual shift that began that day would eventually sweep millions of hungry souls into Jesus's kingdom of righteousness. And these God-stricken Christian ambassadors wouldn't live idly in spiritual defeat. Rather, they would gradually transform society from top to bottom, invading with light and destroying Satan's works wherever they went. Their motto was, "Thanks be to God, who always leads us as captives in Christ's triumphal procession and uses us to spread the aroma of the knowledge of Him everywhere!" (2 Corinthians 2:14). And nothing could stop them, for "neither death nor life . . . nor anything else in all creation, [could] separate [them] from the love of God" which compelled them to service (Romans 8:38-39).

HOLY FIRE FORGOTTEN
AND FORFEITED

Tragically, at some point much of the Christian church lost this victorious, all-or-nothing approach to Christian ministry. We forgot about Jesus's victory over evil and neglected the call to become His agents of reconciliation and world transformation. Think about it—do you *really* think of the church as a force for cultural change? Have you believed it enough to act on it? Most probably don't—but we want to rouse you back to action. Let's recover the story of the victorious church, recounting crucial checkpoints in the church's historical invasion of light.

As you read the next chapter, we challenge you to place yourself in the apostolic story. We often look at "the greats" of Christian history with a false sense of separation. We think to ourselves, "God might have used them like that, but He'll never use me that way." Not so fast! All of Christianity's "heroes" were really only weak believers totally dependent on a powerful Savior. Furthermore, keep in mind that God's will and promises have not changed. "Jesus Christ is the same yesterday and today and forever" (Hebrews 13:8). What He willed for the earliest church, He wills for the latest church. What He did through them, He wills to do through us! The only question is—will we receive God's power, proclaim Jesus's gospel, and invade our dark world with the light of God's kingdom? The choice is ours.

CHAPTER THREE

THE FORGOTTEN INVASION OF LIGHT

Jesus's disciples felt more downtrodden than ever. They had just spent three years promising Christ would take the throne of Israel, declaring *He* was the only way to the Father, and announcing that all who wanted forgiveness of sins must submit to *Him*. They had risked their whole lives for this belief, jeopardizing their reputations, giving up their finances, selling their possessions, leaving their loved ones, and placing their very lives in danger. And now, the unimaginable had come to pass. Jesus Himself had *died*. More than ever, it seemed *darkness had invaded and won a scathing victory.*

One can only imagine their questions and fears. "How did this happen? Where did we go wrong? What about the miracles? What about His incomparable words? And what will come of us now? Will they exile us, ostracize us, or execute us as blasphemers?" No doubt, Jesus's inner circle lay absolutely toppled by His bloody execution.

In a matter of days, Thomas transformed from a radical disciple to a hardened skeptic (John 20:25). Peter the bold groveled in humiliation over his three spineless denials (see Luke 22:62). The whole clan felt such ignominy and trepidation that they hid away "together with the doors locked for fear of the Jewish leaders" (John 20:19). When Jesus died, the disciples' hopes died too.

You can hardly blame them. They had watched the world rebel against God worse than at any other time in history. While they had watched thousands flock to follow Christ, they had also seen most of these budding followers abandon Him in disgust (John 6:66). Despite three years of fervent preaching and miraculous ministry, most of Israel still preferred to live in dead, pharisaical religion instead of the genuine, radical love of God. Outside of Israel, the Gentile world lived excluded from God, growing more unclean by the year (see Romans 1:18-32). And to top it all off, God's own people had just crucified their own Messiah, freeing a vicious criminal (Barabbas) to condemn the God they claimed to worship and obey. The fact is, the world had never sunk so low as it had that Good Friday. And no one in their right mind would have imagined the world was about to change for the better. But the ultimate turning point of world history was shortly on its way.

JESUS RESURRECTED; THE CHURCH EMPOWERED

The book of Luke unveils the story:

> On the first day of the week, very early in the morning, the women [who followed Jesus] took the spices they had prepared and went to [Jesus's] tomb. They found the stone rolled away from the tomb, but when they entered, they did not find the body of the Lord Jesus. While they were wondering about this, suddenly two men in clothes that gleamed like lightning stood beside them. In their fright the women bowed down with their faces to the ground, but the men said to them, "Why do you look for the living among the dead? He is not here; He has risen! Remember how He told you, while He was still with you in Galilee: 'The Son of Man must be delivered over to the hands of sinners, be crucified and on the third day be raised again.'" Then they remembered His words. (Luke 24:1-8)

Soon enough, every disciple witnessed the incredible news first-hand. Darkness had not won. God's kingdom was not canceled. Jesus had risen from the grave! Now, He would rule the world from Heaven, sitting at the Father's right hand until God had made every enemy a footstool for His feet (see Acts 2:34-35)!

While they awaited Jesus's final victory, they must obey Jesus's new mandate to transform the nations through potent preaching and dedicated discipleship. As Jesus commanded them:

> Go and make disciples of all nations, baptizing them in the name of the Father and of the Son and of the Holy Spirit, and teaching them to obey everything I have commanded you. And surely I am with you always, to the very end of the age. (Matthew 28:19-20)

And, thank God, this rag-tag group of disciples wouldn't be left powerless to obey this difficult but crucial commission. Our Lord gave them an incredible promise to sustain their obedience: "You will receive power when the Holy Spirit comes on you; and you will be My witnesses in Jerusalem, and in all Judea and Samaria, and to the ends of the Earth" (Acts 1:8).

Yes, the same Spirit that raised Jesus Christ from the dead would soon dwell in them (see Romans 8:11), and as a result of this world-shaking spiritual power, Jesus's disciples would witness incredible moves of God almost everywhere they went. Through their preaching, Jesus would pierce hearts (John 16:8), unveil the gospel (John 15:26), draw masses to Himself (John 12:32), and work unbelievable miracles (Mark 16:17-18), resulting in a purified people "for His own possession, zealous for good deeds" (Titus 2:14 BSB). And these results would self-replicate like wildfire, for the Holy Spirit would fall on innumerable masses of new believers in every future generation (see Acts 2:17); even on "all who are far off—all whom the Lord our God will call" (Acts 2:39). By giving these "very great and precious promises" (2 Peter 1:4), Jesus guaranteed the disciples' success before they ever spoke a word about His resurrection.

PENTECOST AND FORWARD: SPARKS OF HOLY
REVOLUTION IN THE FIRST DAYS OF THE LAST DAYS

Jesus went up to Heaven, and the disciples went into the prayer closet. Emboldened by Jesus's promises, they gathered together and stormed the gates of Heaven for days on end, committed not to move a finger until the Holy Spirit had fallen upon them (see Acts 1:14). Then, Jesus fulfilled His Word. "A sound like the blowing of a violent wind came from Heaven and filled the whole house where they were sitting" (Acts 2:2). God ignited flames above their heads (Acts 2:3) and flames deep within their hearts. Soon, the flame of the Lord spread from their souls to their lips—for they all "began to speak in other tongues as the Spirit enabled them . . . declaring the wonders of God" (Acts 2:4, 11). Now transformed into a bold witness, Peter stood up before the amazed masses, and the invasion of light began. Emboldened by the Spirit, he declared:

> Fellow Jews and all of you who live in Jerusalem, let me explain this to you; listen carefully to what I say. These people are not drunk, as you suppose. It's only nine in the morning! No, this is what was spoken by the prophet Joel:

> "In the last days, God says, I will pour out My Spirit on all people. . . . I will show wonders in the heavens above and signs on the Earth below . . . before the coming of the great and glorious day of the Lord. And everyone who calls on the name of the Lord will be saved." Fellow Israelites, listen to this: Jesus of Nazareth was a man accredited by God to you by miracles, wonders and signs, which God did among you through Him, as you yourselves know. This man was handed over to you by God's deliberate plan and foreknowledge; and you, with the help of wicked men, put Him to death by nailing Him to the cross. But God raised Him from the dead, freeing Him from the agony of death, because it was impossible for death to keep its hold on Him. . . . Therefore let all Israel be assured of this: God has made this Jesus, whom you crucified, both Lord and Messiah. (Acts 2:14-17, 19-24, 36)

The crowd couldn't believe their ears. They had traveled to Jerusalem to honor God by celebrating the Jewish feast of *Shavuot,* or Pentecost. Now they discovered they had killed God's Son—the very Messiah they had long awaited! The Holy Spirit's promise of conviction kicked into high gear. According to Acts 2:37, Peter's hearers "were cut to the heart," a phrase which means "pierce[d] all the way down . . . deeply (thoroughly) pained . . . [and] emotionally stunned."[1] Unable to contain their grief over sin, thousands cried out at once—"Brothers, what shall we do?" (Acts 2:37). The Holy Spirit testified[2] through Peter immediately: "Repent and be baptized, every one of you, in the name of Jesus Christ for the forgiveness of your sins. And you will receive the gift of the Holy Spirit. The promise is for you and your children and for all who are far off—for all whom the Lord our God will call" (Acts 2:38-39).

The crowd's response was incredible. Only weeks prior, many of the same people cheered as Jesus was dragged off to His brutal death. Now, only moments after the descent of the Holy Spirit, *three thousand* fled their sins to pledge allegiance to Jesus, the New King (Acts 2:41). The invasion of light had begun with shocking success!

And these new believers wouldn't become tepid, timid, part-time disciples. Acts 2:42-47 explains their newfound but radical devotion to the Savior:

> They devoted themselves to the apostles' teaching and to fellowship, to the breaking of bread and to prayer. Everyone was filled with awe at the many wonders and signs performed by the apostles. All the believers were together and had everything in common. They sold property and possessions to give to anyone who had need. Every day they continued to meet together in the temple courts. They broke bread in their homes and ate together with glad and sincere hearts, praising God and enjoying the favor of all the people. And the Lord added to their number daily those who were being saved.

THE INVASION REPLICATES

What began that Pentecost Sunday only continued, replicating in every direction. By Acts 4:4, "Many who heard the message believed; so the number of men who believed grew to about five thousand." In Acts 5:14, "More and more men and women believed in the Lord and were added to their number." In Acts 6:1, "the number of disciples was increasing." In Acts 6:7, "the word of God spread. The number of disciples in Jerusalem increased rapidly, and a large number of priests became obedient to the faith." In Acts 9:31, "The church throughout Judea, Galilee and Samaria enjoyed a time of peace and was strengthened. Living in the fear of the Lord and encouraged by the Holy Spirit, it increased in numbers." In Acts 9:35, "All those who lived in Lydda and Sharon . . . turned to the Lord." In Acts 11:21, "The Lord's hand was with them, and a great number of people believed and turned to the Lord." In Acts 11:24, when the disciple Barnabas preached, "a great number of people were brought to the Lord." In Acts 14:1, "Paul and Barnabas . . . spoke so effectively that a great number of Jews and Greeks believed." In Acts 14:21, Paul and Barnabas "preached the gospel in [Derbe] and won a large number of disciples." In Acts 16:5, "the churches were strengthened in the faith and grew daily in numbers." And in Acts 17:12, "many . . . believed, as did also a number of prominent Greek women and many Greek men."

As a result of this powerful invasion of light, the gospel spread throughout the whole known world in a single generation (see Colossians 1:6, 23). Even nations that never before had access to God now heard and received the glorious news of salvation through Jesus Christ. Wherever the church went, chains were broken, sinners were set free, enemies of God were reconciled to Him, boldness was ignited, and culture shifted. First-century pagans bemoaned this incredible success, complaining, "These men . . . have turned the world upside down!" (Acts 17:6 BSB). Yes, by God's grace, they did turn the world upside down. And of all times, they did it in the "last days." The world would never be the same again.

THE EARLY CHURCH TRANSFORMS THE WORLD

We often complain of the darkness in our generation. Many of us even use this darkness as an excuse for retreat. But our excuses fall to the ground when we consider the victories the early church won in the face of adversity. Their story should grant us faith for battle and zeal for God's modern invasion of light.

You see, few realize that the early church advanced Jesus's kingdom in a society much darker than our own. Their calling must have seemed enormous. The early Christians knew Jesus would transform the world through their witness until His return—Isaiah had promised of Christ: "He will sprinkle many nations, and kings will shut their mouths because of Him. For what they were not told, they will see, and what they have not heard, they will understand" (Isaiah 52:15). But what a task lay before them! When they looked at the world around them, Isaiah's promise must have sounded like music to their ears. The fact is, every day, these holy radicals faced a world so evil that only God could possibly transform it.

Yes, the early church lived within a shocking dystopia. The Greco-Roman world wallowed in almost every moral mire you can imagine—from infanticide and abortion to pedophilia, fornication, adultery, homosexuality, and oppression of the weak, poor, and elderly. Parents killed female or disabled newborns without remorse—some by drowning, some by isolation, others by fiery sacrifice to gods.[3] Society considered the poor and sick as useless and offered them no compassion, charity, or medical help. Even artisans, carpenters, and other low-class manual laborers couldn't legally access medical care when they became sick, for "the sick common people, manual laborers, and the poor 'had no place of refuge.'"[4] Ancient Greeks and Romans mostly gave to causes that would benefit them back—whether by returned favors or increased honor.[5] Slaves often died as gladiators before cheering crowds[6] hungry to see the weak literally cut to pieces for sport.[7] Women had no more rights than slaves. Those who weren't killed in infancy received little education, couldn't leave the house unsupervised, and had to hide in a *women's room* (*gynaeceum*) when the husband's friends visited the house. Under the laws of *manus* and *patria potestas*, every husband legally owned his wife and all of her belongings, and had the legal right to do whatever he pleased with her—including executing the death penalty.[8] Many ancient societies expected the newly widowed to burn themselves alive at their husband's cremation service.[9] Many men flocked to pagan temples to have ritual sex with temple prostitutes.[10] Pedophilia was shockingly widespread and considered culturally acceptable.[11] Fornication, orgies, adultery, pedophilia, and homosexuality were seen as commonplace; so much so that many families had scenes of the shameful acts painted on their daily pottery.[12]

And, honestly, we've only scratched the surface! We've purposely given some of the most grotesque details possible, but the truth is that the ancient world was dark beyond imagination. When reading these gruesome realities, one must ask—how did our world get so much better? Why do today's worst villains seem more moral than antiquity's greatest heroes? The simple and conclusive answer should deeply inspire every modern ambassador of Christ: Jesus radically transformed our world for the better through the church's invasion of light (and He can do it again if we'll fulfill the call!). Faced with such dark conditions, the early church could have easily excused themselves from God's mission, huddling away in retreat to lazily and self-righteously await Jesus's return. Instead, they lived and preached Jesus's message—often at the cost of their lives—and gradually transformed the world from top to bottom. Yes, breathe in this beautiful truth: Christians taught the world to care. Sociologist Alvin Schmidt tells the story in his striking book *How Christianity Changed the World*.

HOW CHRISTIANITY LIT UP THE DARKNESS

Faced with the plight of the newborn, the early church could have retreated. Instead, they preached against this evil, adopted abandoned babies, and raised them in the "the nurture and admonition of the Lord" (Ephesians 6:4 KJV). Once Christianity became legal in 313 A.D., the church founded the world's first known orphanages to care for abandoned children.[13] As Christians gained influence in society, the dark shadow of infanticide retreated more and more. By 374 A.D., Christians abolished infanticide in Rome.[14] With time, even the lost world began to see infanticide as a cruel, harsh treatment of another human being.

Then, they tackled the neglect of the sick and poor. Seeing the world's disdain for the ill, impoverished, and misfortunate, the church could have hunkered down, declaring, "When Jesus makes His final return, He will heal all the sick and bring justice for the oppressed among the righteous! Let's just wait for Him to come!" Instead, they preached against the oppression they saw and did what they could to help the downtrodden. They tended to the sick in their homes. They gave to the poor expecting nothing in return, acting as the sole advocates of widows, orphans, prisoners, slaves, and more.[15] They taught Jesus's strident work ethic, forming the world's first "middle class" and freeing countless families and cultures from the snare of poverty.[16] In times of plague, they tended to and nursed the sick without fear, often losing their lives for the privilege of demonstrating Jesus's love.[17] And once Christianity became legal, they established the world's first hospitals, hospice services, nursing homes, and shelters for sick, dying, or homeless common folk, always sharing the gospel along the way.[18] With this considered, we realize that the modern world's care for the poor, sick, homeless, and dying doesn't stem from innate goodness, or even "liberal ideals." It comes from the gospel's influence on society. It comes from the invasion of light!

And that's only the beginning. The early church's influence eventually stemmed the tide of pedophilia, adultery, fornication, and homosexual practice, as God shaped the world's conscience to the Bible's teaching on sexual purity. Early Christians radically bettered the lives of slaves by treating them as free men,[19] illegally freeing thousands,[20] eventually outlawing the practice of stealing children into slavery, making it legal for citizens to free their slaves,[21] and, by the nineteenth century, laboring successfully to abolish slavery altogether. Christians advanced the cause of female dignity, granting women full, unfettered participation in the church, teaching and baptizing every woman who believed, calling women to testify for Christ, allowing women to hold Christian gatherings in their homes, eventually repealing the oppressive laws of *patria potestas* and *manus*,[22] outlawing the barbaric practice of widow-burning,[23] and so much more.

And that's still only scratching the surface—how much more we would love to tell! The fact is, all the books in the world couldn't contain the glorious history of Jesus's invasion of light. To make a point—one book that tells the story stretches out for 600 letter-sized pages *in about 7-point print* (about half the size of the letters in the print edition of this book).[24] For now, we'll have to leave you with just a few more victories:

- Seeing the world's poor education, Lutheran reformers invented mandatory public schooling, grade systems, and kindergarten for all classes.

- Moved by the truth of God's Word, devoted Christians discovered the scientific method and unveiled most of the fundamentals of science.

- Burdened for the lost masses, Wesley, Whitefield, and the Methodists spearheaded an awakening that saved England from utter destruction.

- Motivated by a yearning for religious freedom, Christian ministers and laymen led the American Revolution[25] and founded the American republic.

- And so much more!

WILL WE INVADE WITH LIGHT IN
THE LAST DAYS OF THE LAST DAYS?

When we read these stories, we can't help but feel stirred and encouraged. The invasion of light has won so many victories, despite great adversity. Now the world has begun to backtrack some of these victories, but that's no reason to quit the battle for righteousness. Friends, it's time to stand on the shoulders of these giants of Christian history and get back to the job.

Could Jesus return soon? Sure. But He could also leave us time to extend the restoration of His kingdom. Does anyone know the day or the hour? (See Matthew 24:36 for the answer). While we await Jesus's return, we must hold the fort and fight for righteousness. Both eternal souls and temporary societies are at stake! After all, if He returns in some other generation, what excuse will we give Him for our laziness and lack of faith?

Seeing these stories, how dare we remain silent for God? Realize—if we excuse ourselves, we do so against the backdrop of two thousand years of Christian advancement. We do so in contrast to millions of saints who fought for God's kingdom to come *despite the fact that they fully knew they lived in the last days.* And we do so knowing full well our negligence will send billions to Hell unwarned and invite God's judgment on the world our descendants must live in (if Christ doesn't return first). It's between you and God if you can stomach that. But we can't. We're going to forge ahead with the invasion of light. If you want to join us, turn to the next chapters, where we'll learn more about the two kingdoms engaged in the battle for souls.

CHAPTER FOUR

THE BATTLE FLAG OF OUR INVASION:
THE KINGDOM OF GOD

So far, we've witnessed the tragic progress of the dark invasion, acknowledged our mission to invade the world with light as Christ's ambassadors, and laid out the biblical and historical case for holy revolution. Now, we want to help you better understand the revolutionary kingdom you serve.

You see, the invasion of light is only possible because Jesus reigns in victory as King over all. Jesus established His kingdom "to destroy the works of the devil" (1 John 3:8 NASB)—so if we want to see transformation and salvation in our world, the very first thing we must do is understand God's kingdom, appreciate it, and align our lives with its cause. That leads us to some important questions. What is the Kingdom of God? What *isn't it*? *Where* is it? What are its battle objectives? We need these answers to fulfill our revolutionary mission. Let's open the Bible to find out more.

THE AMBASSADOR'S MANDATE

In Matthew 6:33, Jesus gave every Christian ambassador a clear mandate: "Seek first the Kingdom of God and His righteousness" (Matthew 6:33 NKJV). Our Lord couldn't have spoken the heavenly call clearer. But today, many believers don't even know what God's kingdom is. It's time for that to change.

You see, God has given the church a primary mission: seek the Kingdom of God—welcome the transforming influence of Jesus's reign in our lives and our world. The original Greek shows the importance of this command: the word translated "seek" is *zēteite* (ζητεῖτε), which means *desire, endeavor, or enquire for*,[1] and the word translated "first" is *próton* (πρῶτον), which means *before, at the beginning, chiefly, at first or first of all.*[2] Jesus commands us to seek, desire, enquire after, and endeavor for the Kingdom of God and His righteousness, and to do it first, chiefly, and before anything else! No longer can we allow the transformative call of God's kingdom to occupy a small part of our lives—it must become our lives! We should be consumed with our pursuit of God's kingdom and its redemptive influence in the world.

And that's exactly the problem. Many of us rarely think of God's kingdom, let alone pursue it before anything else! Truth is, most of us have forgotten we belong to this worldwide revolutionary kingdom, so we see no further than our local churches and denominations. As a result, we waste away the years, devoting our attention solely to our family leisure, hobbies, home church, or personal ministry, and leaving God's worldwide invasion of light to others. We desperately need to recover a vision of God's kingdom so we can experience its redemptive power and spread it to the whole world. That's the ambassador's job description, after all! We want to impart that vision to ignite zeal for the heavenly call. Let's consider some important facts.

NEW TESTAMENT USAGE AND DEFINITION

The phrase "Kingdom of God" appears in the New Testament 69 times in 68 verses. The phrase "Kingdom of Heaven" appears 32 times in 31 verses, all in the book of Matthew. But the Bible refers to the Kingdom by many other names—"the Kingdom of [the] Father" (Matthew 13:43), "the eternal Kingdom of our Lord and Savior Jesus Christ" (2 Peter 1:11), "the Kingdom of Christ and God" (Ephesians 5:5), and "the Kingdom of the Son He loves" (Colossians 1:13). All of these names declare the same basic message: God rules as King over all things.

How can we define the Kingdom of God? The New Testament Greek word for "kingdom" is *basileia* (βασιλεία), which means *royalty, rule, realm, reign, or kingdom.*[3] In other words, the Kingdom is God's rule, reign, and royalty over and across the whole Earth in and through the hearts of His people. To better understand God's rule, we need to consider God's promises to ancient Israel.

A REBELLIOUS PEOPLE; A PROMISED KING

God loved the people of Israel and chose them as His special people. He rescued them from slavery in Egypt and led them into His promised land, working unbelievable victories on their behalf. But again and again, Israel and her kings fell into sin, profaning God's name and inviting His judgment on their land. As a result, they lived under near-constant oppression from the allied nations of the Kingdom of Darkness.

God sent prophets to warn that these oppressions would come—but He also offered a hope that lay at the very foundation of every Jew's worldview. One day, God would forgive Israel's sin, defeat Israel's enemies, take the throne of Israel Himself, and rule over the nations through Israel, ushering in a new world of righteousness, peace, and joy. The King Himself would invade the whole world with pure and holy light! As Isaiah prophesied:

> How beautiful on the mountains
>   are the feet of those who bring good news,
> who proclaim peace,
>   who bring good tidings,
>   who proclaim salvation,
> who say to Zion,
>   "Your God reigns!"
> Listen! Your watchmen lift up their voices;
>   together they shout for joy.
> When the Lord returns to Zion,
>   they will see it with their own eyes.
> Burst into songs of joy together,
>   you ruins of Jerusalem,
> for the Lord has comforted His people,
>   He has redeemed Jerusalem.
> The Lord will lay bare His holy arm
>   in the sight of all the nations,
> and all the ends of the earth will see
>   the salvation of our God! (Isaiah 52:7-10)

Yes, soon the world would have a new king—God Himself! And Jesus Christ is that prophesied king. He came to Earth to begin God's restorative reign—His holy invasion of light—and at the end of days, He will truly "make all things new" for both Israel and the world (Revelation 21:5 NASB).

Yes, after Jesus offered His life on the cross, God the Father "raised Christ from the dead and seated Him at His right hand in the heavenly realms" (Ephesians 1:20). At that time, Jesus paid for the sins of all men, defeated the powers of darkness, and ascended the throne as King over all. According to Paul, Jesus's throne now sits "far above all rule and authority, power and dominion, and every name that is invoked, not only in the present age but also in the one to come" (Ephesians 1:21). Now, every other person, ruler, king, and spiritual power must bow to Him, because "God placed all things under His feet" (Ephesians 1:22).

And Jesus is a kind ruler, desiring salvation, not destruction; light, not darkness; for "God did not send His Son into the world to condemn the world, but to save the world through Him . . . [because] whoever does not believe stands condemned already" (John 3:17-18). As Peter declared, "He is patient with you, not wanting anyone to perish, but everyone to come to repentance" (2 Peter 3:9). Take heart—the merciful God sits on the throne! This is the gloriously good news of the Kingdom of God!

HOW GOD REIGNS ON EARTH

This excellent news leads to a vital question. *How* does God rule and reign on the Earth, thereby transforming souls and societies? After all, the Old and New Testaments attest that the throne of God's kingdom has always been in Heaven. In

Psalm 11:4, David tells us, "The Lord's throne is in Heaven" (NKJV). In Revelation 4:2, John's vision attests the same: "a throne [was] set in Heaven, and One sat on the throne" (NKJV). The author of Hebrews declares that King Jesus is seated "at the right hand of the throne of the Majesty in Heaven" (Hebrews 8:1). It's from Heaven—not Earth—that God the Father rules and reigns (Revelation 3:21), Jesus sits at the right hand of the Father as the King of Kings and Lord of Lords, and the Holy Spirit is dispatched to bring the life and power of the Kingdom of God to Earth (Acts 2:33).

Then how does Jesus bring salvation, healing, and restoration to a sinful world *today*? The answer is simple but startling. Jesus uses *us*, Heaven's worldwide body of ambassadors, to invade the world with the holy light of His reign as we declare and deliver His salvation to lost humanity.

You see, God the Father "appointed [Jesus] to be head over everything for the church, which is His body, the fullness of Him who fills everything in every way" (Ephesians 1:22-23). He is the head of the Kingdom, but *we act on His behalf* as His body. As Peter proclaimed, "You are a chosen people, a royal priesthood, a holy nation, God's special possession, that you may declare the praises of Him who called you out of darkness into His wonderful light" (1 Peter 2:9). And as Revelation 5:10 reveals, "You have made them to be a kingdom and priests to serve our God, and they will reign on the Earth."[4] Yes, in a crucial sense, we are God's revolutionary kingdom! God's Kingdom will take physical form during Jesus's thousand-year reign (see Revelation 21:1-7)—but until then, as Jesus says, "The Kingdom of God is *in you*" (Luke 17:21 KJV).

TEMPLES OF THE KING

Now, that might be a shocking revelation—but it's an undeniable fact. God is King, and you are His "temple" (1 Corinthians 6:19). As temples of the Holy Spirit, Jesus promises to rule and reign inside us if we submit to Him and live out His plan. That's exactly how He invades the world with His marvelous light!

Unfortunately, most of us have totally underestimated our role in God's kingdom. We've hardly begun to grasp our calling as agents of light in the world. Remember, the Bible calls us "a kingdom of priests" (Exodus 19:6, 1 Peter 2:9) and "heirs of God and co-heirs with Christ" (Romans 8:17). God promises we'll one day rule and "reign with" Jesus Christ (2 Timothy 2:12) and "sit with [Him] on [His] throne" (Revelation 3:21). When we bow to Jesus as King, He dubs us Heaven's royalty!

Yes, let that sink in—right now, you are a member of Heaven's royal family. As a result, you have the King's absolute authority to go out and proclaim the gospel of the Kingdom everywhere and anywhere. Oh how different our lives would look if we believed it! This crucial revelation would thrust us out into the world to invade with light in heavenly zeal and confidence!

THE KINGDOM OF GOD IS IN THE HOLY SPIRIT

We've observed that the Kingdom of God is Jesus's spiritual rule in the hearts of committed Christian disciples. So how does Jesus rule in and through us? Paul answers: "The Kingdom of God is . . . *in the Holy Spirit*" (Romans 14:17). It's *in the Holy Spirit* that Jesus rules our hearts, leading us to experience the results of the Kingdom of God—"righteousness, peace and joy" (Romans 14:17). When we experience these spiritual fruits of the revived life, the world can't help but notice and "glorify [our] Father in Heaven" (Matthew 5:16). (We'll discuss this in-depth in Part Three, "How to Walk in the Light: The Ambassador's Character and Crown").

Now, I (Brian) want you to realize something precise but important. The Bible never mentions the "Kingdom of the Holy Spirit"—instead, it declares that "the Kingdom of God . . . is . . . in the Holy Spirit" (Romans 14:17). That's because the Holy Spirit never acts "on His own." As John 16:13 says, "When He, the Spirit of truth, has come, He will guide you into all truth; for *He will not speak on His own authority*, but whatever He hears He will speak" (NKJV). In simple terms, the Kingdom belongs to Jesus, and Jesus accomplishes His royal purposes through the Holy Spirit. As the active agent of the Godhead, He indwells believers and allows us to experience the results of God's kingdom.

As such, the Holy Spirit is our daily partner in the invasion of the light. As we submit to God, Jesus acts through Him to accomplish supernatural things in and through us. As Paul says in Romans 8:11, "The Spirit of Him who raised Jesus from the dead is living in you," and He will "give life to your mortal bodies." We have the revolutionary power of God's kingdom in us, *but it's activated through obedient faith*. For this reason, if we want to walk in the power of God's kingdom, we need to learn to walk in the Spirit. We must heed Paul's warning: "Don't quench the Holy Spirit" (1 Thessalonians 5:19). Otherwise, we'll quench the Kingdom's influence in our lives and gain few victories in the invasion of light.

QUENCHING THE INVASION OF LIGHT

That might sound surprising. Can we really quench the power of God's kingdom in our lives? Can we really stop God's invasion of light from advancing in and through us? Of course—that's why Paul commanded us not to!

Here's an example. Have you ever shrunk back when God asked you to share the gospel with someone? Maybe you got a *holy nudge* that you should serve your neighbor and share the good news with them. You responded to the Lord, "Well . . . I can serve them as a sign of love . . . but I don't want to tell them about Jesus." Or perhaps you saw your neighbor working on their car and felt led to help them and then share the gospel. Instead, you excused yourself, saying, "Maybe later, Lord, but I need to work on my own car today." At that moment, the Holy Spirit wanted to move *through you*, but you wouldn't allow Him. God's kingdom wanted to *come*, but you didn't want to *go*. We're sorry to say it, but we've done it plenty of times, too.

What might God have done if we had obeyed? Is it possible God's kingdom might have come to begin a work of grace in that person's life? Of course—but we refused and chose our own plans instead. By acting this way, we (at least temporarily) flushed out God's invasion of light in that person's life.

All too often, we excuse our negligence by saying, "God can use someone else." But tragically, so many Christians quench the Holy Spirit so often that few around us ever experience a genuine divine appointment. That's part of the reason why the world has fallen into such fierce wickedness!

The plain truth is that the more we quench the Holy Spirit, the less we'll experience the blessings of God's reign in our lives, and the less damage we'll do to the Kingdom of Darkness. But if we'll finally wake up and obey God by the Holy Spirit's power, we'll experience God's kingdom more every day—and so will those we meet. Yes, if we'll simply begin to walk in God's kingdom, Jesus will heal much in our world—person by person, soul by soul. That is society's sole hope of positive change! But if we refuse this heavenly calling, our generation will never find liberty from the deadly clutches of Satan's kingdom.

Now, we'd like to reveal some of the principal objectives of the kingdom we serve. These are the reasons why God sent Jesus to Earth, and why we must go to battle against the forces of darkness.

KINGDOM OBJECTIVE #1: GLORIFYING GOD

The Kingdom's first objective is to glorify God. In Ezekiel 36:22-23, God revealed why He would establish His kingdom:

> This is what the Sovereign Lord says: It is not for your sake, people of Israel, that I am going to do these things, but for the sake of My holy name, which you have profaned among the nations where you have gone. I will show the holiness of My great name, which has been profaned among the nations, the name you have profaned among them. Then the nations will know that I am the Lord, declares the Sovereign Lord, when I am proved holy through you before their eyes.

In Old Testament times, God rescued Israel from slavery and placed them into the promised land to reveal His goodness to the whole world. But rather than demonstrate God's perfect character, Israel rebelled against God, tarnishing His reputation and inviting His righteous judgment on their land. As a result, Israel's neighboring nations likely often saw Yahweh as a weak, powerless, and immoral God who didn't care for His people.

After centuries of this rebellion, God announced He would turn the tables. No longer would He allow Israel and its kings to misrepresent Him! One day, He would take decisive action to show the world how wonderful He *truly is*. He would forgive

Israel's sins, free them from captivity, and reign over them Himself—and the whole world would benefit from His gracious rule. In doing so, He would *glorify Himself*—He would restore His holy reputation in the Earth, winning the praise of billions!

As we discussed, Jesus is that God-king, though His restoration project is still only in its beginning stages.[5] And as our passage declares, God established Jesus's kingdom to restore His glorious reputation in the world. Through our invasion of light, God plans to reveal His beauty, holiness, righteousness, and love to the nations "that in the coming ages He might show the incomparable riches of His grace, expressed in His kindness to us in Christ Jesus" (Ephesians 2:7). Yes, God saves sinners so the joyous songs of His praises might ring louder for all eternity!

This may seem selfish to the undiscerning eye. "Why should I follow a God who does everything for Himself?" But that's a misunderstanding of this biblical teaching. We must realize God doesn't seek His glory *at the expense of His people.* Actually, nothing benefits us more than God's glory. You see, *God is most glorified when we see and experience His goodness.* When God is glorified, the sick are healed, sinners are saved, cultures are transformed, relationships are reconciled, God's church grows, and Heaven fills to capacity. The New Covenant revival advances! But when God isn't glorified on Earth, sickness rules our bodies, sinners rebel without constraint, cultures deteriorate, relationships crumble, the church retreats, and Hell overflows. Put simply—God's glory means the world's redemption. God's absence means the world's destruction.[6]

Think about it this way. One New Testament word for "glory" is *doxa* (δόξα), which sometimes speaks of a bright light ("splendor or brightness").[7] God the Father glorifies Himself through Jesus the Son—"the light of the world" (John 8:12). Jesus alone "shines in the darkness" of our world (John 1:5), "[giving] light to every man" (John 1:9). "In Him we live, and move, and have our being" (Acts 17:28); so without His glory, our world can only fall into gloom and despair. A life without God's glory is like a house without any light. We *desperately need* God to glorify Himself!

Conversely, the more God glorifies Himself, the more wonderful life becomes on Earth and in Heaven. When God glorifies Himself, His attributes ravish our souls, His beauty unraveling before us like a brilliant mountainside sunset. When we witness His infinite glory, our dim souls come ringing back to life as our hearts cry, *"This is why I was created—to know God as He is!"* Yes, the greatest treasure of God's coming kingdom will not be its mansions, jewels, and golden streets. The kingdom's greatest treasure is God Himself! For all eternity, we will glorify God—we'll worship in astonishment of our infinitely glorious, perfect, and loving king, Jesus Christ! Until then, we must make it our life mission to help others join that eternal song of praise.

KINGDOM OBJECTIVE #2: BRINGING
THE KINGDOM TO THE WHOLE EARTH

The Kingdom of Light's second goal is to establish its influence all over the Earth. In Matthew 6:10, Jesus commanded us to pray every day: "Your Kingdom come, your will be done, on Earth as it is in Heaven!" The Greek word here translated "come" comes from *erchomai* (ἔρχομαι), which means *appear, come from one place to another, come to being, arise, show itself, find its place of influence, and be established*.[8] And God wants His kingdom to come on Earth "as it is in Heaven." We'll remind you—God doesn't merely rule parts of Heaven; He rules the whole place! In the same way, God desires for His kingdom to appear, arise, show itself, and be established across the whole Earth, not just in scattered parts.

And with time, God will surely gain this desire through His ambassadors. In Revelation 7:9, God reveals the grand finale of human history—the final result of our invasion of light. When humanity's struggle finally ends, God will fill His eternal kingdom with "a great multitude that no one could count, from every nation, tribe, people and language" (Revelation 7:9). Yes, God is preparing a glorious inheritance for His Son Jesus—an uncountable multitude of perfectly forgiven, wholly-devoted worshippers from every nation, tribe, and tongue! But we must not merely wait for this to happen. Never! Instead, God asks us to work with Him to bring it to pass (2 Corinthians 6:1). Jesus commands: "Go into all the world and preach the gospel to all creation" (Mark 16:15). If you ask us, that's just another way to say, "Let His kingdom be established all across the Earth as in Heaven!"

KINGDOM OBJECTIVE #3: PROMOTING OBEDIENCE TO JESUS THE KING

The third objective of the Kingdom of God is to promote obedience to the King, Jesus Christ. Jesus stated this explicitly in the Great Commission:

> All authority in Heaven and on Earth has been given to Me. Therefore go and make disciples of all nations, baptizing them in the name of the Father and of the Son and of the Holy Spirit, and teaching them to obey everything I have commanded you. (Matthew 28:18-20)

You see, as our Creator, God has every right to rule our lives, and we have no right to rebel. Also, God is our perfect, loving, and wonderful king, and therefore we have *no reason* to rebel. Yes, God truly *deserves* our heartfelt and unconditional obedience, and He created every one of us to enjoy Him through a relationship of obedient love.

Tragically, all of us trampled on God's love by disobeying His commands. But Jesus didn't throw in the towel on us. Extending His love again, He died on the cross to save us from our damnable disobedience: "He died for all, that those who live should no longer live for themselves but for Him who died for them and was raised again" (2 Corinthians 5:15). Yes, Jesus died for us that we would die to ourselves and teach others to do the same. He died to restore us to the relationship of loving obedience He originally intended for us! For this reason, wherever we declare God's glad news of salvation, we must also lovingly warn "that they must turn to God in repentance and have faith in our Lord Jesus" (Acts 20:21).

Many try to invade with light without mentioning this message of repentance and obedience. They much prefer to share soft and cuddly messages—happiness without holiness, revival without repentance, honor without obedience, prosperity without prostration, salvation without self-denial, and God's love without God's law. We know from experience that these messages *feel great* to preach until God teaches you better. After all, who doesn't want to make people feel good? But if we refuse also to clearly declare Jesus's call to obedience, we'll only fill the nations with false converts who profess Jesus but do not follow Him. Tragically, most of those false believers will never open their hearts to the true gospel message again. Whenever a passionate ambassador comes their way with Jesus's true message, they'll smile and say, "Thanks, friend, but I've already checked that box." We shudder at the words they'll hear when they meet the God who demanded loving obedience: "I never knew you. Away from Me, you evildoers" (Matthew 7:23).

KINGDOM OBJECTIVE #4:
RECONCILING THE LOST TO GOD

The fourth objective of the Kingdom is to reconcile the lost to God. Jesus stated this explicitly in Luke 19:10: "The Son of Man came to seek and to save the lost."

The entire unbelieving world is desperately lost. Through sin, they've lost the right to have a relationship with the God of love. Through constant rebellion, they've lost more and more power over their moral character. By stubborn self-rule, they've lost their God-given calling. And if they don't repent, one day they'll lose their souls to the flames of Hell for all eternity. Today, as it stands, they are not children of God, but "children of the devil" (1 John 3:10); "alienated from God and . . . enemies in [their] minds because of [their] evil behavior" (Colossians 1:21). Before Christ, we were too.

The plain truth is that God doesn't *have* to save any of us from our lost condition. We sinned against Him, and as the righteous Judge, He has every right to send us to Hell without intervention. But God's extravagant, eternal love compels Him to move Heaven and Earth to *seek and save* the lost instead. Yes, Jesus went to the greatest lengths to redeem sinful mankind! He became a man, clothing His eternal glory in human weakness. He suffered awful pain and rejection. Finally, He spilled His own blood as a sin offering on the cross. After all He suffered, Jesus rose from the dead and sat as King on His eternal throne of grace. Now, He calls *us* to invade the world with His light, announcing the clarion call of reconciliation through Jesus's blood. Yes, we get to proclaim the glorious news—the Kingdom has come, and the lost can be found! As Paul declared:

> God . . . gave us the ministry of reconciliation: that God was reconciling the world to Himself in Christ, not counting people's sins against them. And He has committed to us the message of reconciliation. We are therefore Christ's ambassadors, as though God were making His appeal through us. We implore you on Christ's behalf: Be reconciled to God. (2 Corinthians 5:18-20)

Yes, lift up the floorboards below every major aspect of salvation, and you'll find this glorious reality: the essence of the good news is our reconciliation to the

Father and adoption into His family. The new believer is "born of God" (1 John 5:1): God gives birth to him anew, becoming his Father! The new believer is baptized "in the name of the Father and of the Son and of the Holy Spirit" (Matthew 28:19)—he is immersed into the very family of the Trinity and takes on the family name. And the new believer receives the "Spirit of adoption as sons by which we cry out, "Abba! Father!" (Romans 8:15). As a result, "The Spirit Himself testifies with our spirit that we are God's children" (Romans 8:16).

These beautiful truths bring our ambassadorial mission into focus. As Christ's ambassadors, our final goal for every soul must be a joyful adoption into God's family. With all of our might, we must declare the danger of sin, warn of the reality of separation from God, and finally joyfully proclaim God's incredible offer of adoption. It's amazing to think—from Heaven's view, evangelism meetings are actually mass adoption ceremonies!

KINGDOM OBJECTIVE #5: DESTROYING THE WORKS OF THE DEVIL

The final objective of God's kingdom is to destroy the works of the enemy. 1 John 3:8 declares: "The reason the Son of God appeared was to destroy the works of the devil" (ESV).

You see, Satan's mission is to destroy everything in his path. As John 10:10 declares: "The thief comes only to steal and kill and destroy." Satan never comes to set things right. He never comes to save, restore, heal, or deliver; He only comes to taint our lives with sin, sickness, separation from God, selfishness, and demonic oppression. His final goal is to drag every life to suffer forever with him in the flames of Hell.

But God's mission is the exact opposite. As Jesus said, "I have come that they may have life, and have it to the full" (John 10:10)! When Jesus came to Earth, He set sinners free, healed "every disease and sickness" (Matthew 4:23), and delivered the demonized (Mark 1:39). Isaiah had prophesied He would walk in an anointing that would destroy all of Satan's works:

> The Spirit of the Sovereign Lord is on Me, because the Lord has anointed Me to proclaim good news to the poor. He has sent Me to bind up the brokenhearted, to proclaim freedom for the captives and release from darkness for the prisoners, to proclaim the year of the Lord's favor and the day of vengeance of our God, to comfort all who mourn, and provide for those who grieve in Zion—to bestow on them a crown of beauty instead of ashes, the oil of joy instead of mourning, and a garment of praise instead of a spirit of despair. (Isaiah 61:1-3)

Yes, Jesus has the authority and longing to set every captive free! And He has given us the same authority by His Spirit. In Luke 10:19, He said, "I have given you authority to trample on snakes and scorpions and to overcome all the power of the enemy!" Now, God wants to use *us* to destroy the works of Satan, as Paul declared: "The God of peace will soon crush Satan under *your* feet!" (Romans 16:20). As we invade with light, we must make this our objective.

When we see the lost, we must preach the gospel of salvation. When we see backslidden Christians, we must declare God's call to repentance and restoration. When we see broken relationships, we must declare Jesus's call to love and forgiveness. When we see the sick, we must reach out in Jesus's love and pray for healing. And when we see the demon-oppressed, we must seek to set the captives free. This is our calling—our divine privilege! The Kingdom of God has enlisted us to destroy the works of the devil. Let us then heed the words of the famous hymn:

> Onward, Christian soldiers,
>   marching as to war,
> With the cross of Jesus
>   going on before!
> At the sign of triumph
>   Satan's host doth flee;
> On, then, Christian soldiers,
>   on to victory!

("Onward Christian Soldier," S. Baring Gould)

CHAPTER FIVE

THE ENEMY OF OUR INVASION: THE KINGDOM OF DARKNESS

You scan the war room with fear. You're a general in the military, and your government just received terrifying intel. A tyrannical foreign enemy has planned an invasion against your nation worse than anything in over a century. Soon, this regime of terror plans to blast your countrymen with all the artillery in their arsenal—gunfire, intercontinental missiles, aerial bombs, chemical weapons, and more—all in an attempt to usurp the presidency and rule your country with an iron rod. Now, you must plot your defensive and offensive strategy. Millions of lives hang in the balance, along with all the values your nation holds dear! The stakes seem higher than ever.

Thankfully, just in time, you receive intel vital to your nation's safety. In a top-secret memo, your nation's spies unveil the enemy's plan in painstaking detail, outlining their organization, resources, weaknesses, and exact battle strategy. With this information, you and your fellow generals can now plan a flawless defense. Having the vital information you need, you set to planning your counterattack. If not for that intel, millions would have perished!

I (Brian) want you to know that this illustration isn't entirely fictional. The truth is, you are in a spiritual battle of epic proportions. The Kingdom of Darkness has plotted mass destruction for the entire human race. They will use whatever artillery they can to destroy lives—lies, temptation, fears, hurts, half-truths, and even the unsavory words and actions of Christians. Their battle plan is to kill, steal, and destroy the lost and to sidetrack the Christian ambassadors who would otherwise oppose their onslaught. Their ultimate goal is to usurp the thrones of men's hearts to rule mankind with an iron fist until they fall together into the depths of Hell. Yes, ours is a battle of eternal stakes—but, thank God, the Holy Spirit knows Satan's plot and promises to "guide [us] into all the truth" (John 16:13), giving us the intel we need to win the war. With His help and wisdom, we can never lose! As David declared before he slew Goliath, "The battle is the Lord's!" (1 Samuel 17:47).

UNAWARE OF HIS SCHEMES

In this chapter, we'll study our enemy in the spiritual battle. We need to know— how has Satan's army organized around us? What methods do they use to invade with darkness? What is their ultimate objective? This enemy intel can often lead to decisive victories in the invasion of light.

Believe me (Brian), Satan would feel much happier if God's church remained oblivious to his battle plan against the souls of men. He doesn't want Heaven's ambassadors to understand his true character, nor the way he works to "kill, steal, and destroy" human lives through the invasion of darkness (John 10:10). Satan knows the truth—if we remain "unaware of his schemes," he may just "outwit us" (2 Corinthians 2:11). He'd love nothing more.

Thank God, the Holy Spirit has a better plan. As the Chief Communications Officer of Heaven's army, the Holy Spirit loves to expose the enemy's battle plans and pinpoint the spiritual principalities and powers that plot against us. Even more importantly, the Holy Spirit loves to deliver God's plan of attack for the battle and dispatch angelic soldiers to assist in obtaining victory. With His help, "The gates of Hell shall not prevail against [us]!" (Matthew 16:18). Satan may have come to steal, kill, and destroy, but Jesus came "that they may have life, and have it to the full!" (John 10:10 NKJV). Jesus won, is still winning, and will always win—and we're on His side!

Knowing God's promise of victory, let's take some time to study our enemy, the Kingdom of Darkness. To accomplish this, we'll conduct a word study on Ephesians 6:12, where the Apostle Paul describes the Kingdom of Darkness with clarity and detail:

> For we do not wrestle against flesh and blood, but against principalities, against powers, against the rulers of the darkness of this age, against spiritual hosts of wickedness in the heavenly places. (Ephesians 6:12 NKJV)

WRESTLING THE KINGDOM OF DARKNESS

The Christian life is not a vacation. According to Paul, every Christian has enlisted in lifelong spiritual combat with the forces of evil. Paul depicts this great conflict as a *wrestling match*—one of the most popular sports of his day. In fact, Bible teacher Derek Prince translated the verse like this:

> For our wrestling match is not against flesh and blood—we are not wrestling against mere human personalities—but against principalities (or rulerships), against authorities, against the world dominators of this present darkness, against spirits of wickedness in the heavenlies.[1]

The days have long passed for sugar-coated pop-theology. We need to begin to see the invasion of light as it truly is. Ambassador of Christ, you are in the battle ring with your diabolical opponent, the devil. His only objective is to pin you to the mat, throw you from the ring, lodge his foot upon your neck, and hold you down until he gets the victory. He wants to steal your fruitfulness, quench your influence, and hold back your invasion of light. You can't let that happen—you must understand your opponent and train to be victorious!

This is the biblical fact, whether we like it or not—Paul teaches that we enter into a new set of *wrestling matches* against the Kingdom of Darkness every day. These one-on-one battles may seem insignificant in themselves, but they play a crucial role within the church's larger conflict against the army of Satan. Whenever a Christian prays, preaches, resists temptation, and casts out demons, he or she wrestles a single demonic soldier to eventually defeat the entire opposing army, blow by blow, warrior by warrior. Satan's kingdom will only fold before us when the whole church engages in hand-to-hand combat with the enemy! Only by persisting in our daily wrestling matches can we push back the invasion of darkness in our lives and others' lives.

FIGHTING THE WRONG OPPONENT

Before unveiling our wrestling opponent, Paul clarifies who we're *not wrestling*. As Derek Prince rendered Ephesians 6:12, "Our wrestling match is not against flesh and blood—we are not wrestling against mere human personalities!"[2] When Paul wrote this passage, he wanted us to know from the start that our wrestling match is not against people. We invade with light *into people's lives*, but we invade *against the Kingdom of Darkness*. The Kingdom of Darkness is the brutal tyrant we fight to dethrone—human souls are the oppressed subjects we fight to liberate! How important to remember!

You see, Satan has often used a diabolical strategy to gain the upper hand in his wrestling match against the church: he convinces us to *wrestle one another*, or even worse, *wrestle unbelievers* with the vehemence of an angry mob. Paul knew this satanic strategy and urged us not to foolishly wrestle the wrong opponent.

Remember, Satan and his coalition of doomed demons have no hope of redemption. Knowing this, their sole objective is "to steal and kill and destroy" as many as possible while time remains (John 10:10). And they've left no method of destruction off the table. Satan would even love to use us as agents in the *invasion of darkness*—meanwhile letting us think we're invading with light!

With this considered, before we can effectively war against Satan, we must appreciate our redemptive mission as Christ's ambassadors in the Kingdom of Light. Jesus is our King, and He sends us to rescue souls doomed in the path of death and darkness. Jesus sends us to declare a faith-inspiring gospel message, not to mow over lost souls with self-righteousness and sanctimony. When we identify our real enemy, it's so much easier to represent Jesus how He wants. Then we can fight our real opponent—the Kingdom of Darkness, not the lost souls Jesus died to save!

Now, let's consider our true enemy, the Kingdom of Darkness.

A HIGHLY ORGANIZED ENEMY

Our spiritual battle is similar to flesh-and-blood wars between nations. Earthly armies organize themselves by various ranks—generals, colonels, captains, lieutenants, sergeants, and more. Each position exercises delegated command over soldiers on different war fronts. Satan's battle strategy is similar, though his warriors use spiritual weapons. Just like earthly armies, Satan has set demonic leaders at various levels of authority and areas of influence. Paul outlines some of the ranks of Satan's army in our verse—"For we do not wrestle against flesh and blood, but against *principalities, against powers, against the rulers of the darkness of this age, against spiritual hosts of wickedness in the heavenly places*" (Ephesians 6:12 NKJV).

Before I unpack each of these ranks, I want to point out that they each war from *"heavenly places"* (Ephesians 6:12 NKJV). Satan's Kingdom is not necessarily associated with earthly countries or rulers, though he often manipulates earthly rulers to accomplish his ends. Therefore, the Christian's battle is not typically against any physical regime but against the spiritual forces that lead people and nations into destruction.

As ambassadors of Christ, God has granted us jurisdictional authority to deliver knockout punches to these destructive, devilish powers here, there, and in the air. Ephesians 2:6 says, "God raised us up with Christ and seated us with Him in the heavenly realms in Christ Jesus." You see, though we physically live on the Earth, God has granted us to sit spiritually with Christ in heavenly places where we can wage war "against spiritual hosts of wickedness in the heavenly places" (Ephesians 6:12). As Jesus promised, "I have given you authority to trample on snakes and scorpions and to overcome all the power of the enemy; nothing will harm you!" (Luke 10:19). With this in mind, we can thrust ourselves into the battle with the confidence of fully equipped and armored soldiers. Glory to God!

Now, let's begin to break down the levels of authority in the Kingdom of Darkness.

DARK AUTHORITY #1: SATAN

We find the dark kingdom's first rank of authority in Ephesians 6:11: "Put on the full armor of God, so that you can take your stand against *the devil's* schemes." Here, Paul clarifies the fountainhead of every evil scheme—the devil himself. As the commander-in-chief of the Kingdom of Darkness, Satan sits in his war room and plots the surest ways to lure mankind from God's grace. Then he delivers his maniacal plan to his demonic inferiors who execute his attacks wherever possible.

The Greek word most often translated "devil" is *diabolos* (διάβολος) which means *false accuser* or *slanderer*.[3] We derive the English word diabolical from this satanic name—and the adjective describes him perfectly. The devil truly is *diabolical*. He never fights fairly, regardless of his opponent. In fact, he's the dirtiest fighter in all of creation! All he does is lie, steal, cheat, slander, accuse, tempt, and deceive. That's why the Apostle John called the devil the "accuser of the brethren" (Revelation 12:10 NKJV), and Jesus called him "a liar and the father of [lies]" (John 8:44 NKJV). He and his minions have no consideration for human life or dignity—they only "[prowl] around like a roaring lion looking for someone to devour" (1 Peter 5:8). Yes, like hungry, savage lions, they prowl, plan, and go for the kill!

Speaking of this, Jesus declared, "The thief comes only to steal and kill and destroy" (John 10:10). Steal! Kill! Destroy! *That* is Satan's sole battle plan—and his ultimate goal for the invasion of darkness. And don't be deceived—you are in his sights. He has zeroed in his flaming arrows of harrowing hate and dastardly deception right on your heart. His prized mission is to destroy you and every other humble and holy ambassador of Christ, and he'll stop at nothing to achieve it.

SATAN'S INFERIORITY TO JESUS

It's crucial to understand our enemy and his schemes, but more than that, we must dwell upon God's world-shaking power. Satan's armory can never match the Lord's! When compared, Jesus's might is like an intercontinental ballistic missile and Satan's power is like a mere firecracker. For this reason, Satan's army can't even operate outside of God's permission (for example, see Job 1:6-12). Fear not, saint of God—"Greater is He who is in you than he who is in the world"! (1 John 4:4 NASB).

Yes, our God is infinitely greater than every other being in creation, including the former archangel Lucifer we now call Satan. And He has empowered us against the Devil's wily, deceitful, and sinister methods of destruction. Breathe this in, ambassador of Heaven—compared to Christ in us, Satan is no more than an imp! His wicked ways are no match for King Jesus and His faithful and humble warriors.

God's light always dispels demonic darkness as we faithfully invade our world with the light of the gospel. Knowing this, we must fight Satan with extraordinary tenacity and focus—not as mean, hateful warriors, but as triumphant soldiers in God's army, holding up the banner of Jesus: "I came that they may have life and have it abundantly!" (John 10:10 ESV).

AUTHORITY #2: PRINCIPALITIES

Now, let's discuss the second level of satanic authority mentioned in this passage. Ephesians 6:12 says, "We do not wrestle against flesh and blood, but against principalities..." (NKJV). The Greek word here translated "principalities" is *archē* (ἀρχή), which also means *magistrate, power, or rule*.[4] According to dictionary.com, a principality is "a state ruled by a prince, usually a relatively small state or a state that falls within a larger state such as an empire."[5] Likewise, in the Kingdom of Darkness, Satan acts as king (though he's actually only "the prince of the power of the air," Ephesians 2:2 NKJV), and principalities act as under-princes and magistrates.

What and where do Satan's principalities rule? Quite simply, each demonic prince rules from the heavenly region over a piece of land (not mistaken for the highest Heaven where God's throne dwells). I believe a distinct demonic principality dwells over every single municipality worldwide, and every principality has a plan of attack for the municipality it governs. We see these principalities in action in Daniel 10.

In this passage, we find a humble saint, Daniel, fasting and praying for God's restoration in dark times. On Daniel's first day of fasting, God heard his prayer and sent an angel to deliver the answer (Daniel 10:12). But while the answer traveled, a dark spiritual being fought fiercely to delay the execution of God's response. As God's messenger angel explained, "The *prince of the Kingdom of Persia* withstood me twenty-one days," so he couldn't fulfill his assignment from Heaven (Daniel 10:13 NKJV). In other words, Daniel's answer had been delayed by the satanic prince in authority over his country of residence.

And this prince was no earthly being. An angel of any stature could defeat an earthly prince with a flash of their brilliant light. But the messenger angel explains the only way he could get free from the grasp of the demonic principality: "Michael, one of the chief princes, came to help me" (Daniel 10:13 NKJV). Clearly, the demonic principality over Persia did not want Daniel to receive God's message, and apparently would never allow it except by battle with a spiritual prince of equal or greater power—in this case, Michael, the archangel of God's heavenly armies, one of the chief prince angels of God's Kingdom. And realize—*the heavenly victory never came until Daniel finished his intercessory responsibility*. The Prince of Persia released the messenger after exactly twenty-one days of battle—the exact duration of Daniel's fast (see Daniel 10:3 and 13). Talk about spiritual warfare!

This story suggests a shocking principle: some principalities have greater influence over their municipalities because of the complacency of God's praying people. This is why some regions have more significant problems with certain sins than others. For example, Sodom and Gomorrah were overtaken with sexual immorality (including homosexual practice) and were destroyed for their lack of repentance. Why had Sodom and Gomorrah become so widely perverse? We can't be sure, but I (Brian) believe the satanic prince over Sodom fought hard to ensnare those two cities in perversion. With less than ten righteous people in the entire vicinity, Satan's kingdom could invade citizens' lives with little or no resistance.

In the same way, I believe many local moral crises arise through the initiation, influence, and implementation of satanic princes. When God's people back down in prayer, Satan's army boldly steps up to establish a stronghold in a community. To avoid this, we must organize our ranks to constantly agonize in prayer for the lost world and backslidden church. What wonders can take place if we learn to resist Satan's plans through prayer! (We'll discuss how to do this in Chapter Fourteen, "Prevailing Prayer: The Ambassador's Mightiest Weapon").

Yes, rather than retreat, God calls His ambassadors of light to war against these principalities—to "have no fellowship with the unfruitful works of darkness, but rather expose them" (Ephesians 5:11 NKJV). With this in mind, we must begin to obey God, organize the agonizers, pray in the Holy Spirit, and preach God's truth openly. And we must never fear to openly speak God's truth about cultural idols like abortion, homosexuality, and pornography. It's the only way to push back these principalities and rescue the perishing from the wiles of evil! Church, now is the time to push back the invasion of darkness! Let's gather forces and do it.

AUTHORITY #3: POWERS

Now let's consider the next battlefield arena Paul unveils—"powers." The Greek word here translated "powers" comes from *exousia* (ἐξουσία), which means *authority, jurisdiction, liberty, power, right, and or strength*, and here infers a demonic delegated influence. In other words, this rank consists of delegated authorities—we might call them officers or soldiers—with jurisdictional authority to invade with darkness in a particular region or among certain types of people.

In Colossians 1:16, Paul seems to describe the realm of spiritual authority in descending order—"thrones or dominions or principalities or powers" (NKJV). To us, this suggests that *powers* operate below the authority of *principalities*. If so, the prince of every municipality employs lesser demons, or *powers*, to attack individuals, families, and Christian leaders within the area. Perhaps a principality might even delegate power over neighborhoods and boroughs.

Likewise, many evil agents dedicate their efforts to a single temptation, illness, or incapacitation—anger, addiction, adultery, homosexuality, lust, lying, rebellion, witchcraft, and many more. This is why scripture often names demons by the afflictions they bring—for example, the Bible mentions a "deaf and dumb spirit" (Mark 9:25 NKJV), a "spirit of divination" (Acts 16:16 NKJV), an "unclean spirit" (Mark 1:26 NKJV), "deceiving spirits" (1 Timothy 4:1), a "spirit of infirmity" (Luke 13:11 NKJV), and more.

The only force that can stop these satanic powers is an authority with greater power and influence. King Jesus is that authority—and no evil force can resist His power! And here's the amazing news: Jesus has delegated His power and authority to us, His blood-washed people. In fact, while these forces of evil are called *exousiai* (ἐξουσίαι)—powers and delegated authorities—God has granted us *exousian* (ἐξουσίαν)—power and delegated authority—over all the forces of evil:

> Then He called His twelve disciples together and gave them power and authority (*exousian*) over all demons, and to cure diseases. He sent them to preach the Kingdom of God and to heal the sick. (Luke 9:1-2 NKJV).

> Behold, I give you the authority (*exousian*) to trample on serpents and scorpions, and over all the power of the enemy, and nothing shall by any means hurt you. (Luke 10:19 NKJV)

Therefore, we never need to fear when we encounter the Kingdom of Darkness at work before our eyes. Instead, we should simply remember our authority as ambassadors of God's kingdom and use our *exousian* to put these *exousiai* to flight in the name of Jesus. On with the invasion of light!

AUTHORITY #4: THE WORLD-DOMINATORS OF
THE DARKNESS OF THIS AGE

Next, let's consider the third ranking Paul lists—"the rulers of the darkness of this age" (Ephesians 6:12 NKJV). At first, it might seem Paul is merely mouthing off a high-sounding religious term—but we believe the original language suggests he spoke with intent. The Greek word here translated "rulers" is *kosmokrator* (κοσμοκράτωρ)—a combination of *kosmos*, which here likely means *world*,[6] and *krateo*, which means *to have power of, master, rule, seize, or hold*.[7] To us, this title suggests a global level of demonic authority. In other words, it seems Paul points to rulers who, under Satan, have power of, master, rule, and seize the whole unbelieving world, holding the lost masses firmly in their evil grip. In harmony with this thought, Derek Prince translated *kosmokrator* as "world-dominators."[8]

What role do Satan's *kosmokrator* play in the invasion of darkness? It's impossible to know for sure, but it would seem they govern *principalities* much like *principalities* must govern *powers*. Most likely, Satan has granted these world-dominators to organize his attack over *countries*, *continents*, or *hemispheres*; or, perhaps, to organize attacks across the whole globe *in respect to certain sins and infirmities*. Could there be a world-dominator of lust who gives battle orders to principalities about how to organize the powers of uncleanness at different times? Could there be a world-dominator over the United States of America who gives battle orders to the principalities over every state, county, city, or neighborhood? We believe that's the most likely possibility, though it's unfruitful to speculate any further.

Paul is the only biblical author who explicitly mentions these *world-dominators*, so I (Brian) can't help but wonder how he learned about them. Did he see them during his experience in the heavenly realm? Speaking of himself, Paul wrote, "I know a man in Christ who fourteen years ago—whether in the body I do not know, or whether out of the body I do not know, God knows—such a one was caught up to the third heaven" (2 Corinthians 12:2 NKJV). Could he have first witnessed these spiritual world-dominators as he passed through the realms of spiritual authority on his way up to the third heaven? It's certainly possible!

It's easy to tremble at the thought of these massive powers of darkness—but Paul announces a higher call. When Satan's armies approach, we must not fear but "put on the full armor of God" (Ephesians 6:13). If we'll only armor up and train for battle, then "when the day of evil comes" we'll "be able to stand [our] ground" against the Kingdom of Darkness (Ephesians 6:13). Satan's greatest authorities are no match for a born-again Christian filled with the Holy Spirit of God! (We'll discuss how to use our spiritual armor in Chapter Fifteen, "Suit Up! The Invasion Requires Armor," and Chapter Sixteen, "The Ambassador's Weapons of Warfare: The Armor of God").

Now, let's discuss the goals of Satan's kingdom.

SATANIC GOAL #1: STEAL, KILL, AND DESTROY

Satan's first objective is "to steal and kill and destroy" (John 10:10). As we've stated, Satan never comes to set anything right. He hated God's perfect creation in the Garden of Eden, and to this day he takes every opportunity to destroy all that is good, true, and beautiful.

For this reason, it's never hard to tell when Satan steps onto the scene. To put it plainly—he spreads disaster wherever he goes. When darkness invades, Satan brings disorder in place of order, sin in place of holiness, sickness in place of health, fear in place of security, temptation in place of victory, confusion in place of clarity, and most importantly, spiritual blindness in place of heavenly encounter.

Satan uses all of these devices with one dark goal in mind—to steal the glorious and holy life God wants you to live in Jesus Christ. Why? So ultimately, he can kill you, dragging you down to Hell with him to be tormented forever by his side. Yes, hellfire is Satan's target, and tragically he has excellent aim. The Bible tells us "the whole world is under the control of the evil one" (1 John 5:19); "For wide is the gate and broad is the road that leads to destruction, and many enter through it!" (Matthew 7:13).

While Satan often treads loudly, he also knows how to invade on tiptoe. He feels perfectly glad to leave sinners healthy, wealthy, happy, sane, and even generally moral as long as he can divert their attention from the salvation of Jesus Christ. At the end of the day, He doesn't care how he buries you—whether in rags or robes, as a pastor or a pimp. He just cares *that he* buries you, keeping you in his clutches until you stand unforgiven before the Throne of God's judgment! Nothing would please him more!

SATANIC GOAL #2: BLIND TO THE GOSPEL

Satan's second objective is to blind the world to the gospel of Jesus Christ. Remember, Satan isn't in the market for new slaves—he already owns every unbeliever alive. As "the god of this world," he already has "the whole world . . . under his control" (2 Corinthians 4:4 NASB, 1 John 5:19). In light of this, his one great objective is to *keep them under his oppressive regime.*

Satan didn't always have to fight so hard to keep souls in his grasp. He had free rein to wreak havoc upon the world before the cross. For almost four thousand years, his army invaded with darkness almost wherever they pleased and rarely suffered a loss. But then God's kingdom came. Christ died and rose again, setting the captives free and "spoil[ing] principalities and powers . . . triumphing over them" through the cross (Colossians 2:15 KJV). Christ won and Satan lost! This is the gospel of the Kingdom! And this glorious message of Christ's victory carries with it all the might of Heaven's armies—even "the power of God that brings salvation to everyone who believes" (Romans 1:16). It's the one pesky weapon Satan's armies cannot defeat. That's why Satan hates it so much.

You need to realize something. *Satan fears the gospel.* He knows this message has eternal power to set lost sinners free. He knows it alone can "open [sinner's] eyes and turn them from darkness to light, and from the power of Satan to God, so that they may receive forgiveness of sins and a place among those who are sanctified by faith in [Christ]" (Acts 26:18). Even worse, Satan knows that whoever sees and receives the gospel falls from his evil clasp until further notice, having been "rescued . . . from the domain of darkness, and transferred . . . to the Kingdom of [God's] beloved Son" (Colossians 1:13 NASB). Once a sinner believes this gospel and deeply repents of all sin, Satan can't lay his evil fingers upon them any longer, because Jesus "keeps them safe, and the evil one cannot harm them" (1 John 5:18)!

Knowing this, Satan's army dedicates most of its efforts to *blinding the world* to God's plan of redemption. As Paul declared, "The god of this age has blinded the minds of unbelievers, so that they cannot see the light of the gospel that displays the glory of Christ, who is the image of God" (2 Corinthians 4:4). And Satan will use whatever weapons he must to keep sinners in the dark about this eternity-shifting message. His range is vastly diverse.

In many cases, he'll first seek to keep us oblivious to spiritual realities altogether. If he fails there, he often tries to mislead us into false worship and idolatry, or else to derail our spiritual desire through the pleasures of the world. If this fails, he attempts to inoculate our consciences through pride, legalism, and false standards so we won't see our need of a Savior. If this fails—and we find our consciences awakened to the reality of sin—he does whatever he can to make sure we don't seek or understand the gospel message. In the end, he wants to ensure he can keep sinners in his grasp by all means possible! Knowing this, we must fight with all our might for the souls of mankind, never shrinking back from preaching God's Word! On with the invasion of light!

SATANIC GOAL #3: DECEIVE AND INOCULATE THE CHURCH

Satan's final goal is to *deceive the church*. You see, the devil will always first seek to prevent your salvation—but when this becomes impossible, he'll try to keep you from *spreading salvation to others*. In this battle, his attack is often three-fold.

First, he uses intimidation, fear, shame, and guilt to silence the church's witness. With some, he shoots stinging darts of accusation: "You're not worthy to preach salvation! You're too sinful! Clean up your act, and then you can testify of Jesus . . . maybe." To others, he stirs up social fears: "You can't preach the gospel that way—people will dislike you! You don't want to lose respect—then no one will ever listen to you preach again!" Then, he beats those same people down with guilt for not obeying Jesus's Great Commission: "You sinner! You're too afraid of preaching the gospel! You'll never get it right!" This heavy cloud of guilt and confusion keeps many from witnessing out of the freedom of love.

Second, if Satan can't keep us silent, he'll seek to mislead us into false teaching. He leads some into a message without grace; others into a message without repentance. Satan cares not which error we embrace—either will prove fatal to our invasion of light and crucial to his invasion of darkness.

Finally, if Satan cannot mislead us into false teaching, he'll seek to steal our intimacy with God or compromise our witness through sin. This way, our words will fall on deaf ears, either by lack of spiritual power or by the stench of blatant hypocrisy.

You must remember that Satan never plays easy with God's saints. Jesus warned Peter—"Satan has asked to sift all of you as wheat" (Luke 22:31). Likewise, Satan has asked to sift *you* as wheat, tempting and trying your faith until the day he loses you to Heaven forever. Knowing this, you must prepare yourself for the spiritual war.

Suit up and stand strong, soldier of God! As Paul declared: "It is for freedom that Christ has set us free. Stand firm, then, and do not let yourselves be burdened again by a yoke of slavery!" (Galatians 5:1). No matter what fiery trials come your way, remember Who is on the throne, and remember Jesus's blood shed for you on the cross! And above all, remember the Lord's encouraging words to you: "In the world you will have trouble. But take heart! I have overcome the world" (John 16:33).

SATAN'S FINAL FATE

Yes, thank God, Jesus has overcome the world, and Satan's day of judgment quickly approaches! Soon John's vision will become sweet reality: "The devil, who deceived them, was cast into the lake of fire and brimstone where the beast and the false prophet are. And they will be tormented day and night forever and ever" (Revelation 20:10 NKJV). Until then, the dark kingdom will battle God's people with all the fury it can muster. Hell's hordes will stop at nothing to steal the masses into Hell, for lost souls are Satan's treasured spoils. But thank God, the Light of the World leads our army into battle. And as the Apostle John declared, "The light shines in the darkness, and the darkness did not comprehend it" (John 1:4-5 NKJV).

Do not fear, ambassador of Heaven—God's light is piercing the darkness, and with patient obedience, your invasion of light will succeed. In the next section, we'll study God's Word to learn how to effectively fight Satan's armies and invade our world with gospel light. Let's consider God's pathways to victory!

Part 2.

*How to Invade with Light
(The Ambassador's Armory)*

CHAPTER SIX

THE CALL OF THE INVASION: THE MINISTRY OF RECONCILIATION

We know *what* God wants to do—invade with light. We know *who* He wants to do it through—us, Christ's ambassadors. We know the glorious flag we carry in this battle—the banner of the Kingdom of Light. And we know the brutal enemy we must face—the Kingdom of Darkness. Then one crucial question remains before we can move from theory to reality. How does God want to use us to defeat the Kingdom of Darkness, extend the influence of the Kingdom of Light, and invade our society with King Jesus's restoring power? The answer is simple. God has given us a clear battle plan for this spiritual war—the ministry of reconciliation through the Great Commission (2 Corinthians 5:18, Mark 16:15-18). If we obey this heavenly calling in the Earth-shaking prayer-power of the Holy Spirit, God will use us to welcome His kingdom in our surroundings, and as a result, we may very well witness positive change in our societies. If we disobey, the lost masses can only continue racing toward judgment. The choice is up to us.

UNDERSTANDING THE MINISTRY OF RECONCILIATION

God's primary strategy in the invasion of light is the ministry of reconciliation. Paul unveils it in 2 Corinthians 5:18-21:

> All this is from God, who reconciled us to Himself through Christ and gave us the ministry of reconciliation: that God was reconciling the world to Himself in Christ, not counting people's sins against them. And He has committed to us the message of reconciliation. We are therefore Christ's ambassadors, as though God were making His appeal through us. We implore you on Christ's behalf: Be reconciled to God. God made Him who had no sin to be sin for us, so that in Him we might become the righteousness of God.

The ministry of reconciliation is the divine mission to reconcile the lost to God the Father through the message of Jesus the Son by the Holy Spirit's power. Through the gospel, God is "reconciling the world to Himself in Christ" (2 Corinthians 5:19), thereby forgiving sinners, freeing captives, and transforming lives. But He doesn't want to reconcile the world alone—He has enlisted us as His agents of reconciliation, and has "committed to us the message of reconciliation" (2 Corinthians 5:19)! Now, it's our job to advance the ministry of reconciliation by faithfully proclaiming the message of reconciliation from a thriving relationship with God. Yes, when we preach the gospel of reconciliation, Paul says it's "as though God were making His appeal through us" (2 Corinthians 5:20). In other words, God's voice comes through our lips and touches the hearts of our hearers! As Jesus explained, "It will not be you speaking, but the Spirit of your Father speaking through you!" (Matthew 10:20).

GOD'S APPEAL THROUGH US

Listen closely, and mark this down. God's divine appeal through us is the greatest key to our invasion of light. Alongside prayer, it's the very engine that pushes the victory of God forward in the Earth. When an on-fire Christian speaks up for Jesus, God's voice through them often acts like a wrecking ball, crushing every lie, excuse, and false idea, powerfully revealing Jesus's loving offer of salvation, and sending the lost running to God in deep repentance and joyous faith. In Jeremiah 23:29, God asked, "Is not My word like fire . . . and like a hammer that breaks a rock in pieces?" *That* is what people encounter when we allow God to speak through us! And *that* is what the world misses when we refuse to speak. What an opportunity—and a responsibility!

You see, as Christians, we can do many great deeds without saying a word—but our good example alone can never lead souls to eternal life. Before the lost can receive Christ, *God must speak through us*, awakening hearts from slumber and unveiling the urgency of salvation. As Jesus declared, no one comes to Him "unless the Father . . . draws them" (John 6:44)—and He draws through teaching, not force.[1] That's why Jesus promised, "When the Advocate comes . . . the Spirit of truth Who goes out from the Father—He will testify about Me. *And you also must testify*" (John 15:26-27). Yes, God promises to testify to the lost about His message of reconciliation, but He doesn't want to do it alone—He wants to teach human hearts by sending heavenly words through human voices! He wants to use you as His herald.

What a glorious privilege—God calls us to become conduits for His voice! This reality should profoundly challenge and encourage us. We should feel challenged by the urgency of the call—for "how can they believe in the one of whom they have not heard? And how can they hear without someone preaching to them?" (Romans 10:14). Yet we should take courage at God's willingness to appeal through us, for God's words never fail! As God promised in Isaiah 55:11: "So shall My word be that goes forth from My mouth; It shall not return to Me void, But it shall accomplish what I please, And it shall prosper in the thing for which I sent it" (NKJV). Praise the Lord, this promise takes effect whenever a faithful ambassador preaches the gospel of Jesus! With this considered—how desperately we need to recover the message of reconciliation and again approach the ministry of reconciliation with reverence, honor, and joyful obedience!

THE MESSAGE OF RECONCILIATION

What is the message of reconciliation, then? Paul tells us clearly: "That God was reconciling the world to Himself in Christ, not counting people's sins against them . . . God made Him [Jesus] who had no sin to be sin for us, so that in Him we might become the righteousness of God" (2 Corinthians 5:19, 21). The message of reconciliation declares that *on the cross, Jesus made a way for every soul to be reconciled to God*, and pleads with souls to be reconciled to God. To clearly share this message, it helps to break it down into three easy-to-memorize ideas—*the problem, the promise, and the practicals.* Here, we'll briefly unveil the essential elements of the gospel of reconciliation, but we'll discuss how to effectively share these truths in the chapters immediately following. Let's dive in to master the central message of God's invasion of light.

THE PROBLEM: SIN, JUDGMENT, & SEPARATION

First, to effectively invade with gospel light, we must soberly warn of the problem— that all have sinned and have therefore earned God's righteous judgment both now and for all eternity. After all, what good is it to offer reconciliation with God if our hearers don't truly understand they are *separated from Him*?

Here's the plain truth about our spiritual problem. God is our Creator, and therefore has an absolute right to rule our lives. He created us to glorify Him through a relationship of obedient love, and gave us a law (the Ten Command- ments) to reveal what obedience looks like. But all of us have broken God's law—we've lied, stolen, de-prioritized God, mistreated others, dishonored our parents, taken God's name in vain, looked with lust, exercised greed, lived by selfish principles, and so much more. Not only have we sinned—"All men have "[drunk] in evil like water" (Job 15:16), guzzling down as much evil as conscience can bear without losing self-respect. That's why so many excuse themselves, say- ing, "It's not *that* bad!"

God is the righteous Judge of the Universe and cannot let these crimes go unpunished. His very nature requires Him to punish every sin with perfect justice, for "will not the judge of all the Earth do right?" (Genesis 18:25). For this reason, after we die, each of us must stand before God's throne for judgment. He will review each of our sins, assigning a righteous penalty to every one (see Revelation 20:12).

And God's Word tells us the final verdict ahead of time: all who have sinned "will be consigned to the fiery lake of burning sulfur" (Revelation 21:8). In that terrible place, "their worm does not die, and the fire is not extinguished" (Mark 9:48 NASB). Forever, those who neglected Christ's salvation will cry, "I am in agony in this fire!" (Luke 16:24 NASB). The righteous penalty we deserve is so terrible that

God doesn't want *anyone* to suffer it: "The Lord is . . . not willing that any should perish but that all should come to repentance" (2 Peter 3:9 NASB).

What awful news—but we must help our hearer understand these truths before they will truly appreciate the good news. As we declare these truths, Jesus has promised to help our hearer understand his plight: "[The Holy Spirit] will convict the world concerning sin and righteousness and judgment" (John 16:8 NASB). When the Holy Spirit convicts the conscience, they'll inwardly cry, "How can I be saved from this terrible fate?" That's exactly where the promise comes in—and in most cases, not a moment sooner.

THE PROMISE: TOTAL SALVATION IN JESUS CHRIST

What is the promise, then? That King Jesus died and rose again to pay the penalty for our sins, reconcile us to God, and welcome us to join His Kingdom of Light. You see, God could have righteously left us in our sins and allowed us to sink down to Hell for all eternity—but in His great love, He chose to sacrifice His own Son Jesus on the cross to pay for our sins, release us from the penalty we deserved, reconcile us to Himself, and secure our place in His kingdom.

But death couldn't hold the Son of God down! Jesus Christ rose from the dead, defeating every evil power and proving God the Father had accepted His payment for our sins. Now, He sits at the right hand of the Father as King of Kings and Lord of Lords, and He has extended His loving arms to the human race, offering to invade their lives with His light, erase their sins in His blood, accept them into His family, and joyfully reconcile them to Himself so they can enjoy a life-changing relationship with Him now and for all eternity. As Jesus declared, "God so loved the world that he gave His one and only Son, that whoever believes in Him shall not perish but have eternal life" (John 3:16). What glorious news! And when we declare it, Jesus promises to make it real to the broken sinner's heart: "When the [Holy Spirit] comes . . . He will testify about me" (John 15:26).

THE PRACTICALS: REPENTANCE AND FAITH

Once our hearer has understood and appreciated this glorious news, we must proceed to the *practicals*. It's no good to tell a thirsty man we have water—we must offer him to *drink*! In the same way, we'd be unwise to proclaim the problem of sin and the promise of salvation but stop short of leading others to practically respond to Christ's offer.

We see *the practicals* in action in Acts 2. On the Day of Pentecost, after Peter preached the problem and the promise, the broken crowds cried: "Brothers, what shall we do?" (Acts 2:37). Many preachers today would reply, "Nothing! There's nothing you can do to receive salvation!" Not Peter. Peter gave the same clear directions we must give to every lost soul:

> Repent and be baptized, every one of you, in the name of Jesus Christ for the
> forgiveness of your sins. And you will receive the gift of the Holy Spirit. The

promise is for you and your children and for all who are far off—for all whom
the Lord our God will call. (Acts 2:38-39)

Yes, to be reconciled to God, we must believe God's promise of salvation through
Jesus Christ, bow the knee to Jesus in repentance (whenever possible, expressing
repentance through water baptism), and welcome the transforming power of God's
Holy Spirit into our lives. When we do, Paul's promise will become our reality:

If anyone is in Christ, the new creation has come: The old has gone, the
new is here! All this is from God, who reconciled us to Himself through
Christ and gave us the ministry of reconciliation: that God was reconciling
the world to Himself in Christ, not counting people's sins against them! (2
Corinthians 5:17-19)

Amen! Now that we know the basis of our invasion of light, let's consider
God's strategy for advancing the ministry of reconciliation. We find this strategy
in the Great Commission.

CHAPTER SEVEN

THE BATTLE PLAN OF THE INVASION: THE GREAT COMMISSION

Before Jesus returned to Heaven, He gave His disciples crystal clear instructions on how to advance the invasion of light through the ministry of reconciliation. In the Great Commission, He instructed them *how to invade, where to invade, what signs they should expect as they invade, and the harvest they'll reap as they invade.* As Jesus outlined in Mark 16:15-18:

> Go into all the world and preach the gospel to all creation. Whoever believes and is baptized will be saved, but whoever does not believe will be condemned. And these signs will accompany those who believe: In My name they will drive out demons; they will speak in new tongues; they will pick up snakes with their hands; and when they drink deadly poison, it will not hurt them at all; they will place their hands on sick people, and they will get well.

Jesus didn't only leave these commands for His inner circle. He gave the Great Commission as a blueprint for the invasion of light in any age of history. You see, when we bowed the knee to Jesus Christ, God dubbed us "the light of the world" (Matthew 5:14). Jesus transformed our lives, reconciled us to God, and has now entrusted us with the "light of the gospel of the glory of Christ" (2 Corinthians 4:4 NKJV). But Jesus didn't grant us His glorious light just to use it on ourselves. As He exhorts us in the Sermon on the Mount:

> You are the light of the world. A town built on a hill cannot be hidden! Neither do people light a lamp and put it under a bowl. Instead they put it on its stand, and it gives light to everyone in the house! In the same way, let your light shine before others, that they may see your good deeds and glorify your Father in Heaven. (Matthew 5:14-16)

Yes, God bestowed this glorious light so we would shine it in the darkness! He doesn't want us to sit tight until the whole world sinks to Hell—"He has committed to us the message of reconciliation" (2 Corinthians 5:19), and has called us to "proclaim the excellencies of Him who called [us] out of darkness into His marvelous light!" (1 Peter 2:9 ESV). Let's unpack Jesus's words to learn how best to fulfill this heavenly calling to invade with light.

WHAT WE MUST DO WITH THE LIGHT: GO

To invade our world with light, the first thing we must do is *go*—we must take up the light, go where souls suffer Satan's darkness, and shine the light for all to see. The invasion of light rarely advances through a stationary Christian! As William Booth so powerfully exhorted, we must "go straight for souls, and go for the worst!"

The word "go" encapsulates the call to invade with light more powerfully than almost any other. In only one syllable it rallies God's armies to movement and momentum. Without an ounce of eloquence it forever condemns complacency and passivity. And it's a command, not a suggestion; a required course, not an elective. When Jesus called us to go, He meant *we must forge the invasion of light*, not just *wait for God to do it*. No excuses will do—He said *go*, which means the invasion of light depends upon our action!

In fact, the very definition of "invade" implies going. According to encyclopedia. com, to invade is to "enter a country or region so as to subjugate or occupy it."[1] To invade with light, we must *boldly go* into Satan's territory to push back the invasion of darkness by Jesus's authority. Only, contrary to the common meaning of *invade*, we don't go to gain power and subjugate human souls. Rather, we invade the strongholds of Satan to reclaim what belongs to God—to liberate Satan's captives and win back those God created for His glory! We invade the darkness as liberators and emancipators, not as rulers and taskmasters; as agents of light and freedom, not of darkness and oppression! And as we approach Satan's citadels, we can always surge forward with confidence in Jesus's promise—we're God's church, and "the gates of Hades shall not prevail against" us (Matthew 16:18 NKJV)! Satan's kingdom cannot withstand the advances of a Christian empowered by the Holy Spirit!

In the Great Commission, the word translated "go" is *poreuthentes* (πορευθέντες), which means *to depart*.[2] As kingdom ambassadors, God requires us to depart to another place to represent His kingdom. As you invade, God may not require you to depart from your country or even your city—but believe us, He will require you to depart from your comfort zone. To live as a faithful ambassador, you must leave behind comfortable living, go to those who disagree with and dislike you, and represent God's kingdom the way God reveals in the Bible. If you will, you can rest assured that God will shine His light through you. If you won't, don't expect to see God move in your surroundings. There's no other way to fulfill this heavenly call!

WHERE WE MUST GO WITH THE LIGHT:
INTO ALL THE WORLD

Next, Jesus tells us where to invade with light—we must "go into all the world" (Mark 16:15). Remember, God wants His kingdom to come and His will to be done all over the Earth, not just here and there. As of now, "the whole world is under the control of the evil one" (1 John 5:19). To complete our redemptive mission, then, we must reach every geographical location with Jesus's message of liberation.

Tragically, the modern church has lost its way in this regard. For centuries, the church sent out its best workers to evangelize the former frontier lands of Central America, South America, Africa, and the like. By martyrs' blood and gospel preaching, our spiritual ancestors gradually discipled entire continents to Jesus Christ. How powerful to see the invasion of light in motion! But at a certain point, Heaven's ambassadors decided to put down their tents and go no further, drowning certain people groups in light and leaving others to suffer in darkness. To this day, 96.7% of Christian missionaries labor in those prior "frontiers," which now have very few unreached people at all. Meanwhile, the unreached world has only 1 Christian missionary for every 216,300 people.[3] So much for going into the whole world!

These harsh realities force us to face an uncomfortable truth—the church should not send another two thousand mission teams to Guatemala, Nicaragua, or Uganda this year. Of course, God will continue to send out strategic messengers to those areas; we would never deny that, and we don't mean to devalue any work you've done there, as we've labored in some of those vineyards too. We simply mean that the church must radically shift its resources towards those who have never yet heard Jesus's name, forging invasions of light in the regions that have most suffered satanic darkness. Jesus commanded us to do everything in our power to send the gospel to every person in the world—and if we don't submit to Jesus's worldwide plan, we're sinning and standing in His way! As Heaven's ambassadors, we all must play a role in this crucial shift—by going, giving, or praying. It's time to invade the world's darkest places with light!

HOW TO SHINE THE LIGHT:
BY PREACHING

Then how do we shine the light of Christ? Jesus tells us—"Go into all the world and *preach*" (Mark 16:15). Psalm 119:130 declares, "The unfolding of your words gives light; it gives understanding to the simple." As we discussed, when we preach God's Word, the Holy Spirit shines His light on human hearts, showing them the way to salvation, freedom, and reconciliation with God. The Lord invades our world with light when we go into dark places and speak forth the light of His Word! As Paul declared, "We are therefore Christ's ambassadors, as though God were making His appeal through us" (2 Corinthians 5:20). What a glorious gift—yet so often neglected!

We'll tell you the sad truth: most who do go into all the world only do social work when they get there. We've personally witnessed that many missionaries preach very little, though they offer all kinds of charitable services. This is both a terrible tragedy and a fundamental neglect of God's blueprint for personal and societal transformation. Jesus explicitly commanded: "Go into all the world and preach the gospel to all creation" (Mark 16:15). As Heaven's ambassadors, whatever public service we offer must lead to the clear proclamation of the message of salvation and reconciliation. If we deny that call, God will have to use someone else to shine His Word in our surroundings. Any ambassador who refuses to clearly preach the good news has officially excused himself or herself from God's invasion of light.

What does it mean to *preach*, then? The New Testament Greek word for "preach" is *kérussó* (κηρύσσω), which means "to herald, publish, or proclaim."[4] In the first century, political officials called heralds would travel to busy areas and raise their voices high to announce good news from their king. In the same way, Jesus requires us to go into the public square and passionately announce good news about His kingdom to dying souls. This is the only way the masses can receive liberation from Satan's clutches! As Paul declared:

> How, then, can they call on the one they have not believed in? And how can they believe in the one of whom they have not heard? And how can they hear without someone preaching to them? (Romans 10:14)

Many of Christ's ambassadors openly reject this high and lofty call, retorting—"Preach the gospel, use words when necessary!" This catchphrase isn't necessarily bad in itself—the Bible agrees we should be "zealous for good works" (Titus 2:14 NKJV), and sometimes God can use our good deeds to soften hearts to the good news. But make no mistake—good works are a terrible excuse for evangelistic silence. Remember, the word "preach" always implies "speech"; and not only dead words, but passionate proclamation! You can speak without holy passion, but you can't proclaim or herald without it. Knowing this, be sure to offer yourself as an instrument of God's truth wherever He places you. You'd be surprised what powerful things God can do through even the weakest testimony!

THE LIGHT TO SHINE: THE GOSPEL

Next, Jesus tells us *what we must preach* to effectively invade with light: "Go into all the world and *preach the gospel*" (Mark 16:15). We must always remember what light God calls us to carry—"the light of the gospel of the glory of Christ" (2 Corinthians 4:4 NKJV). God has called us to "open their eyes and turn them from darkness to light, and from the power of Satan to God, so they may receive forgiveness of sins and a place among those who are sanctified by faith in [Jesus]" (Acts 26:18). Yes—you are called to "open their eyes and turn them from darkness to light!" To do this, you must share the message of salvation and reconciliation— the only message that allows people to "receive forgiveness of sins and a place among those who are sanctified by faith in Jesus."

Paul declared that God "gave us the ministry of reconciliation . . . and has committed to us the message of reconciliation" (2 Corinthians 5:18-19). The Greek word here translated "gave" comes from *didōmi* (δίδωμι), which means *to bestow upon, to grant, to yield,* or *to deliver*.[5] The gospel is no mere trinket, but a sacred gift God has *bestowed* upon every believer for their personal invasion of light. For this reason, we must *never* make it secondary to other messages and ideas. Like Paul, we must cherish it as "of first importance" (1 Corinthians 15:3) and joyfully proclaim it to all who will listen.

You see, as soldiers of God, we must lose our maverick mindset and learn to obey orders. God never called us to declare whatever spiritual ideas pop into our little hearts. Rather, He specifically called us to "preach the gospel" (Mark 16:15). The gospel—the message of salvation and reconciliation through Jesus—is the great force behind every genuine invasion of light. It alone is "the power of God to salvation for everyone who believes" (Romans 1:16 NKJV). No other message can save souls, transform lives, restore rebellious societies, and defeat the Kingdom of Darkness! Then what a tragedy if we fail to preach it! As we invade with light, we must lay every other message to the side and preach the gospel with laser focus. (We discuss how to do this in the following several chapters.)

Tragically, very few have learned to prioritize this all-important message. All too often, Christians sidetrack the lost with other themes, riffing passionately on pet doctrines, non-essentials, cheap inspirational talk, and spiritual self-help. They speak at length about how to improve your marriage, how to get more money, how to improve your family relationships, how to receive divine healing, and so much more. While some of these teachings may have value for sincere believers, it's usually misguided to preach such things to the unsaved. God didn't call us to go into all the world and preach good marriage, good finances, and good family—He called us to go into all the world and preach good news! As Oswald J. Smith declared, "Our work is to preach the gospel, and we must not be sidetracked!" Then let us get to the work, and never allow Satan to divert our invasion strategy again.

THE PROOF OF THE LIGHT:
DEMONSTRATIONS OF GOD'S POWER

Next, Jesus commands us to demonstrate the truth of the gospel by carrying His miraculous power. In Mark's record of the Great Commission, Jesus makes a shocking promise: "These signs will accompany those who believe: In My name they will drive out demons; they will speak in new tongues; they will pick up snakes with their hands; and when they drink deadly poison, it will not hurt them at all; they will place their hands on sick people, and they will get well" (Mark 16:17-18). Yes, Jesus promises to work wonders we never imagined for His glory as we invade with the light of the gospel! And His promise implies a command—we must seek to become vessels of His miraculous power. Jesus sends us out much like He sent the twelve: "As you go, preach, saying, 'The Kingdom of Heaven is at hand.' Heal the sick, cleanse the lepers, raise the dead, cast out demons. Freely you have received, freely give" (Matthew 10:7-8 NKJV)!

Miracles, healing, and demonic deliverance are very controversial themes in the modern church, but they shouldn't be. As the late Derek Prince often pointed out, the New Testament offers no example of ministry without miracles. Jesus worked miracles. The apostles worked miracles. "Everyday" Christians were even used by God to work miracles (remember when God used regular-old Ananias to restore Paul's sight in Acts 9:10-18?). Church history fails to record a time when miracles ceased! Christian history is the history of miracles. Why should it all stop now?

We don't write this to win a theological debate, but to point back to the biblical blueprint for the invasion of light. Miraculous ministry is part of the Great Commission and is therefore crucial to our mission. Miracles are not fireworks for super-Christians. They are signs of Jesus's saving power, meant to draw attention to the most important message in the Universe: King Jesus died and rose again to save all men from sin and judgment and reconcile them to the God of love. Therefore, we should seek to operate in divine healing, deliverance, word of knowledge, and other biblical gifts whenever God provides opportunity as a testimony to the salvation message.

With that glorious truth considered—have you ever tried praying for a sick person? Maybe that step seems too frightening for you. Why not study the Bible's teaching about God's miraculous power with an open heart? If you seek God for His power and study God's Word for His methods, He will surely give you His blessing in due time. We've not provided an in-depth study of the Bible's approach to miraculous ministry in this book, but we plan to tackle it in future publications.

It's inevitable that some of our readers don't believe in the continuation of the gifts of the Spirit today. If that's you, let's at least agree on this—God wants to invade our world with light, He often invades in miraculous ways, and those acts of God testify wonderfully to Jesus's love and power. Knowing that, let's be bold and trust God to do amazing things to reveal His power to the lost world. Can it hurt to pray big prayers?

HOW TO SEAL THE INVASION: BAPTIZE NEW BELIEVERS

Sixth, Jesus tells us how to liberate those who want to escape the slavery of Satan—we must baptize them in water. In Matthew 28:19, Jesus says, "Go and make disciples of all nations, baptizing them in the name of the Father and of the Son and of the Holy Spirit." In Mark 16:16, Jesus promises that "whoever believes and is baptized will be saved, but whoever does not believe will be condemned." The truth is clear—if we don't baptize new believers, we've failed to obey the Great Commission.

The New Testament teaches that baptism is an important part of becoming a Christian. Therefore, it must play a prominent role in the modern invasion of light. On the Day of Pentecost, Peter told the masses how to receive salvation: "Repent and be baptized, every one of you, in the name of Jesus Christ for the forgiveness of your sins. And you will receive the gift of the Holy Spirit" (Acts 2:38). When Ananias led Paul to Christ, he exhorted him clearly: "Get up, be baptized and wash your sins away, calling on his name" (Acts 22:16). In Romans 6,

Paul pinpoints the moment we begin a new life in Christ: "We were . . . buried with Him through baptism into death in order that, just as Christ was raised from the dead through the glory of the Father, we too may live a new life" (Romans 6:4). It seems the modern church has seriously overlooked the importance of baptism in our mission.

Now, we'll be clear. Water cannot save you; only blood—the blood of Jesus. But in baptism, we make "an appeal to God for a good conscience—through the resurrection of Jesus Christ" (1 Peter 3:21 NASB). Baptism is the biblical "sinner's prayer." For this reason, whenever we win someone to the Lord, we should seek to baptize them in the name of the Father, Son, and Holy Spirit as soon as possible. Only, we should make sure the new believer enters the water in true repentance and faith, trusting God to cleanse their conscience and renew their inner man. Anyone can baptize—an everyday believer baptized the Apostle Paul. What stops us from leading someone to Christ biblically?

Perhaps you'll enter situations where it's impossible to conduct immediate baptisms. For example, perhaps you lead someone to Christ from a distance or on a plane, making baptism impossible. Or maybe you find yourself on a fast-paced mission trip from village to village, and your schedule doesn't permit you to baptize personally. In these cases, we suggest you urge new believers to seek baptism in their new home church as soon as possible. In missional settings, we suggest you communicate with local pastors ahead of time who can contact new converts and baptize them as soon as possible. This way, you can continue preaching the good news, and the new believers can experience a "normal Christian birth."

HOW TO ESTABLISH THE INVASION: TEACHING
THEM TO OBSERVE ALL JESUS COMMANDED

Finally, as we invade with light, Jesus commands us to establish His movement long-term by discipling those who receive Christ. God doesn't only want us to lead people to reconciliation with Himself—He wants us to teach people how to walk in reconciliation. That's why Jesus commands us, "Go and make disciples of all nations . . . teaching them to obey everything that I have commanded you" (Matthew 28:19-20).

In the late 1800s, Evangelist William Booth warned, "The chief danger that confronts the coming century will be religion without the Holy Ghost, Christianity without Christ, forgiveness without repentance, salvation without regeneration, politics without God, Heaven without Hell." Booth sure got it right. In the last century, Christian missionaries have exported a powerless gospel more than ever before. This gospel omits the call to repent of past sins and follow Jesus in obedience by life or by death. It offers peace, joy, and happiness, but doesn't warn of persecution, temptations, and trials. As a result, the world has more professing Christians than ever—but in many places still has shockingly few fiery disciples of Christ. This will never do! To forge a biblical invasion of light, we must not only win converts but disciples—true Christians who have died upfront, choosing to spend their lives learning how to follow Jesus Christ.

Perhaps we've forgotten this call more than any of the others. Today, if you begin to teach Jesus's commands, many cry, "Legalist!" If you focus too much on the Sermon on the Mount, others cry, "You're giving us law, not grace!" But if we would obey the Great Commission of our Lord, we must teach new believers "to observe all that [Jesus] has commanded" (Matthew 28:20). Of course, we must ground our hearers in the love and grace of God—but we must also show them how to properly respond to God's grace: "I appeal to you . . . brothers, by the mercies of God, to present your bodies as a living sacrifice, holy and acceptable to God, which is your spiritual worship" (Romans 12:1 ESV). If we don't, we'll never successfully push back against the invasion of darkness—the darkness will always creep back in among our ranks.

Many shy from personal discipleship because of its difficulty. It's dirty. It takes time, patience, and wisdom. Even more, it requires consecration. To teach another obedience to Christ, you must first obey Christ. If you don't, your disciples will quickly see through the ruse and lower their expectations for holiness. Therefore, perhaps the Great Commission contains an eighth, hidden command: Give your all to Jesus. Follow Him day in and day out. Let His hope and light restore you. Let His Word transform you. Soon, you may find it hard to keep His glorious message hidden away!

THE HARVEST GUARANTEED

We've unpacked the ministry of reconciliation and revealed Jesus's basic strategy for the invasion of light. Then what results should we expect when we follow His battle plan? What will happen when we invade our dark world with the message of reconciliation? Jesus tells us plainly: "Whoever believes and is baptized will be saved, but whoever does not believe will be condemned" (Mark 16:16). In other words, if you biblically invade with light, *the harvest is guaranteed*. Yes, some will reject Christ and receive the judgment they've earned—but others will receive Christ and experience glorious salvation by grace. Every Christian should take great comfort in this truth.

You see, many ambassadors of Christ draw back from sharing the gospel because they fear no one will respond. Likewise, Christians often refuse to follow up on spiritual encounters with loved ones because *they didn't seem to respond*. Instead of drawing back, we should remember God's promise: "At the proper time we will reap a harvest if we do not give up" (Galatians 6:9).

Christian history proves the truthfulness of this divine promise. The Prophet Jeremiah saw very little fruit in his day, but now God's words through him have transformed millions of lives. Jesus died rejected, scorned, and martyred, but soon His gospel changed the whole world. Many frontier missionaries never won a single convert—but their prayers, preaching, and pious example paved the way for national awakening in future generations. God crafted these powerful examples to help every sincere ambassador grasp His promise: "My word that goes out from My mouth . . . will not return to Me empty, but will accomplish what I desire and achieve the purpose for which I sent it" (Isaiah 55:11). It's with such figures in mind that Tertullian declared, "The blood of the martyrs is the seed of the church." Truly, God often turns earthen failure into heavenly success. Knowing this, we should boldly invade the darkness with gospel light, never fearing how people will respond.

It also helps to remember that *no one* has ever heard the gospel without responding. Every person who has ever heard the gospel has responded with either a "yes" or a "no"—for God doesn't accept "maybe" as an answer. All who answer "maybe" actually answer "not now"—and Jesus declared, "Whoever is not with Me is against Me, and whoever does not gather with Me scatters" (Matthew 12:30). For this reason, Paul declared, "The message of the cross is foolishness to those who are perishing, but to us who are being saved it is the power of God" (1 Corinthians 1:18).

Ultimately, we must remember that conversion does not depend on the ambassador but on the hearer and the Holy Spirit. Jesus said, "No one can come to Me unless the Father who sent Me draws them, and I will raise them up at the last day" (John 6:44). Only God can draw men to Himself; but God's Word spoken God's way will convict the hearts of men and women, shine the light of the gospel, and drive home the call to repent and be reconciled to God. Once God has done this special work, people can only say "yes" or "no." As Heaven's heralds, we only have to hear God's missionary call and obey at all costs. Take heart—if you faithfully invade with light, God will grant you fruit sooner or later!

MINISTERING FROM GOD'S HEART OF RECONCILIATION

Now, let's shortly consider the heart we need as we pursue this ministry of reconciliation. You see, though only God can draw men to Himself, you can get in God's way if you don't minister with His heart. Unbiblical preaching and living can act as roadblocks to the invasion of light. If God is love (1 John 4:8), He will not bless us if we speak with hatred. If we live like the devil, people will not believe what we say about God. That's why Paul declared, "We put no stumbling block in anyone's path, so that our ministry will not be discredited" (2 Corinthians 6:3).

If you preach the gospel in a condemning attitude or without a clear call to reconcile with God, you'll very likely put a stumbling block before many. For this reason, we need to see people with God's eyes of reconciliation no matter how they respond to us. We can't count their sins against them by thinking of them as merely alcoholics, drug addicts, adulterers, liars, or thieves. Rather, we must see them as lost sinners whom God wants to find and reconcile to Himself. We must preach the message of reconciliation with God's heart of reconciliation and plead with them to repent and "be reconciled to God" (2 Corinthians 5:20).

In Peru, I (Brian) once met a man named Jesús. One day, he came up to us staggering drunk, and mumbled—"I want to work." At that time, I said to him, "Jesús, if you come back tomorrow sober, we will get you a job." We shared the gospel with him, cleaned him up, and he seemed to follow the Lord for a time. But after many years, I saw him again—and this time he had fallen into drunkenness once more. When I saw him stumbling around from alcohol use again, I had a choice: I could see him as Jesús the drunk, or I could see him as Jesús, the man who needs Jesus.

The truth is, we all have people like Jesús in our lives, and we need to bring *Jesus* to them. Remember, your first calling isn't your job or your education but your heavenly mandate as Jesus's ambassador. For this reason, we must learn to drop what we're doing to proclaim to each person with God's heart of urgent love. After all, your hearer may never have a chance to respond to Christ again. Do you want to thwart their last chance by a bad attitude, an ungodly life, or an apparent lack of urgency?

THE AMBASSADOR'S MOTIVATION

Now, let's discuss motivation. What should motivate us as we invade with light, boldly heralding the message of God's kingdom? What will shoot us forth as arrows from God's quiver? What will help us keep our hand to the plow as we dedicate our lives to destroying the works of Satan through the ministry of reconciliation? Here I (Brian) want to present two biblical motivations for our mission.

GOD'S LOVE SUSTAINS US

The first motivation Paul prescribes for Heaven's ambassadors is *God's love for us*. Many try to minister to others without truly experiencing a love relationship with God for themselves. But Paul teaches us that we must experience God's love before we can share God's love. In 2 Corinthians 5:18, he says that "God . . . reconciled us to Himself through Christ and gave us the ministry of reconciliation."

You see, when we surrender our lives to Jesus Christ, God reconciles us to Himself by wiping away all of our sins and making us a new creation. At that very moment, we are born again into the Kingdom of God, and we can experience the fruit of Jesus's victory over sin and death. This is wonderful news, but few believers understand it by personal experience. If we want any success or endurance in the ministry of reconciliation, we need to understand and experience the gospel of reconciliation for ourselves by spending quality time with the Lord. After all, Jesus gave His very life for us on the cross to make us friends with God. Are you running on empty as an ambassador for Christ? Maybe you need to return to your first love by seeking the Lord in a fresh way (see Revelation 2:1-7).

CHRIST'S LOVE COMPELS US

The second motivation Paul prescribes for Heaven's ambassadors is *Jesus's love for the lost*. In 2 Corinthians 5:14-15, Paul says, "For Christ's love compels us, because we are convinced that one died for all, and therefore all died. And He died for all, that those who live should no longer live for themselves but for Him who died for them and was raised again."

I want you to realize that God must release something very important into your life before you can effectively serve as an ambassador of Christ's kingdom—the love of Christ. His love alone will give you the strength to fulfill your divine mission to invade with light. His love alone will compel you to go after the lost and hurting of this world.

I (Brian) live in Florida, where NASA launches space shuttles into space from Cape Canaveral. Fairly often, NASA used to send astronauts up to work on the space station, and then they would come back in the same ship. One day, the Lord spoke to me as I watched the shuttle rise into the air. I realized that just as the spaceship needed the correct fuel to leave the atmosphere, I needed the right fuel to leave my comfort zone and reach the lost. The Lord seemed to say to me: "Only My love will compel you to go out into the world. Only My compassion will compel you to keep reaching out to the lost. Even when you're rejected, you won't give up if you are truly compelled by My love." I realized it was *love* that propelled Jesus through His great sufferings till He finally cried out, "It is finished." In the same way, we must receive Jesus's love for others to finish the work God has set out for us.

A CHALLENGE TO GOD'S AMBASSADORS

As God's ambassadors, we must be brave and stay true to our heavenly call. We must not be like little princes and princesses, who have the royal name but no royal authority or royal deeds. Many reading now are ambassadors of Jesus Christ by name—but are you walking it out? If not, it's not very useful to call yourself His ambassador!

I want to ask you some questions as an ambassador of Jesus Christ. Are you ready to present the gospel to someone? When was the last time you preached the full message of reconciliation to an unbeliever? Have you studied the Word to sound the depths of this glorious message of salvation? God has committed the message and ministry of reconciliation to you, and you need to take His call seriously. You can't expect someone else to fulfill *your role* in God's invasion of light. Now is the time to step up into your destiny as an ambassador of God's kingdom—and the following chapters will help you do just that. Be bold, trust God, seek the Spirit's power, and step out on a limb for the truth of Jesus Christ. You'll never regret it!

CHAPTER EIGHT

THE MESSAGE OF THE INVASION: 5 Ps OF BIBLICAL EVANGELISM

Several years ago, an American ministry planned a mission of historic size to a Latin American country. They spent copious amounts advertising their events, declaring everywhere that God would save *the whole country*. National news organizations welcomed the mission leaders on national television. Renowned Christian leaders endorsed their efforts. Hundreds of native church leaders gathered to fast and pray for months in advance. A speaker for the movement declared to a room of cheering Christian ministers: "This nation will never be asleep again!" No matter where they spoke, they gave a clear, singular message: this team would forge a historic invasion of light that would change the nation's destiny.

Finally, the day came. Thousands of missionaries invaded the country, claiming to bring a message of "purpose and identity." Christians flooded every public school in the nation, singing happy songs, performing funny skits, and sharing what they called an "inspiring message" to every young person in the land. Not only so—many evangelists hit the streets to proclaim this "inspiring message" in the open air and through personal witness. To the average onlooker, this would seem like a tremendous opportunity. Through this giant crusade, the entire country could hear the gospel in mere days!

Unfortunately, it turned out as a missionary tragedy. Why? Because for the most part, this massive mission team preached a shallow, unbiblical gospel—self-esteem rather than salvation, and prosperity rather than penitence toward God. Their online evangelism training videos revealed a self-centered message almost devoid of Jesus's name (I [JJ] wept as I watched). I have a friend who ministers in that country, and he felt just as grieved at what he witnessed at an outdoor crusade. He told me:

> They did everything but preach the gospel. They didn't talk about Jesus hardly at all. They were almost like false prophets. What they did is promise [the country] that God was about to prosper them—that God didn't forget about them—but the problem is that most of [this country] is in idol worship and the worship of demons. So their prosperity ideas gave all of [the country] a false hope.

The mission came to its climax in this country's largest stadium. In the two-hour event, the preacher dedicated only ten minutes to the gospel message[1]—and though he likely meant well, he explicitly denied the biblical reality of God's wrath, neglected to clearly mention the danger of Hell, and didn't issue forth the urgent call to repent of sin. Despite his neglect, he announced his confidence that the whole country was on the brink of awakening. The zealous leader boldly declared: "Today is the first day of a new [country]!" Yes, today was a new beginning for the nation. From this day on, God would prosper them and bring them into His perfect plan. The Kingdom of God had come to the nation, and a brilliant future was to come! Or was it?

Fast forward ten months, when tragedy befell the land. In the spring, thousands filled the streets to protest this government's abusive policies. In response, the nation's leaders turned on many of its own people. Many were shot, thousands were injured, and several hundred were killed. The nation's economy continued to rush towards collapse, and the people's hopes ebbed to a historic low. The promised "new day" had not come (nor has it come to this day, as I write). *The nation had not been saved as promised.*[2]

THE FATAL FLAW

I have to ask—what happened to the shining message declared by those thousands of missionaries? What happened to the promises that God would prosper the nation? I want you to realize *exactly* where this invasion of light failed. This team received millions in missionary funding, spent hours in missionary training, and partook in detailed missionary planning. They even spent months in missionary fasting and prayer. Without a doubt, they had tremendous missionary sincerity—I'd never question that! But when their feet got on the ground, many of them failed the Lord of the Harvest by compromising the missionary message. Therefore, the people did not have the *good news* of salvation they would need in the trying times ahead. Instead, they had a message of *false comfort* that would *disappoint many* when trials and tribulations came.

What does this teach us? You can have all the planning in the world. You can have all the prayer in the world. You can have all the fasting in the world. Your outreach may produce miracles, tears, cheers, letters of recommendation, TV interviews, and best-selling worship albums. But if you compromise the message, you will inevitably leave sinners disappointed and souls streaming to Hell unwarned. I want to help you not to make that mistake. In the next few chapters, I will show you how to give a successful biblical gospel presentation anywhere in the world, therein forging your own genuine invasion of light.

I want to warn you ahead of time that I don't mean to merely provide a cut-and-dry evangelism script. While I will provide evangelism methods you can use in your invasion of light right away, I primarily intend to show powerful biblical principles you can apply in your own way by the Holy Spirit's leading.

Also, keep in mind that the Holy Spirit may lead you to apply these principles quite differently in various contexts—for example, from a pulpit, with a stranger, and with a lost spouse, friend, or family member. For example, He may lead you to speak very plainly and quickly with one, and guide you to a more gentle and long-term approach with another.

Finally, realize that the coming chapters offer an array of evangelism principles—a few of which may seem a bit advanced at this moment. That's all right; just apply what you can for now and begin winning souls. You don't have to cross every "t" and dot every "i"—just grasp the most crucial principles (reflected by the chapter titles themselves), and let God remind you of the others when needed. In time you'll master it all with prayer and practice. Finally, as you read each chapter, consider how you can wisely apply the principles to forge a successful invasion of light by God's power. Let's open the Bible to learn more about the crucial theme of biblical evangelism.

GOD'S MAP OF EVANGELISTIC SUCCESS

When we consider tragedies like the one we've discussed, we can't help but ask—where is the map to evangelistic success? If thousands of man-hours in prayer and fasting don't guarantee a true harvest; if millions of dollars in funding doesn't guarantee a true harvest; if the widespread support of evangelicals doesn't guarantee a true harvest; and if open doors in every part of a country don't guarantee a harvest—then what *will* guarantee a harvest? What will send throngs of souls genuinely running to the Savior, never to leave Him all their days? The answer is simple. *God's biblical promises* guarantee a harvest. To see the harvest God has promised, we need to act in accordance with His promises, not follow our own whims and ideas.

You see, the entirety of biblical evangelism is based on a principle: God is the one who saves souls, but we work along with Him in that process. As Jesus proclaimed, "No one can come to Me unless the Father who sent Me draws him; and I will raise him up on the last day" (John 6:44 NASB). Yet, as Paul declared, "We are God's fellow workers [in] God's field" (1 Corinthians 3:9 NKJV); "We are therefore Christ's ambassadors, as though God were making His appeal through us . . . Working together with Him, then, we appeal to you . . ." (2 Corinthians 5:20 NIV, 6:1 ESV). Yes, God saves souls through His divine appeal to the heart—but He wants to issue that divine appeal through you and me. Therefore, to evangelize successfully, we must lay aside *our own ideas about what the invasion of light should look like,* and instead study how *God has promised to appeal* through His ambassadors. Then, we must follow the breadcrumbs of His promises, pray for God to fulfill His Word, and appeal to the lost with the appropriate truths "in such a manner that a large number of people believe" (Acts 14:1 NASB).

I (JJ) don't teach this as an armchair theologian, but as one who has deeply studied the topic because I *needed* to find the Bible's teaching about effective evangelism. When I was a teenager, the Lord poured out a tremendous burden for lost souls over me—and compelled by His Spirit, I *had* to know how to reach them for Christ. Following this heavenly urge, I spent years devouring the best books on biblical evangelism I could find and constantly mining God's Word for the truth about effective soul-winning. I believe God has revealed some of those crucial principles to me, though I don't claim to have a corner on the subject. And both alone and alongside my dad, I've had the undeserved privilege to apply these principles by preaching the gospel to thousands around the world.

As we've applied these principles, we've often seen throngs of souls come to the Savior and enter into discipleship with local churches. (And other times, of course, we saw few results at all. That's ministry for you!). I've had the shocking privilege of seeing whole rooms flock to the altar, weeping in repentance and receiving Jesus's mercy. I've even seen pastors reconcile with other pastors, unreached village chiefs spontaneously proclaim their allegiance to Jesus, and timid teenagers suddenly open up like social butterflies after radically encountering the God of grace. I haven't only seen these truths in the Bible—I've seen them with my own eyes, and I firmly believe those results had nothing to do with me and everything to do with God's promises. In other words, God will use you to achieve the same results as you invade your surroundings with Jesus's light—though it may look quite different as God expresses Himself through your personality, gifts, and calling.

FIVE STEPS TO A GREAT HARVEST

Jesus gave four crystal-clear evangelism promises that I want to unpack in the coming chapters. These promises lead us to *five elements of a successful gospel presentation*; five steps towards a great harvest, or a successful invasion of light, if you will. They are as follows: First, the Holy Spirit will give us power. In Acts 1:8, Jesus promised: "You will receive power when the Holy Spirit has come upon you; and you shall be My witnesses both in Jerusalem, and in all Judea and Samaria, and even to the remotest part of the Earth" (NASB). Second, the Holy Spirit will convict of the problem of sin. In John 16:8, Jesus promised: "when [the Holy Spirit] has come, He will convict the world of sin, and of righteousness, and of judgment" (John 16:8 NKJV). Third, the Holy Spirit will testify of the promises of salvation in Jesus Christ. In John 15:26, Jesus promised: "When the Helper comes, whom I will send to you from the Father, that is the Spirit of truth who proceeds from the Father, *He will testify about Me*" (NASB). And fourth, by these divine appeals the Holy Spirit will draw men to practically respond to the gospel of Jesus Christ. Jesus promised, "I, if I am lifted up from the Earth, will draw all men to Myself" (John 12:32 NASB). In other words, Christ has promised to give every human being a sincere opportunity to respond to Him if we'll only faithfully proclaim the gospel.

From these promises, we can deduce five crucial parts of a successful gospel presentation or outreach. (You can also use a modified version of these five Ps when laboring for revival among backslidden Christians.)[3] I've organized them to all begin with the letter P as follows:

1. Receive God's <u>power</u>

2. Come to understand the <u>person</u>

3. Reason about the <u>problem</u>

4. Testify of the <u>promise</u>

5. Advise in the <u>practicals</u>

Let's dig into the scriptures to learn more in the following five chapters.

CHAPTER NINE

P #1: RECEIVE THE *POWER* OF THE HOLY SPIRIT

First, to pull in a great gospel harvest, we *must* receive the power of the Holy Spirit. If we fail here, our invasion of light will prove futile no matter how convincingly we speak. Remember, *God* is the one who appeals to the heart through our voices. Our words can have no effect if He hasn't taken powerful residence within us.

PENTECOST FIRST

The disciples felt more anxious to proclaim Jesus's truth than ever. They had just seen their Messiah rise from the dead, and Jesus had spent forty days with them unfolding the mysteries of the Kingdom of God. Now, they saw clearly that Jesus had come to show mercy to the whole world, emancipating souls from slavery to sin, liberating souls from their well-deserved judgment in Hell, welcoming souls into God's eternal family, and teaching every new believer to spread the blessing on all sides. The Messiah was not dead—He had risen again to restore the world from Heaven's throne! They wanted to tell every living soul the excellent news.

But Jesus forbid them from speaking yet. He told them:

This is what is written: The Messiah will suffer and rise from the dead on the third day, and repentance for the forgiveness of sins will be preached in His name to all nations, beginning at Jerusalem. You are witnesses of these things. I am going to send you what My Father has promised; but stay in the city until you have been clothed with power from on high. (Luke 24:46-49)

Yes, soon the disciples would powerfully announce Jesus's message of repentance toward God and restoration through the cross; but first, they needed to receive God's special equipment for the task. Jesus had promised it before His ascension: "You will receive power when the Holy Spirit comes on you; and you will be My witnesses in Jerusalem, and in all Judea and Samaria, and to the ends of the Earth" (Acts 1:8). Yes, when the Spirit came upon them, God would ignite their words with holy fire from Heaven; "for it will not be you speaking, but the Spirit of your Father speaking through you" (Matthew 10:20). No longer would their appeals spring from their own hearts and minds; they would speak "the very words of God" (1 Peter 4:11)! This could only result in either powerful harvest or radical upheaval, for God had declared, "'Is not My word like fire,' declares the LORD, 'and like a hammer that breaks a rock in pieces?'" (Jeremiah 23:29). Yes, soon, the Holy Spirit would send God's blazing word *through their lips* to "convict the world of sin, and of righteousness, and of judgment," "testify of [Christ]," and "draw all men to [Christ]" (John 16:8 NKJV, 15:26, and 12:32 NASB).

The results were well worth the wait. Only weeks before, Peter feared to testify of Christ before a little girl (see Luke 22:55-57). But as soon as the Spirit descended, God's boldness filled him, and He testified with piercing words to thousands complicit in Jesus's crucifixion (see Acts 2). As a result of this heavenly power, three thousand sinners fled to the Savior that day, so deeply convicted of sin and awakened to the reality of future judgment that they couldn't contain the cry, "Brothers, what shall we do?" (Acts 2:37). And the results didn't stop there. From that day on, "the Lord added to their number daily those who were being saved" (Acts 2:47), extending the harvest in every direction. As this victorious church continued in God's power, they invaded the whole world with light and transformed society as we know it.

Ah! What a glorious history. But it leaves me asking. Where is that power today? Where are the preachers who live as God's mouthpieces and welcome God's throne-room glory into our midst? Where are the messages that pierce hearts with unbearable conviction, stripping away every false hope and sending the lost fleeing to the Savior who loves them? Where are the heralds who preach Christ's message with heavenly clarity, striking eternal hope in the darkest hearts and setting souls ablaze with love for God? Where are the baptismal pools full of new believers who go down weeping in repentance and come up weeping for joy in God's salvation? Where are the altars full of souls flocking to the Savior in genuine surrender and faith? As Dr. Michael Brown asked in his book of the same title, "*Whatever happened to the power of God?*"

What is the source of our lack? It doesn't come from a change in God's power itself, for "Jesus Christ is the same yesterday and today and forever" (Hebrews 13:8). It doesn't stem from a change in God's promise, nor a change of dispensation, for "the promise [of the Holy Spirit] is for you and your children and for all who are far off—for all whom the Lord our God will call" (Acts 2:39). It surely doesn't come from a lack of activity, for the last two generations have had more activity than ever, but far weaker results (in the West at least). No, the true source of our lack is inside. *We have not sought the true power of God.*

God wants to move in the same power today as He did through the apostles, the early church, the reformers, and the revivalists of the two Great Awakenings. He has promised to "pour out [His] Spirit on all people" (Acts 2:17), bringing fruit where there is no fruit and more fruit where there is fruit—salvation for the lost, and revival for the saved. He revealed this unequivocally when He promised—when "the Spirit is poured on us from on high . . . the desert becomes a fertile field, and the fertile field seems like a forest" (Isaiah 32:15). He is ready, willing, and able to grant heavenly, historic power to our invasion of light! But first, we must see our lack, and seek His fire.

Do you find yourself too scared to witness? You need God's power. Do you find your words leave little effect on your hearers? You need God's power. Does your witness leave the lost feeling complacent instead of convicted? You need God's power. Do your encouraging words leave others feeling depressed instead of refreshed? You need God's power. Do you find you can't overcome the daily moral and mental battles you face? You need God's power. The Holy Spirit is the key to victory in our invasion of light. He sharpens our swords, trains our fingers for battle, fills us with heavenly light, and opens wide the doors of revival. With Him, we have no lack. Without Him, we have no life. God's Spirit transforms the weakest vessels into weapons of mass salvation!

HOW TO DRINK GOD'S LIVING WATER

Then how do we receive this glorious gift of God? We'll lay it out simply here. Both Dad (Brian) and I (JJ) have had the privilege of helping many encounter and receive the Holy Spirit, whether for the first time or for special refreshing. Here, I want to share simple truths we've used to lead others into God's powerful presence.

You see, Jesus made one promise that most clearly reveals how to receive the Holy Spirit's power so we can successfully invade the world with light. Speaking of the Holy Spirit, Jesus proclaimed: "If anyone is thirsty, let him come to Me and drink" (John 7:37 NASB). In this promise, we find three important keys to receiving the Spirit—whether for the first time, for refreshing, or for renewed spiritual impact. First, you must be thirsty—you must genuinely desire more of God and His power. Second, you must come to Jesus—you must believe Jesus wants to fill you now, surrender your life to His transforming power, and ask Him to immediately fulfill His promise and pour out His Holy Spirit. Third, you must drink—you must posture yourself to receive the Holy Spirit now by faith.[1] Only then will you have the power you need to push back the invasion of darkness. Let's dive deeper into these sacred conditions of personal revival and empowerment.

BE THIRSTY FOR GOD

First, *you must be thirsty for God.* In Psalm 42:1-2, David cried, "As the deer pants for streams of water, so My soul pants for you, My God. My soul thirsts for God, for the living God. When can I go and meet with God?" Many come to God to find something other than God Himself—perhaps happiness, a better family life, wealth, or some miraculous intervention. But to truly encounter the Holy Spirit, we must come to God for His own sake. Like David, we must pant after God's presence and renewing power, yearning to fathom the depths of His grace. In the same breath, we must yearn that He glorify Himself through our witness by drawing many souls to Himself. That kind of hunger for God's glory through the harvest is what drove John Knox to pray, "Give me Scotland or I die!"

Perhaps your thirst for God isn't as it should be. For now, don't overthink the depth of your desire. Simply ask this question—"Do I genuinely yearn for more of God's power and glory in my life? Also, do I genuinely desire to invade with light and win more souls to Jesus?" If so, then take heart—Jesus has promised you can come to Him and drink. If not, consider what's blocking your yearning for God. What act of lawlessness has made your love grow cold (see Matthew 24:12)? Repent at once and get it right. Then seek God's powerful presence again.

COME TO JESUS, THE BAPTIZER

Next, you must come to Jesus, the Baptizer. This implies three things: faith, repentance, and prayer.

First, you must *believe* Jesus is ready to fill you with fresh power from Heaven NOW. No obstacle exists on His side. The only obstacle is our own sin, unbelief, laziness, or lack of thirst. In Luke 11:13, Jesus revealed His infinite willingness to pour out the Holy Spirit on every needy soul: "If you then, though you are evil, know how to give good gifts to your children, how much more will your Father in Heaven give the Holy Spirit to those who ask Him!" (Luke 11:13). And Paul declared that we receive the Holy Spirit by "hearing with faith" (Galatians 3:2 NASB). If you would receive God's power, you must hear Jesus's promise and believe He meant it *for you. Right now*, Jesus is waiting to pour out His Spirit into the vessel of your heart. Believe it now, remove the obstacles you've placed in the way, and prepare to receive! Think of this like placing your heart as a cup under Jesus's barrel of living water.

Second, you must come to Jesus in *repentance*. You must *surrender your life* to Jesus, repenting of all sin, casting upon Him all your cares, forgiving all who've sinned against you, and adopting a desire for God to supernaturally transform you however He pleases. If you skip this crucial step, you can expect nothing from God's hands. Remember, God only gives "the Holy Spirit . . . to those who obey Him" (Acts 5:32). As Jesus promised: "If you love Me, keep My commands. And I will ask the Father, and He will give you another advocate to help you and be with you forever—the Spirit of truth" (John 14:15-17). The Holy Spirit comes to connect us with the Father, transform our lives, and give us power for witness. Why would God fill you if you don't desire to walk close to Him, live a holy life, and speak up for Jesus? With this considered, whenever I help someone receive the Holy Spirit, I lead them in a short prayer of absolute surrender toward God and forgiveness toward others. Think of this as removing waste from the vessel of your heart so Jesus can fill you to the top.

Third, *ask Jesus to immerse you in God's power*. Speaking of the Holy Spirit, Jesus promised, "Ask and it will be given to you; seek and you will find; knock and the door will be opened to you" (Matthew 7:7). Jesus later said, "If you then, though you are evil, know how to give good gifts to your children, how much more will your Father in Heaven give the Holy Spirit to those who ask Him!" (Luke 11:13). And as Acts 4:31 tells us, "*After they prayed*, the place where they were meeting was shaken. And they were all filled with the Holy Spirit and spoke the word of God boldly." Why don't many experience the Spirit's refreshing power? "You do not have because you do not ask God!" (James 4:2-3). As Isaiah 40:31 declares, "Those who wait for the LORD Will gain new strength; They will mount up with wings like eagles, They will run and not get tired, They will walk and not become weary!" (Isaiah 40:31 NASB). If you want the Holy Spirit to empower you to invade with light, then get alone with God, believe Jesus's promise, repent of your sins, and *pray for Jesus to fill you*. If you ask Him for the Holy Spirit, He won't give you a snake or a scorpion (i.e., a demon—see Luke 11:13). He'll give you the authentic Holy Spirit, with whom you can "trample on snakes and scorpions and . . . overcome all the power of the enemy" (Luke 10:19).

DRINK DEEP OF THE SPIRIT

There's only one more condition of receiving the Holy Spirit's empowerment for the invasion of light. You must drink—you must receive the Holy Spirit by faith. Many get stuck *right here*. They thirst after God, believe Jesus wants to give them living water, remove the inner obstacles so He can fill their cup, and pray for Jesus to pour out the Holy Spirit—but there's one problem: they leave a cap on the vessel of their heart. They *hope* Jesus will fill them at some point down the road, but don't take a drink for themselves right now! Instead, we must come to Jesus in an attitude of immediate expectation, opening our hearts wide and preparing for the heavenly downpour! Ambassador of God, don't just pray for rain—step under the Niagara of God's love and power!

Remember, God has been waiting for all eternity to fill you with the Spirit, "for He chose [you] in Him before the creation of the world to be holy and blameless in His sight" (Ephesians 1:4). Now, it's *your prerogative* to receive. As God commanded in Isaiah 55:1—"Come, all you who are thirsty, come to the waters; and you who have no money, come, buy and eat! Come, buy wine and milk without money and without cost!" I have seen this time and again—when we come before God in bold faith and open our hearts to Jesus's immediate refreshing, He often comes swiftly to heal, strengthen, refresh, and empower. Come on, Christians, let's dive into the refreshing power of the Holy Spirit! It's time to receive all we need for the battle for souls!

NEW HORIZONS IN GOD'S POWER

God will very likely fill you in some measure the very first time you call on His name. If so, you have the equipage to begin a more powerful invasion of light. But as you continue your mission, don't stop crying out for God's power. God wants to draw you closer, bring you deeper, fill you higher, and ignite your flame hotter.

He wants to saturate your words with more gospel power, ignite your heart with more gospel passion, and use you to win more gospel disciples so He can gain more gospel glory through the invasion of light. Oh, that we would live under the waterfall of God's glorious power; always amazed; always astonished; always passing "from glory to glory" (2 Corinthians 3:18 NKJV) in holiness, witness, and wisdom—all for the glory of the Lord alone!

A story from D.L. Moody's life shows the importance of continually seeking new horizons in God's power. Wesley Duewel recounts in *Ablaze for God*:

> Dwight L. Moody had already been greatly used by God in Chicago. Two humble Free Methodist women prayed faithfully for him during his Sunday services. At the close of the service they would say to him, "We have been praying for you." "Why don't you pray for the people?" Mr. Moody would ask. "Because you need the power of the Spirit," was the reply. "I need the power! Why," he said in relating the incident afterwards, "I thought I had power. I had the largest congregation in Chicago, and there were many conversions!"

> One day Moody said to them, "I wish you would tell me what you mean." And they told him about the definite infilling of the Holy Spirit. So he asked them to pray with him and not merely pray for him . . . Moody's own words were: "I was crying all the time that God would fill me with His Spirit. Well, one day, in the city of New York—oh, what a day!—I cannot describe it . . . I can only say that God revealed Himself to me, and I had such an experience of His love that I had to ask Him to stay His hand. I went to preaching again. The sermons were not different; I did not present any new truths; and yet hundreds were converted. I would not now be laced back where I was before that blessed experience if you should give all the world—it would be as the small dust of the balance."

Do you see what glorious power God desires to exercise through His ambassadors? So many of us are barely scraping by, but Jesus wants to accomplish "far more abundantly beyond all that we ask or think, according to the power that works within us"! (Ephesians 3:20 NASB). We must press into God's promise and receive greater and greater power from on high. We'll never succeed in spiritual battle in our own strength. We can forge a victorious invasion of light—but "'not by might nor by power, but by My Spirit,' says the LORD Almighty" (Zechariah 4:6). Amen!

CHAPTER TEN

P #2: UNDERSTAND THE *PERSON*

Once we've received the power of the Spirit, we're prepared to invade with light by the powerful proclamation of God's message. But we must not merely stand before the people and cast random spiritual ideas into the air. As Proverbs 11:30 declares, "He who wins souls is wise" (NKJV). In other words, *it takes wisdom to witness effectively*. And the wisdom of soul-winning begins with rightly understanding the person we speak to. As a skilled farmer studies soils, we must study souls. Only then can we properly remove obstacles, break up hard soil, sow liberally, water wisely, and reap a successful harvest.

In the parable of the sower, Jesus represents the evangelist as a sower (or farmer) and the lost world as *soil*. You've probably heard plenty of powerful messages about this parable, ranging on subjects from biblical evangelism, to sanctification, to rightly receiving God's Word. But if I preached a message about this passage, I (JJ) would title it, "How an Unwise Farmer Wasted Most of His Seed." Think about it—in this parable, the sower doesn't use an ounce of wisdom!

Sure, he casts some of his seed on good, tilled soil. Good job, brother. But then he does what any farmer would consider unthinkable. He leaves his farm and casts some seed beside the road (are you lost, there, sir?). Then he finds some rocky soil and throws it there for some reason. Then he finds a thorn bush, and says, "I think I'd like to see some wheat grow up here!" I wonder if Jesus told the story to make us laugh—because any of us would chuckle if we watched it in real life.

The farmer sowed a comedy but reaped a tragedy (how much like modern ministry!). Because he refused to wisely steward the seeds God granted—because he cast seed in every direction without understanding the soils—most of his seed produced no long-term fruit.

THREE-FOURTHS A FAILURE

Some have used this parable to suggest we should only expect one-fourth of Christian converts to stay true to God. According to this thinking, every invasion of light must always turn out three-fourths a failure! I simply can't buy that idea. If that's correct, why did the earliest church grow so powerfully and have so few quitters?[1] On the contrary, this parable suggests how to steward our seed well, evangelize wisely, and obtain a massive harvest. It teaches us a crucial message: *Only one type of soil bears fruit*, and as wise gospel farmers, we shouldn't waste our time throwing gospel seeds on rocks, thorns, and roadsides. If we "throw [our] pearls before swine . . . they will trample them under their feet" (Matthew 7:6 NASB), and we'll never see God move in salvation through our invasion of light.

Of course, in a way, we *ought* to broadly scatter seed, expressing God's Word in small statements wherever we go throughout the day without respect to the type of soil. And God's invasion of light definitely has plenty of room for building relationships, getting to know people, and sharing bite-sized truths along the way. But eventually, we must get to the more extensive work of *personally dealing with souls* with the intention of winning them to Christ. Once we do, instead of casting our seed in wasteful ways, we need the wisdom to identify *what obstacles exist in the soil*, "break up . . . fallow ground" by the Law of God (Hosea 10:12 NASB), and soon cast the supernatural seed of the gospel, which is "the power of God for salvation" (Romans 1:16 NASB). If we will, we have Jesus's own promise to back up our preaching: "And I, if I am lifted up from the Earth, will draw all men to Myself" (John 12:32 NASB). By God's grace, our invasion of light will succeed, and many will turn from sin to the loving Savior!

EXAMINING THE SOIL

Every soul is different, and therefore every soil is different. When we come into an evangelism encounter, we must ask—is the soil hard or soft? What obstacles, stones, and thorns stand in the way? And how, by God's power, can I remove them so my invasion of light can bear genuine fruit?

There are a few questions we might consider. First, what is their doctrine? What do they already believe about God, life, death, morals, the Bible, and the afterlife? Do they have any biblical context at all? If we fail to consider this, our seed will often die on the rocks. For example, if you preach a typical evangelistic message in the 10/40 Window, you'll leave people's heads spinning. Most there have never heard biblical words like Jesus, Heaven, Hell, cross, resurrection, repentance, faith, and salvation—so if you preach without explaining the ABCs, they won't have a clue what you mean. To reap a harvest there, you need to slow down, back up, and define your terms.[2]

Next, we might discern their state of religious devotion. Evangelist Steve Hill gave us a wonderful grid we can use to identify our audience. He taught that every audience holds only four types of people: on-fire Christians, backsliders, religious but unsaved persons, and unbelievers. In short, on-fire Christians need encouragement and activation; backsliders need the message of repentance and revival; religious but unsaved persons need to see through their false conversion or religion and come to the true Jesus; and unbelievers need to come to Christ for salvation, plain and simple.[3] These four categories prove incredibly helpful for both personal witness and mass evangelism.

Then, we might sometimes even consider the audience's emotional condition. Are they weary and war-torn, or pretty and puffed up? Have they had overly negative experiences with professing Christians? Have they experienced some particular trauma that Jesus wants to heal? These answers could radically change how you invade with light among different people groups and personalities.

THE MOST IMPORTANT QUESTION

But one question holds more relevance to our invasion strategy than any other. Does our hearer see their desperate need of Jesus's salvation?

You see, Jesus said, "The seed falling on good soil refers to someone who hears the word and *understands it*" (Matthew 13:23). What must they profoundly understand and respond to? "That Christ died for our *sins* according to the Scriptures" (1 Corinthians 15:3-8). Sinners will never *truly understand* this good news of *salvation, freedom*, and *reconciliation by grace* until they painfully understand the bad news of *damnation, slavery, and separation by sin*. Therefore, before we cast the happy seed of the gospel, we must test the soil for the hardness of self-righteousness and moral blindness.

We must discern—do they believe they're good enough for God, or do they see themselves as the sinners they truly are (just like us without Jesus)? Do they believe they've lived great lives and earned Heaven, or lived sinful lives and earned Hell? Do they believe God is pleased with them in their current state, or do they see they can never please God by their own merits? Are they deeply broken over their sins, or untouched by the conviction of the Holy Spirit? Do they desire freedom from the bondage of sin, or do they feel comfortable living in the mire? Do they see God or themselves as the great sovereign of their lives? Do they see Jesus's salvation as a life-saving necessity, or an unnecessary frivolity? Finally, are they willing to obey God, or are they continuing in rebellion against Him?

The answers to these questions will quickly show us the quality of the hearer's heart-soil. Once we know these facts, the Holy Spirit can guide us how to leverage God's Word to shatter the rocks (Jeremiah 23:29), remove the thorns, and break up the fallow ground of our audience's soul-soil (Hosea 10:12), preparing the way for the miraculous and joyous seed of the gospel. If we remove those obstacles and sow the gospel seed, "at the proper time we will reap a harvest if we do not give up" (Galatians 6:9). Take heart, ambassador of Christ—God will make your invasion of light a heavenly success if you only keep your hand to the plow of evangelism.

FINNEY TESTS THE SOIL AND REAPS A HARVEST

Nineteenth century evangelist Charles G. Finney knew the supreme value of understanding his audience. In fact, he believed no invasion of light could succeed without a thorough understanding of the people, their spiritual needs, obstacles, excuses, confusions, and convictions. For this reason, everywhere Finney preached, he talked with the common people so he could adapt his gospel presentation to their spiritual maladies. As a result, he often saw God move in historic power to save sinners and revive saints. One story from his life especially reveals the potential harvest power of *understanding the person.*

Nineteenth century lawyers were often hardened to the gospel. Most hid behind the deceptive refuge of intellectualism, atheism, and agnosticism. But Finney didn't feel intimidated when he received an invitation to preach a series of evangelistic meetings to men of the law. He was ready to invade with light! You see, Finney knew this hardened soil; he once studied law himself, and knew perfectly the excuses, refuges, and objections the law-trained mind would suggest against the gospel. As he recounted:

> I understood pretty well [lawyers'] habits of reading and thinking, and knew that they were more certainly controlled by argument, by evidence, and by logical statements, than any other class of men . . . I have often been very much affected, in conversing with members of the legal profession, by the manner in which they would consent to propositions, to which persons of ill-disciplined minds would have objected.

Understanding his law-trained audience, he took a fascinating approach quite different from his usual habit. Rather than burst right into the gospel, he began from *square one* of God's truth and logically reasoned his way into the salvation message, line upon line, precept upon precept. In his *Memoirs*, he recounted:

> I began my course of lectures to lawyers by asking this question: "Do we know anything?" To this question I gave an answer, and followed up the inquiry by lecturing evening after evening.[4]

He continued his ministry, tackling a new question with irrefutable logic every week. Soon, he approached pertinent spiritual issues, such as *the existence of God, the sin of man, the righteousness of God's judgments, the atonement of Christ,* and *unconditional surrender to God.* Every week interest deepened, and the Holy Spirit's conviction grew more profound.

Before long, a leading judge came to him in private, predicting Finney would *never* successfully resolve his objections. But Finney expounded God's truth with irrefutable clarity, and God sent waves of conviction over the judge and the whole audience. Soon, Finney had answered every reasonable doubt, and no one could bear to reject the Savior any longer. God's invasion of light was advancing in that courtroom, and none could deny it! Finally, the prominent judge quit resisting the Holy Spirit and publicly announced his desperate need of salvation in Jesus Christ. When the audience saw this, the whole room finally broke before God. Finney reported:

> When I announced to them what [the judge] said it produced a wonderful shock. There was a great gush of feeling in every part of the house. Many held down their heads and wept; others seemed to be engaged in earnest prayer. [The judge] crowded around in front of the pulpit, and knelt immediately down. The lawyers arose almost en masse, and crowded into the aisles, and crowded around the open space in front, wherever they could get a place to kneel, and as many knelt around Judge Gardiner as could. As the movement had begun without my requesting it, I then publicly requested that any who were prepared to renounce their sins and give their hearts to God, and to accept Christ and His salvation, should come forward—that they should get into the aisles, or wherever they could, and kneel down. There was a mighty movement. The congregation was moved to its profoundest depths, and the movement was among the principal citizens of Rochester.[5]

Yes, Finney studied the soil to identify every obstacle in the way of salvation. Then, he confidently invaded with light and reaped a massive harvest among one of New York's toughest classes. Praise God, some of those lawyers even left the courts to preach the gospel full-time! What a powerful Savior we have in Jesus!

Fast forward to today. Can you imagine a room full of hardened agnostics flocking to the altar in twenty-first century America? Why couldn't God achieve the same through a wise, empowered ambassador? "Jesus Christ is the same yesterday and today and forever" (Hebrews 13:8 NASB). The problem is simple: to this day, "the harvest is plentiful, but the workers are few" (Matthew 9:37 NASB). It's time to dream as big as God's power. Together, let's receive God's call, love souls, understand our hearers, and invade with light, preaching God's Word in the wisdom and power of the Holy Spirit.

QUESTIONS TO TEST THE SOIL

Now, you may say—"I want to successfully invade my surroundings with the light of the gospel. But before I plant the miraculous gospel seed, how can I measure the soil of the heart?" Well, evangelists have studied soul-soils in many meaningful ways, but I want to suggest a few tools often used to much success. These are simple, interesting questions that immediately reveal if our hearer is *humble or proud before God*; if they *see the reality of their sin* or not; if their soil is hard and patted down, needing raking, or open and broken, ready for gospel seed. They are as follows:

1. "Do you mind if I ask you an interesting question? If you died today, where would you go? To Heaven, or to Hell? Why do you say that?" Or…

2. "Do you mind if I ask you an interesting question? Do you see yourself as a good person? What about by God's standard? Do you believe you've kept the Ten Commandments?"

Sometimes I struggle to witness just as much as you might. But through the years, I've had the opportunity to personally ask these questions to hundreds of people—and I've almost always seen the same results. About 90% who respond to the first question say, "Of course—interesting question! I would go to Heaven because I'm a good person." And about 90% who respond to the second question say, "Of course I'm a good person! And yes, I believe God is pleased with me."

And there you go. I've tested the soil, and I already know what obstacles I must remove before I can effectively invade with the light of the good news.

Why? Because the Bible promises that *no one can receive salvation by being a good person*. Instead, "As many as are of the works of the Law are under a curse; for it is written, 'Cursed is everyone who does not abide by all things written in the book of the Law, to perform them" (Galatians 3:10 NASB). Yes, "by the works of the Law no flesh will be justified in His sight" (Romans 3:20 NASB), "for the Law brings about wrath" (Romans 4:15 NASB). Jesus died to save them from their sin, but they are blissfully unaware and unbothered by their rebellion against God and its terrible eternal consequence. I've tested the soil and have seen that my hearer has the hardened topsoil of *self-righteousness*; a subtle but fatal malady which only God's law can cure—for "through the Law comes the knowledge of sin" (Romans 3:20 NASB). Which leads me to the next step toward a successful invasion of light.

CHAPTER ELEVEN

P #3: REASON ABOUT THE *PROBLEM* OF SIN

Once we've received God's power and analyzed our soil, we can begin working the ground to prepare the way for the miraculous gospel seed. Before we can effectively invade with the light of the good news, we must simply and clearly reason with our hearer to help them understand the following spiritual problems:

1. They've sinned against their Creator.

2. They're enslaved to sin.

3. They live under the power of the Kingdom of Darkness.

4. God is just and must punish each of their crimes for all eternity—or else He wouldn't be just at all.

5. God is holy and can't have fellowship with sinners. Therefore, they're separated from God and can't know Him until they receive Jesus's cleansing.

What crucial tool has God granted to convey these truths? What spiritual instrument has God bestowed upon us to convict of sin, righteousness, and judgment, open blind eyes, awaken sleeping consciences, shut every proud mouth, and prepare the sinner for the glorious message of God's grace in Jesus Christ? Paul answers in Galatians: "*The Law* has become our tutor to lead us to Christ, so that we may be justified by faith" (Galatians 3:24 NASB). Do you want to invade with light and lead men to Christ? Prepare the soil of the conscience with God's law—the Ten Commandments, the universal moral precepts of the Old Testament, and Jesus's commands. Our hearer will never flee to Jesus's grace in grateful repentance until they feel the weighty problem of God's law and its righteous penalty.

THE LAW: UNPOPULAR BUT ESSENTIAL

The Law is not a popular tool these days. Just like the unwise sower, many of Christianity's most popular preachers prefer to ignore the soil and scatter gospel seed in all directions. They may mean well, but at the day's end, they're professional nice-guys for Jesus. They can't bear to take out the rake and break up hard ground in a compassionate and loving way—a solution that would actually produce long-term fruit and do their hearers some good. As a result, our generation has witnessed the very same tragic false harvest Charles Finney warned of:

> Evermore the Law must prepare the way for the gospel. To overlook this in instructing souls is almost certain to result in false hope, the introduction of a false standard of Christian experience, and to fill the church with false converts. Time will make this plain.[1]

Think about it. When we preach a lawless gospel, should we feel surprised at a lawless "church"? Modern Christians decry our lack of true growth, yet often refuse to preach the very messages that sent the lost running to Christ in sincere repentance throughout history. We must stop this travesty at all costs. Souls hang in the balance! We must not simply follow the trends of modern Christianity, but the promises of God Himself! And God has promised to use the Law in world-shaking harvest power as we invade the world with light. Without the bad news, the good news reads like yesterday's news.

THE BIBLICAL FUNCTIONS OF THE LAW

Consider some of the biblical functions of the Law. Do you really want your invasion of light to miss out on these shocking scriptural promises?

Through the Law, God silences every proud mouth and holds the whole world accountable. As Romans 3:19 declares, "Whatever the Law says, it says to those who are under the Law, so that every mouth may be silenced and the whole world held accountable to God."

Through the Law, God makes every blind sinner aware of his rebellion. As Romans 3:20 teaches, "Through the Law comes the knowledge of sin" (NASB).

Through the Law, God causes our awareness of trespasses to increase, making the message of grace sweeter. As Romans 5:20 says, "The Law was brought in so that the trespass might increase. But where sin increased, grace increased all the more."

Through the Law, God brings understanding of sin, for Paul says, "I would not have come to know sin except through the Law, for I would not have known about coveting if the Law had not said, 'You shall not covet'" (Romans 7:7 NASB).

And it's through the Law that God convicts us of sin: When the Law is preached, we're "convicted by the Law as lawbreakers" (James 2:9).

No wonder Paul saw the Law as an essential part of His gospel— saying, "the Law is . . . according to the glorious gospel of the blessed God" (1 Timothy 1:8-11 NASB):

> The Law is good, if one uses it lawfully, realizing the fact that law is not made for a righteous person, but for those who are lawless and rebellious, for the ungodly and sinners, for the unholy and profane, for those who kill their fathers or mothers, for murderers and immoral men and homosexuals and kidnappers and liars and perjurers, and whatever else is contrary to sound teaching, according to the glorious gospel of the blessed God, with which I have been entrusted!

THE MASS-HARVEST POWER OF GOD'S LAW

The scriptures drip heavy with accounts of the mass-harvest power of God's law. You can hardly find a biblical invasion of light that lacks it! When King Josiah first heard the words of the Law, "he tore his robes [and cried] 'Great is the Lord's anger that burns against us because those who have gone before us have not obeyed the words of this book!'" (2 Kings 22:11, 13). When the Prophet Nathan preached the Law to King David, he cried, "I have sinned against the Lord!" (2 Samuel 12:13). When John the Baptist preached the Law, the convicted crowds cried, "Then what shall we do?" (Luke 3:10 NASB). When Peter declared the crowds had committed idolatry and murdered Christ, "they were cut to the heart and said to Peter and the other apostles, 'Brothers, what shall we do?'" (Acts 2:37). When Jesus revealed the rich young ruler's greed and covetousness, "he went away grieving; for he was one who owned much property" (Matthew 19:22 NASB). When Paul "reasoned about righteousness, self-control, and the judgment to come, Felix was afraid" (Acts 24:25 NKJV). When Paul preached the Law to backsliders in the church of Corinth, they "were made sorrowful . . . to the point of repentance" (2 Corinthians 7:9 NASB).

All of these stories share a common thread—a preacher waxed bold enough to obey God, explain the reality of sin, and lovingly warn of impending judgment, invading with the piercing light of God's holy standard. As a result, God struck the hearer's conscience like a morning bell, disrupted their comfortable spiritual slumber, and forced them to face the question, "How can I be saved?" Those who then submitted to God treasured His eternal mercy as the glorious gift it truly is. What glorious testimonies of God's convicting power! And God will use us in the same ways if we humbly invade our world with the light of His holy law. The only question is—will we drop our fears and join God's army of faithful witnesses, or shrink back in fear of what others might say?

CO-LABORING FOR CONVICTION

Billy Graham famously said, "It's God's job to judge, the Holy Spirit's job to convict, and my job to love." I have tremendous respect for Billy Graham, so I don't mean to speak a word against him. But many Christians have taken his quote way too far. Whereas Billy likely meant we should lovingly preach the truth and leave the results to God, many abuse this quote to excuse their refusal to preach the hard truths of Jesus's message. This is a fatal mistake. Why? According to the scriptures, we *co-labor with Christ for conviction.*

Jesus gave a tremendous promise: "When [the Holy Spirit] has come, He will convict the world of sin, and of righteousness, and of judgment" (John 16:8 NKJV). Many assume this promise excuses them from preaching difficult truths as they invade with light. "If He will convict, I can just preach the love of God, right? He's on the job, so I don't need to speak any hard truths." Whoa, whoa, not so fast! Believe it or not, in a way, *God commands you to convict.* In 2 Timothy 4:2, Paul commanded: "Preach the word; be ready in season and out of season; <u>reprove</u>, rebuke, exhort, with great patience and instruction" (NASB). The Greek word here translated "reprove" comes from *elegcho* (ἐλέγχω)—the same exact root word as "convict" in John 16:8.[2] In other words, God commands *you* to play a role in His promised conviction. He will *convict* of sin, but you must *converse* about sin. To see God's conviction break up hard-soil, we must lovingly speak the truth so God will pierce the heart. That's one of your crucial roles in the invasion of light!

The author of Acts well understood our calling to co-labor for conviction. Though he hadn't yet read John's gospel,[3] he'd inevitably heard of Jesus's promise to "convict of sin, and of righteousness, and of judgment" (John 16:8 NKJV). Yet the author of Acts conveyed another crucial agent in the process of conviction—the Christian ambassador. Speaking of Paul, he said: "He reasoned about righteousness, self-control, and the judgment to come" (Acts 24:25 NKJV).

Yes, Paul reasoned about righteousness, self-control, and the coming judgment, and as a result, the Holy Spirit convicted of sin, righteousness, and judgment. What happened next in this invasion of light? "Felix was afraid and answered, 'Go away for now; when I have a convenient time I will call for you'" (Acts 24:25 NKJV). You see, Paul co-labored for conviction, so Felix had a genuine opportunity for conversion. Unfortunately, as far as we know, he rejected Christ and suffered eternal condemnation—but at least he had a chance. What if Paul had excused himself, saying, "It's God's job to judge, the Holy Spirit's job to convict, and my job to love?"

REASONING FOR REVIVAL

Now, you may ask, "How can I follow in Paul's footsteps and reason about righteousness, self-control, and the judgment to come? In my invasion of light, how can I reason to bring about revival like Paul?" We all know Paul preached with great power, winning great masses of souls almost wherever he went. But what in particular did he preach to spark such great invasions of light by God's power?

The book of Romans grants us a window into Paul's fiery evangelistic message. There, we see at length how he reasoned about sin, righteousness, and judgment. His law presentation to the Romans looked something like this:

1. First, he explained the fact of God's judgment.

2. Second, he explained the *manner* of God's judgment—that God would judge us by our deeds, by the measure of His law.

3. Third, he tested his hearers with God's law to reveal how they would fare on judgment day.

4. Fourth, he declared the obvious truth—without Christ, all of us deserve God's righteous punishment for sin.

Let's open Romans to consider some key points in Paul's presentation of the Law.

HOW PAUL PREACHED THE LAW

First, Paul established that God would judge all mankind by their deeds. Quite shocking to many, he began his presentation by expounding the heavy theme of God's wrath:

> The wrath of God is revealed from Heaven against all ungodliness and unrighteousness of men who suppress the truth in unrighteousness! (Romans 1:18 NASB)

Second, he explained the manner of God's judgment. He took pains to show that God will righteously judge us by our deeds, measuring us by His perfectly holy law. He revealed that God will grant each person an exacting punishment for their crimes against Heaven, and even explained the nature of that judgment, saying:

> In the day of wrath and revelation of the righteous judgment of God, [He] will render to each person according to his deeds: to those who by perseverance in doing good seek for glory and honor and immortality, eternal life; but to those who are selfishly ambitious and do not obey the truth, but obey unrighteousness, wrath and indignation. There will be tribulation and distress for every soul of man who does evil, of the Jew first and also of the Greek, but glory and honor and peace to everyone who does good, to the Jew first and also to the Greek. For there is no partiality with God. (Romans 2:5-11 NASB)

As Paul continued, he made no buts about God's holy standard. In all sobriety, he declared that God will judge absolutely everything we've done—even our secrets!

> For all who have sinned . . . will also perish . . . on the day when, according to my gospel, God will judge the secrets of men through Christ Jesus. (Romans 2:12, 16 NASB)

Third, he plowed his audience's hard soil. He asked if they had kept the Law, literally passing from commandment to commandment like the strike of a rake upon fallow ground:

> You who preach that one shall not steal, do you steal? You who say that one should not commit adultery, do you commit adultery? You who abhor idols, do you rob temples? You who boast in the Law, through your breaking the Law, do you dishonor God? (Romans 2:21-23 NASB)

Finally, he declared that all are condemned for their sin, and therefore need the salvation freely offered in Jesus Christ. He openly declared:

> There is none righteous, not even one; There is none who understands, There is none who seeks for God; All have turned aside, together they have become useless; There is none who does good, There is not even one. (Romans 3:10-12 NASB)

> For all have sinned and fall short of the glory of God, being justified as a gift by His grace through the redemption which is in Christ Jesus. (Romans 3:23-24 NASB)

I have to ask—does your evangelistic message sound anything like Paul's? If not, it's time to count the cost and imitate his example. In our invasion of light, we do well to "Follow [Paul's] example, as [he followed] the example of Christ" (1 Corinthians 11:1).

THE SAVIOR AND THE SINNER

Jesus took a similar approach in His invasion of light. I'd remind you that the entire Sermon on the Mount was a commentary on the Law of God—He preached the Law to prepare His hearers for the coming message of grace. But one passage in particular unveils how Jesus preached the Law in individual encounters. Consider this shocking interaction between the Savior and a sinner from the book of Luke.

Once a rich young ruler approached Jesus, asking, "Good teacher, what must I do to inherit eternal life?" (Luke 18:18). Jesus tested his soil and observed he needed the rake of the Law, not yet the seed of the gospel. In love, He started to break the young man's hardened ground, testing him by the Ten Commandments to open his eyes to the danger of sin. He said to the young man:

> You know the commandments: "You shall not commit adultery, you shall not murder, you shall not steal, you shall not give false testimony, honor your father and mother." (Luke 18:20)

At first, the young man didn't experience any conviction of sin. Blind to his need of God's grace, he responded: "All these I have kept since I was a boy!" (Luke 18:21). But Jesus didn't give up. He continued plowing with the Law until the man saw his own covetousness and lack of surrender toward God.

Jesus said to him: "You still lack one thing. Sell everything you have and give to the poor, and you will have treasure in Heaven. Then come, follow me" (Luke 18:22). Finally, the rake of God's law fulfilled its sacred function, and God's conviction settled into the freshly broken soil. The young man "became very sad" (Luke 18:23) as he realized his covetousness and greed. He now finally understood He was not righteous enough to inherit eternal life. He had broken God's laws, and as the righteous judge, God must punish his crimes and expel him from the coming kingdom. The scriptures don't tell us if he ever received the gospel of God's forgiveness and liberation from sin, but one thing is for sure—if he heard it, he would have jumped for joy.

Do you want to *reason for revival*—to preach in such a way that souls will run to the Savior and bear genuine fruit of love for God? Receive the power of God, understand your audience, then follow Paul and Jesus's example by using the Ten Commandments to bring the knowledge of sin. Place your hearer in God's courtroom. Establish the reality of divine judgment. In simple words, explain that their day in Heaven's court is coming, that God will judge them strictly by His law, and that He will punish every sin with perfect justice. Then kindly test them by the Ten Commandments. Recite a commandment, then ask if they've kept it. Finally, ask if they'd be innocent or guilty if God judged them by this law today. Then say, "God is a righteous judge. If He judges you righteously, would He send you to Heaven, or to Hell?" Graciously and plainly reason with them about God's justice, holiness, and wrath against sin until they realize their eternal plight without Jesus Christ. Let me tell you a true story about my invasion of light to show you how it might look.

A SINNER WHO HAD NEVER SINNED

Once I spoke to a young man who had given himself to a partier's lifestyle of drugs, drunkenness, fornication, pornography, and debauchery. Yet as I spoke with him, I learned something that shocked me—he believed he had never sinned.

I was on a mission trip in Latin America, and one night, we set up our tent outdoors for an outreach to the locals. We played worship songs and performed skits, and when night began to fall, we finally preached the gospel. My brother in Christ preached with incredible passion, pleading with tears streaming down his face that souls would flee to Jesus. In his message, he talked about sin, God's judgment, the glorious salvation offered from the cross, and the call to repent and believe in Jesus Christ. It was a better message than you'd hear in most churches today, that's for sure, and a spirited invasion of light! But, probably by accident, he omitted one crucial element from his presentation—the Law. He spoke at length *about* sin, but he didn't use the Ten Commandments to *grant the knowledge of sin* to his hearers. As I would soon find out, this mistake single-handedly sterilized his message—at least for one hearer.

During the entire sermon, a young man leaned against a food shack, seemingly rapt with attention. My eyes kept returning in his direction (often when this happens, you know the Holy Spirit is prodding you to start a spiritual conversation). I figured he must have been under the Holy Spirit's conviction, so I decided to practice my Spanish and ask him about his soul. My, was I surprised with what happened next.[4]

"Hey, how are you doing tonight?" I asked.

"I'm doing all right." He replied.

"Cool. I saw you paying a lot of attention to the message. What did you think of what my friend said?"

He shrugged with absolute, stone-cold disinterest. "It was good."

I was a little surprised at his cool-headedness. Wasn't he listening closely the entire time? How could he be so unbothered?

"Well, what do you say to my friend's question? If you died today, where would you go, to Heaven or to Hell?"

"Uh, I think I would go to Heaven," the young man responded.

"Why do you say that?" I asked.

His answer shocked me to the core:

"Because I don't do anything wrong. I'm a good person. I've never sinned or anything like that."

I stood in awe. How could he think he had *never sinned*? Does anyone really think like that? An urgency came upon me from Heaven.

"You've never sinned? Are you *sure* of that?"

"Yeah. I've never sinned."

Seeing my opportunity, I decided to co-labor for conviction by testing him with the Ten Commandments.

"Well, you and I might be good by our own standards, but when we stand in God's courtroom after death, He will judge us by *His standard of good*. Do you know what His standard of good is? The Bible says, 'The Law is holy, and the commandment is holy, righteous and good' (Romans 7:12). Do you believe you've kept the Ten Commandments?"

"Of course," he said, his voice ringing with confidence.

"Well, let's see if you have or not. God's law commands, 'You shall not lie.' Have you ever told a lie?

"Um, well . . . yes."

"I'm not judging you—I have, too. But let's be honest—what does that make you and I?"

"Liars."

"Yes, and it means you *have* sinned, just like the rest of us. On the day of judgment, you'll have to answer to God for each of your lies. Let's try another. God's law commands, 'You shall not steal.' Have you ever stolen anything—even something small?"

The teen started to get uncomfortable.

"Yes, I have stolen things."

"What does that make you?"

"Um, I guess it makes me a thief."

"All right, let's try another. God's law prohibits all sexual sin. Have you ever had sex outside of marriage, looked with lust, or watched pornography?"

"Yes, I've done all those things!"

I continued in this way for quite a while until the young man willingly admitted his whole laundry list—drunkenness, drugs, fornication, pornography, lying, disobedience to parents, and more! Then I said to him,

"Friend, you could die at any time. I've had multiple friends who died suddenly before the age of twenty-five. If you died right now and God judged you by these commandments, would you be *innocent or guilty*?"

His head began to hang in shame.

"I would be guilty."

"Would you go to Heaven, or to Hell?"

He knew he had done wrong, but he was still holding onto a false hope.

"Well . . . I hope I would go to Heaven, because God would forgive me."

I looked him in the eyes with urgency and compassion. I had heard this false hope likely hundreds of times, and I knew I had to reason with him about God's righteousness to show him the truth.

"Hm. Let's test that by your basic sense of justice. Imagine if you had committed hundreds of thousands of crimes against your country's law. The judge discovered every single one of your misdeeds and called you to court. Then imagine you suggested that to the judge. 'Sir, I know I've broken the Law, but I also know you're a merciful judge, and I believe you will forgive my crimes.' What would the judge say to you?"

A look of clarity came upon his face. He knew his hope had no logic to it.

"Well . . . the judge would send me to prison."

"Exactly. And not because he's a mean judge, but because he's a good and righteous judge. In the same way, God is the righteous judge of all the Universe, and the Bible promises He will always judge rightly. Now again, if you died today and God judged you by the Ten Commandments, would He reward you in Heaven, or would He have to punish your crimes in Hell?"

He paused a second and faced the painful truth.

"When you put it that way . . . God would have to send me to Hell."

I exhorted him with urgent concern for his soul.

"Friend, does that concern you? Do you really want to risk your eternal soul for a short season of pleasure?"

"It deeply concerns me. I don't want to go to Hell."

"It should concern you! As Jesus asked, 'What does it profit a man to gain the whole world, and forfeit his soul?' (Mark 8:36 NASB). The fact is, if you died today, you would lose your soul, my friend. And not only do you face the danger of eternal judgment—right now, you are separated from God and enslaved in the mire of sin. God did nothing but good to us, but we stirred up His perfect anger by dishonoring Him all our lives. It breaks my heart to say that if someone doesn't do something to save you, you're in deep trouble!"

I continued in that vein for a while, "with many other words warning and pleading with him to be saved from this corrupt generation" (see Acts 2:40) with an urgency I've scarcely experienced in personal witness. Suddenly, my urgency and severity turned to joy.

"Look, I know the things I've been saying are pretty tough. The truth of God's justice and holiness can shake us to the core. But I only share these truths so I can show you your need of God's extravagant love. Would you like to know what God has done to reveal His amazing love and save you from the judgment you deserve?"

"Yes, please!" he responded.

I then shared the good news of Jesus's crucifixion and resurrection with him. Afterward, he kneeled down on the spot and committed to flee his life of drugs, alcohol, fornication, pornography, and sin, and serve Christ until God called him heavenward. Because I took the time to plow the ground of his heart by God's law, co-laboring with the Spirit to teach him the fear of the Lord, he received the miraculous gospel seed with joy and committed to a life of obedient faith in Jesus Christ.

Do you think you could follow that simple evangelistic method in a heart of love, but a tone of urgency and sobriety? Of course you can! With the Holy Spirit's power surging within, it will be much easier than you realize. Before you know it, you could find yourself leading souls to Christ left and right, advancing the invasion of light with power and accuracy, all to the glory of Almighty God.

THE AWAKENER'S ATTITUDE

Now that we've discussed how to use the Law, I'd like to suggest *in what manner* you should use it. With what attitude should we awaken souls from their spiritual slumber? I believe this information will guard you from destructive pitfalls.

AWAKEN AUTHORITATIVELY

First, we should preach the Law authoritatively. Do not skimp around the issue and say God *may* judge the wicked. Do not beat around the bush and say they might have sinned. Also, don't lighten the language, saying your hearers have made "mistakes" and will experience only "separation from God." No, tell the truth, and tell it in God's vocabulary. Boldly declare that all have sinned, crucifying the King of the Universe, and thus will receive eternal judgment in the Lake of Fire. As you study God's Word, He'll grant you interesting, unique, and profoundly convicting ways to explain these difficult themes.

AWAKEN SIMPLY

Secondly, we should preach the Law simply. Don't get carried away with fancy terms, big words, and overly complex illustrations. Preach God's law as simply as you can. Abandon all attempts at eloquence—unless God's given it to you as a gift—and instead reason in plain English, much like a concerned friend, or a lawyer before a citizen jury.

AWAKEN URGENTLY

Thirdly, we should preach the Law urgently. Jude 1:23 commands, "Save others, *snatching them out of the fire*" (NASB). Whatever you do, don't let the lost feel they have time. Show that eternity is at the door—and if they refuse God's solution, they may very soon plunge into the depths of Hell. Let them see the sands of time winding down before their very eyes. This is the only truth, and we lie if we give any other impression.

AWAKEN SOBERLY

Fourth, we should preach the Law soberly. Some preach the Law in a way that comforts rather than convicts. Could you imagine saying with a giggle, "You have cancer, and could die within days?" What folly! We must adapt our manner to our message. Speak with exuberant, even overwhelming joy when you declare the gospel, but speak soberly and with great concern when you warn of God's judgment.

AWAKEN TO GOD'S HOLY NATURE

Fifth, preach God's law in the context of God's holiness. Don't merely set your hearer before a calm and collected judge with a powdered wig in some court in the sky. Place them before the immediate throne of the Holy God whose very presence caused Israel's most righteous prophets to cry, "Woe is me, for I am ruined! Because I am a man of unclean lips!" (Isaiah 6:5 NASB). Emphasize God's moral perfection, infinite glory, unwavering justice, and righteous eternal wrath against wrongdoing. Then warn that they may face Him this very day to review every detail of their moral lives. Help them see that our best deeds are like filthy rags compared to His infinite righteousness (see Isaiah 64:6). I suggest you deeply study God's holiness and ask God to teach you how to bring it to bear upon the lost. I've found that no other theme so deeply convicts the human heart, often leaving sinners broken to the depths and crying out for mercy from on high.

AWAKEN COMPASSIONATELY

Sixth, we should preach the Law compassionately. Paul commands us to "reprove, rebuke, and exhort . . . with great patience" (2 Timothy 4:2 NASB). We must be as Richard Baxter, who declared, "I preach as a dying man to dying men!" Many warn of God's judgment in a critical spirit—but we must instead preach with a bleeding heart of care and love. If we're full of God's Spirit, our hearers will sense we're giving a loving warning, not a hateful scolding. We warn humbly, realizing we would also be trapped in the desert of sin if not for Jesus. We must "save others, snatching them out of the fire; and on some have mercy with fear, hating even the garment polluted by the flesh" (Jude 1:23 NASB).

AWAKEN WISELY

Finally, we must preach the Law wisely. Paul commands us to "reprove, rebuke, and exhort . . . *with great . . . instruction*" (2 Timothy 4:2 NASB). Many barely touch the Law because it hurts to do so, and they feel as if they're hurting others. Others preach the Law to the neglect of the gospel because they fear their hearers will take advantage of the good news. These are both fatal errors. Like a farmer analyzing his soils, we must assess our audience and determine how much breaking up they need before they're likely to receive the gospel seed fruitfully. Then, we must plow until the soil is ready for seed. Once we have, we can finally set upon the joyous task we've anticipated all along—we can cast the gospel seed and testify of God's promise of salvation in Jesus Christ. Which brings us to the next step toward a successful invasion of light.

CHAPTER TWELVE

P #4: DECLARE THE *PROMISES* OF SALVATION

You've faithfully plowed your hearer's soul-soil with the Law of God, removing rocks and thorns, and breaking up fallow ground. The Holy Spirit has awakened their conscience to the depth of their sin, and a holy fear of God has begun to settle upon their heart. They finally see that God is holy, and their sins are a stench in His nostrils. They see He is just and must punish their every crime. They see He's separate from sinners and can't fellowship with them as they are. And they see, above all, that they're covered in moral mud and desperately need cleansing. You might even see concern on their face, or in their slightly bowed head, or in something they say, or you might even feel God's weighty glory fill the air around you. One thing is for sure—God is at work, invading with light and plowing the soil as promised. Right now, by His grace, their heart burns and bursts with one all-consuming question—"How can I escape this awful fate?"

Now, God has granted you the privilege of a lifetime. You get to tell that broken soul the best news they will *ever hear*. You get to proclaim the message prophets waited to hear for centuries, searching to try to understand God's coming redemption in Christ (see 1 Peter 1:10-12); the divine realities into which *"even angels long to look"* (1 Peter 1:12)! Rejoice, ambassador of Christ—now is the time to invade with the gospel of salvation, reconciliation, and transformation in Jesus the Savior!

I can't overstate how crucial it is that you preach the message God has ordained at this point. Remember that now you're finally casting *seed*: *"the seed is the Word of God"* (Luke 8:11). As in real life, the seed you cast will determine the plant that grows. God has only granted *one type of seed* that will bear fruit for eternal life—the gospel message. As Paul declared, "the gospel . . . is the power of God for salvation to everyone who believes" (Romans 1:16 NASB); "the message of the cross . . . *is the power of God* . . ." (1 Corinthians 1:18). When we plant the powerful gospel seed, God invades with His light and grows the glorious fruit of new life: "For you have been born again, not of perishable seed, but of imperishable, through the living and enduring word of God" (1 Peter 1:23). What does that mean for you, the sower? Quite simply, if you want your hearer to reap "a hundred, sixty or thirty times what was sown" (Matthew 13:23), you must assure he "hears . . . and understands" the promises of the gospel (Matthew 13:23). Without this crucial step, your invasion of light can never succeed.

PROMISING FOR PISTIS

Earlier, you reasoned for revival and co-labored for conviction. Now, God calls you to promise for *pistis*—the New Testament Greek word for faith. The Holy Spirit longs to grant salvation through your invasion of light, and He has already promised to testify of Jesus's grace to your hearer's heart (John 15:25). But one thing remains undone: "*You also must testify*" (John 15:27). The Holy Spirit doesn't want to testify of Christ through a mystical voice in the air. Neither does He prefer to testify through a vague lyric sung during a worship event (at least, not as a total replacement of your verbal witness).[1] Rather, He wants to use your words to ignite faith in your hearer so they can have a sincere opportunity to turn to Christ and receive salvation.

You see, God has clearly revealed how He saves human souls—"by grace you have been saved *through faith*" (Ephesians 2:8 NASB). The author of Hebrews declares, "*Without faith* it is impossible to please God, because anyone who comes to Him must believe that He exists and that He rewards those who earnestly seek Him" (Hebrews 11:6). Then how does God's grace *inspire faith*? How do sinners come to trust in the Savior? Paul tells us: "Faith comes from hearing, and hearing by the word of Christ" (Romans 10:17). Paul's meaning is obvious. The lost can never believe the gospel until they hear it. And as he later asked, "how will they hear without a preacher?" (Romans 10:14 NASB).

I want you to realize a crucial principle of effective evangelism. Your audience can only believe in the Jesus you proclaim. In fact, your proclamation will often represent the high watermark of your hearer's faith. In other words—if you preach Jesus as Savior, they can trust Him and be saved. If you preach Jesus as Sanctifier, they can trust Him and advance in sanctification. If you preach Jesus as Healer, they can trust Him and be healed. If you preach Jesus as Baptizer in the Holy Spirit, they can trust Him and receive the Holy Spirit's empowerment. If you preach Jesus as Deliverer, they can trust Him and be delivered from demonic oppression. But if you don't declare some aspect of the "manifold grace of God" (1 Peter 4:10 NASB), it's unlikely they'll trust Jesus for that particular grace at that time.

Don't get me wrong. Jesus loves to show up in unexpected ways. God suddenly saves, heals, delivers, and empowers souls during messages that don't clearly explain those promises all the time. As the Psalmist declared, "Our God is in the heavens; He does whatever He pleases!" (Psalm 115:3 NASB). But as Christ's ambassadors, we should seek to preach messages that *inspire the faith that welcomes God*. Why should we settle for *popcorn* moves of the Spirit? I don't want to see one or two healed, saved, delivered, or empowered—much less by a *heavenly exception*. I want to preach in a way that inspires faith in the masses, leading to plentiful harvests of salvation, healing, deliverance, and spiritual empowerment!

With exceptions aside, this general rule of harvest remains: If you don't preach the promise, your hearers can't yet believe the promise, and therefore, they can't benefit from the promise. But if you will clearly and comprehensively preach the promises of Christ's salvation, your words can become like fiery arrows in the Holy Spirit's quiver, burning down all doubt and unbelief, and igniting human hearts with passionate love for Jesus Christ. On with the invasion of light!

THE FLAMING ARROWS OF FAITH

The book of Acts paints many powerful portraits of the flaming arrows of faith that God longs to shoot through the lips of His humble ambassadors. We find one in the life of Peter.

In Acts 10, this godly messenger preached a simple message about forgiveness of sins in Jesus Christ. Peter placed Himself as a bow in God's hands, opening his mouth to proclaim God's promises. As a result, God set the arrow, stretched back His arm, perfected His aim, and *thwip!* The Holy Spirit testified so powerfully that Peter's whole audience trusted Christ before he had a chance to finish his message!

And God didn't wait for Peter to wrap up his sermon with a tidy ribbon before He sent the saving fire of Heaven. Having inspired true faith, God would not delay His saving power! Thank the Lord of the Harvest, Peter's message received a divine interruption—God poured out the Holy Spirit upon the whole group at once, unleashing the joyous sounds of salvation: "For they heard them speaking in tongues and praising God" (Acts 10:46). Yes, it was just as Paul declared in Ephesians: "You also, when you heard the word of truth, the gospel of your salvation, and believed in Him, were sealed with the promised Holy Spirit" (Ephesians 1:13 ESV). Peter preached, God testified, the hearers believed, and the promised Holy Spirit fell as a seal of salvation![2] Glory to God, the invasion of light advances!

Another story from Acts powerfully demonstrates the Spirit's flaming arrows of faith. On one occasion, Paul and Barnabas "spoke in such a manner that a large number of people believed, both of Jews and of Greeks" (Acts 14:1 NASB). I'd ask you not to skip past this verse in fear of pragmatism. Rather, consider what it openly explains about Paul and Barnabas's invasion of light. We observe that God drew "a large number of people" to Christ at this location. But what instrument did the Holy Spirit use to reap such a harvest? The verse states it clearly—God used the clear and powerful manner in which Paul and Barnabas preached the good news! This fiery gospel duo made themselves available to the Spirit's wisdom, and under God, their timely, urgent, and confident words hit the bullseye, destroyed doubt, and ignited faith in Christ.

In both of these cases, the clarity and divine power of their gospel preaching directly influenced the quality of the harvest. First, they proclaimed the promises clearly, joyously planting seeds of truth in every heart. Then, the Holy Spirit testified to their audiences' hearts clearly, confirming the Word and producing a profound spiritual impact. As a result of this holy partnership, many believed the Word of Christ and turned to God in heartfelt repentance. The invasion of light was a success!

And I believe God wants to do the same thing through Christ's ambassadors today. You may say, "JJ, that was in the book of Acts! We're in the twenty first century now, and God's way has changed." But is it so? Must our invasion end in defeat? Must our preaching save so few? Does Christ now long that none should be saved and that few should come to the knowledge of the truth? (See 1 Timothy 2:4 for the definitive answer). Of course not! God wants to send waves of salvation into the world through us just like He did in the book of Acts. But if we want to see an Acts awakening, we must know the Acts God, live the Acts life, and preach the Acts gospel. It's time to invade with light!

Like Paul, Barnabas, and Peter, we must partner with the Holy Spirit to inspire faith in our hearers by clearly proclaiming the salvation promises of God. Let our lips be the bow through which the Holy Spirit shoots His fiery arrows of faith! Who knows—if we do, we might also experience the divine interruptions of God's Spirit. "You can pause your message, little Peter. My promises have done their perfect work, and I'm saving souls!"

PREACHING THE PROMISES OF THE GOSPEL

Now that we've considered how God uses His promises to ignite saving faith, I want to consider some of the gospel promises we must proclaim, and some other vital aspects of gospel preaching. My guidance is as follows:

1. Preach the everlasting love of God.

2. Preach the salvation story.

3. Preach the promises of salvation—forgiveness, reconciliation with God, personal transformation, and eternal life.

4. Preach Christ Himself as the prime jewel of salvation.

5. Preach the freeness of salvation.

THE SAVING LOVE OF GOD

First, we must proclaim the promise of God's *saving love*. Charles Finney said, "There are always, in a genuine revival, deep convictions of sin, and often cases of abandoning all hope."[3] If the Holy Spirit has deeply convicted of sin, our hearer may doubt God could ever love or save them. We must demolish this lie of Satan, echoing the cry of God's heart: "I have loved you with an everlasting love!" (Jeremiah 31:3). We must proclaim that God doesn't desire to destroy us, for He promises, "I take no pleasure in the death of the wicked, but rather that they turn from their ways and live" (Ezekiel 33:11). Rather, He longs to wash us clean and draw us into a life-giving relationship with Himself—"for God so loved the world that He gave His one and only Son, that whoever believes in Him shall not perish but have eternal life . . . that they know . . . the only true God, and Jesus Christ" (John 3:16, John 17:3). Yes, we have grossly rebelled against our Creator, but "God demonstrates His own love for us . . . while we were still sinners" (Romans 5:8). His love toward us never changes, and His offer of mercy never expires during our life on Earth. Compelled by love, God did something incredible to save us from the judgment we deserve and draw us near to His side forever!

THE SALVATION STORY

Next, we must declare the salvation story. While God loves us and wants the best for us, He can't simply let us off the hook for our sins. We sinned against God's government and earned the righteous penalty of God's law, for "cursed is everyone who does not continue to do everything written in the Book of the Law" (Galatians 3:10). In fact, God would be *infinitely unjust* if He didn't punish our crimes. "Will not the Judge of all the Earth do right?" (Genesis 18:25). Then how can we be saved? The answer lies in the shadow of the cross of Christ.

God could have justly left us in our sins, but He loved us so much that He gave everything for our salvation. God the Son stooped down to us, leaving Heaven's glory to live as a man. Jesus Christ lived the perfect life we couldn't, obeying God's law without fail and perfectly representing the Father's heart. But by the time Jesus completed three years of public ministry, His enemies had enough. Moved by hatred, these "wicked men . . . put Him to death by nailing Him to the cross" (Acts 2:23), forcing Him to face unspeakable pain, dishonor, and death before the mocking crowds.

Those murderous detractors intended to stop Jesus's kingdom in its tracks. But who can stop the Lord of glory? By nailing Jesus to the cross, they actually helped Him secure the redemption He'd promised. Yes, the cross was God's kingdom plan all along! You see, while Jesus had promised to restore lives through the Kingdom of God, one great obstacle stood in the way—man's sin. But on the cross, Jesus paid the penalty for our sins to wipe our record clean, reconcile us to the loving God, and transform us by His kingdom. We owed an infinite debt to Heaven which neither we nor the most glorious angel could ever pay—but right in our moment of helplessness, God the Son Himself stooped to Earth in eternal love and paid our debt in His own blood. Prisoners go free when their fine is paid—and Jesus paid our fine on the cross!

As Paul declared,

> Christ redeemed us from the curse of the Law, having become a curse for us—for it is written, "Cursed is everyone who hangs on a tree"—in order that in Christ Jesus the blessing of Abraham might come to the Gentiles, so that we would receive the promise of the Spirit through faith. (Galatians 3:13-14 NASB)

Yes, this is the message of the cross: "He was pierced for our transgressions, He was crushed for our iniquities; the punishment that brought us peace was on Him, and by His wounds we are healed" (Isaiah 53:5). And as Paul declared: "God made Him who had no sin to be sin for us, so that in Him we might become the righteousness of God" (2 Corinthians 5:21). In other words, on the cross, Jesus took *your* place so *you could take His place.*

I often like to put it like this. Jesus experienced what *you* deserved so you could experience what *He* deserved. On the cross, Jesus bore your *Hell* so you could experience His *Heaven*. He bore *your curse* so you could experience *His blessing.* He bore your *separation from God* so you could experience His *relationship with God.* He bore the *wrath of God* you deserved so you could experience the *love of God* He deserved. Jesus wore *your sin* so you could wear *spotless righteousness.* God condemned sin in Jesus's flesh so you could walk in the holiness of God's Spirit (see Romans 8:3). Jesus took your place—now leave behind your life of sin and receive His life of righteousness! What a glorious substitution this is, don't you agree? As the famous hymn declares,

> Bearing shame and scoffing rude,
> In my place condemned He stood;
> Sealed my pardon with His blood.
> Hallelujah! What a Savior!

("Hallelujah, What a Savior!" Phillip P. Bliss)

But the gospel story doesn't end with the bloody cross of Calvary. No, death could not hold down the very Creator of life! Three days after the bloody cross, history and prophecy reached their climax in a stone tomb outside Jerusalem. Jesus's lungs filled with air and His veins pumped with blood. His muscles loosed, His eyes opened wide, and His soul filled with joy.[4] Jesus *rose from the grave*—not as an undead spirit, but as a *living person* in His *own body.* The King was alive!

By rising from the dead, Jesus placed the final nail in the coffin of Satan's reign. At that moment, "He disarmed the rulers and authorities and put them to open shame, by triumphing over them in Him" (Colossians 2:15 ESV). Yes, through His sacrificial death and glorious resurrection, "He . . . render[ed] powerless him who had the power of death, that is, the devil" (Hebrews 2:14 NASB), "abolished death and brought life and immortality to light" (2 Timothy 1:10 NASB)!

Now, Jesus sits on the throne of Heaven as the merciful King of salvation, for God the Father has "seated Him at His right hand in the heavenly places, far above all rule and authority and power and dominion, and every name that is named" (Ephesians 1:20-21 NASB). None of Jesus's enemies stand a chance, for God has already "put all things in subjection under His feet" (Ephesians 1:22 NASB). One day all the forces of evil and sin will *finally* "be made His footstool" forever (Hebrews 10:13). Jesus is not dead—He is alive and well, and gloriously reigning from the throne of Heaven, restoring every soul that receives Him! The King has taken the throne, and His kingdom is invading the Earth through the gospel! This is the story of salvation! What glorious news indeed. And what does the salvation story mean for our hearers? In a word, a *totally new life.*

THE PROMISES OF SALVATION: PARDON

First, by Jesus's victory, all people can receive absolute and immediate pardon for their sins. Jesus didn't establish a credit system we could use to gradually pay off our crimes against Heaven. No, on the cross, Christ paid for *all sins,* of *all sorts,* for *all men,* for *all time,* once for all. As Hebrews 9:26 declares, "He has appeared once for all at the end of the ages to *put away sin by the sacrifice of Himself*"! (ESV). If our hearer submits to God, Christ will *put away* the weight of their sins at once; His blood will perfectly cleanse them, leaving them "holy in His sight, without blemish and free from accusation" (Colossians 1:22). Yes, whenever a sinner surrenders to the Savior, Paul's words become their supreme reality: "He forgave us *all our sins, having canceled the charge of our legal indebtedness,* which stood against us and condemned us; he has taken it away, nailing it to the cross"! (Colossians 2:13-14). How brilliant the light of the gospel!

And Jesus didn't die only for some sinners, leaving our hearer unsure if he can confidently receive Christ's sacrifice. God's Word clearly declares, "He Himself is the propitiation for our sins; and not for ours only, but also for those of *the whole world*" (1 John 2:2 NASB). Yes, Jesus died for the sins of the *whole world,* paying our debt with His own life—a sacrifice of eternal value. Because Jesus's sacrifice has eternal value, His offer of forgiveness can never be exhausted. Hypothetically, if every man from every age truly repented and received Christ's forgiveness, emptying Hell forever, infinite worlds to come could still avail themselves of His blood. Yes, Christ's atoning sacrifice is sufficient to wipe away all sins of all people from every era—and that with a single word from the throne of grace! Then I must ask, "Cannot Christ's blood forgive your sins, o you of little faith?"

FREEDOM FROM SIN

Second, Christ's victory means all people can receive absolute and immediate *emancipation* from the power of sin. When our hearer experiences true conviction, they realize they don't only need forgiveness, but also an *entire practical overhaul of their moral character.* Thank God, the gospel amply provides for this heavenly renewal.

Matthew 1:21 declares, "You shall call His name Jesus, for He will save His people from their sins" (NASB). This prophecy clearly announces Jesus does *not* save people *in their sins* but *from their sins.* He won't merely cover our dirty souls with clean white robes, leaving us filthy to ourselves but clean before God. Instead, He promises to send the Almighty Holy Spirit to live within us, cleansing our souls and "sav[ing] us . . . by the washing of regeneration and renewing by the Holy Spirit, whom He pour[s] out upon us richly through Jesus Christ our Savior" (Titus 3:5-6 NASB). If our hearer welcomes this transformation, God will save their soul without delay.

Yes, we must clearly promise our hearer that if they receive Jesus Christ, the Holy Spirit will come to live inside them *at once*, and they will be "set free from sin and . . . become slaves to righteousness" (Romans 6:18), no longer having any obligation to obey the desires of their flesh (see Romans 8:12). Instead, now their lives can be ruled by the all-encompassing principle of love to God. Yes, when they genuinely entrust their soul to Jesus, God will save them from sin, break their chains of selfishness, and ignite them with a passionate yearning to love God with all of their heart, soul, mind, and strength. God's New Covenant promise will overtake them by faith:

> I will cleanse you from all your filthiness and from all your idols. Moreover, I will give you a new heart and put a new spirit within you; and I will remove the heart of stone from your flesh and give you a heart of flesh. I will put My Spirit within you and cause you to walk in My statutes, and you will be careful to observe My ordinances. (Ezekiel 36:25-27 NASB)

Utterly transformed by the love of God, they'll become "God's handiwork, created in Christ Jesus to do good works, which God prepared in advance for [them] to do"! (Ephesians 2:10). The inner transformation will be unmistakable. Awed by God's power, they will declare—"I am in Christ, and now 'the new creation has come: The old has gone, the new is here!'" (2 Corinthians 5:17).

FREEDOM FROM DEMONIC POWERS

Third, Jesus's victory means all people can receive freedom from demonic powers. The enemy comes to steal, kill, and destroy, tormenting our lives with anxiety, addiction, excessive temptation, fear, overwhelming sorrows, demonic encounters, and more. In the West, we mostly experience demonic power in subtle ways—but in Eastern cultures, demons often act right in the open, appearing as ghosts, working through shamans, causing demonic illnesses and curses, acting like malevolent gods, and more. Every soul needs freedom from the power of Satan, whether we've encountered him through the mind and body (as typical in the West), or through open spiritual manifestation (as typical in the East). No matter how Satan has oppressed and enslaved our hearer, Christ's victory on the cross has made a sure way of freedom.

Colossians 1:13 promises every soul that receives Christ, "He has rescued us from the dominion of darkness and brought us into the Kingdom of the Son he loves" (Colossians 1:13). When we receive Christ, God turns us "from darkness to light, and from the power of Satan to God" (Acts 26:18). As a result, Jesus "keeps [us] safe, and the evil one cannot harm [us]" so long as we abide in the loving protection of His holy will (1 John 5:18). Jesus delivered many from demonic oppression during His earthly ministry, and He has no desire to stop. Our world needs freedom from evil powers just as much as Jesus's world did, and Christ still longs to set every captive free into the liberty and safety of the sons of God. What lacks? Only that we submit to the Deliverer, Jesus Christ!

RECONCILIATION TO GOD

Fourth, and most importantly, Jesus's resurrection victory means all people can be immediately reconciled to God now and for all eternity. You see, our hearer has one problem greater than any other. Though God created them for fellowship with Himself, they are "alienated from God and . . . enemies in [their] minds because of . . . evil behavior" (Colossians 1:21). As God warned them through the prophet Isaiah:

> Your iniquities have made a separation between you and your God, and your sins have hidden His face from you so that He does not hear. For your hands are defiled with blood, and your fingers with iniquity; your lips have spoken falsehood, your tongue mutters wickedness. (Isaiah 59:2-3 NASB)

As a tragic result, God declares to every unclean soul—"when you spread out your hands in prayer, I will hide My eyes from you; Yes, even though you multiply prayers, I will not listen. Your hands are covered with blood!" (Isaiah 1:15 NASB).

Then what's the solution? How can sinful man have a relationship with the Holy God—the very relationship God created him for? Paul answers: "Now [God] has reconciled you by Christ's physical body through death to present you holy in His sight, without blemish and free from accusation"! (Colossians 1:22). Yes, in Jesus Christ, God washes the blood from our hands so we can experience perfect communion with Him again. When we trust Jesus's blood, God utterly reverses the curses of Isaiah 1 and 59, now declaring—"Your hands are cleansed of all blood. Now, when you spread out your hands, I will not hide My eyes from you; and in all your many prayers, I will hear you! The blood of Jesus has created a perfect union between you and Me, and His mercy has turned My face towards you so that I will hear!" What glorious news—Jesus wants to destroy the barrier between our hearer and God. If they'll obey His call, they can "approach God's throne of grace with confidence, so that [they] may receive mercy and find grace to help . . . in [their] time of need" (Hebrews 4:16).

And this glorious union with God isn't just for our earthly life—it lasts into all eternity! As Jesus declares:

> In My Father's house are many dwelling places; if it were not so, I would have told you; for I go to prepare a place for you. If I go and prepare a place for you, I will come again and receive you to Myself, *that where I am, there you may be also.* (John 14:2-3 NASB)

Yes, if our hearer will submit to Jesus, Christ Himself will prepare a place for them in His eternal kingdom. God will commute their eternal death sentence in Hell and grant them the privilege to dwell in the inexplicable joy of Jesus's presence for all eternity! One day, they'll experience God's heavenly promise:

> Behold, the tabernacle of God is among men, and He will dwell among them, and they shall be His people, and God Himself will be among them, and

> He will wipe away every tear from their eyes; and there will no longer
> be any death; there will no longer be any mourning, or crying, or pain; the
> first things have passed away! (Revelation 21:3-4 NASB).

CHRIST: THE PRIME JEWEL OF SALVATION

When we preach the promises of salvation, we must place special emphasis on this
incomparable gift of reconciliation to Jesus Christ. Do *not* shortly tack friendship
with God onto the end of your presentation, as if Christ Himself is a lesser blessing than forgiveness, freedom, and our eternal home. Rather, seek to inspire in
your hearers the same exclusive love of Christ that Paul testified of when he said:

> I count all things to be loss in view of the surpassing value of knowing Christ
> Jesus my Lord, for whom I have suffered the loss of all things, and count them
> but rubbish so that I may gain Christ! (Philippians 3:8 NASB)

Christ has pre-eminence in all things (Colossians 1:18)—but does He have
pre-eminence in our preaching? In our gospel message, do we declare Him as
the meaning of life, or only as a means to new life? Do we mainly proclaim Him
as the way to forgiveness, freedom from addiction, purpose, a wonderful plan,
and Heaven; or do we proclaim Him as the prime jewel of salvation—the *very
reason for living*; the wondrous treasure for which we should willingly surrender
our hearts, possessions, relationships, schedules, and very lives?

We often hear preachers say Jesus is the Way. Amen, brother. But what is He
the way to? To God's gifts? Well, yes, but not primarily. More importantly than
anything else, Jesus is the way to *God Himself*. Jesus declared, "I am the way and
the truth and the life. No one comes *to the Father* except through Me" (John 14:6).

Sure, Jesus is the Way to receive pardon. Of course, through Jesus we obtain
a heavenly inheritance and walk in freedom from evil deeds. But it's very easy
to preach at length about forgiveness, freedom, Heaven, and other benefits of
God's kingdom, all the while forgetting to declare why these gifts are glorious
at all. Remember, forgiveness is glorious because it grants us access to the glorious King of Heaven. Freedom from sin is glorious because it grants us deeper
communion with the glorious King of Heaven. And Heaven is glorious simply
because the glorious King of Heaven is there! We often equate "eternal life" with
"going to Heaven"—but Jesus declared, "This is eternal life: that they know you,
the only true God, and Jesus Christ, whom you have sent" (John 17:3). In other
words, the knowledge of Jesus is the centerpiece of salvation. He is the glory of
revelation; the very sun of the soul, without which we live in utter darkness! As
Charles Spurgeon said, "No Christ in your sermon, sir? Then go home, and never
preach again until you have something worth preaching."[5]

SEEING JESUS: THE MARK OF A TRUE CHRISTIAN

The modern church has exported a self-centered gospel around the world for
several generations now. As a result, many tend to measure faith by faulty

standards. Some say a Christian is someone with the right doctrine. Others say a Christian is one with the right behavior or spiritual feelings. Still others say a Christian is one with the right external blessings. But the Bible teaches us that a Christian is one who *sees, knows, and obeys Jesus.* Paul explains the new birth this way: "God, who said, 'Let light shine out of darkness,' made His light shine in our hearts to give us the light of the knowledge of God's glory displayed in the face of Christ" (2 Corinthians 4:6). Here, Paul explicitly states that every genuine Christian personally encounters the glory of Jesus—furthermore, to Paul, this revelation is the very essence of the new birth! Then are we leading people into that glorious encounter with Jesus Christ Himself? If not, we're placing our hearers on shaky ground. Remember, Jesus warned:

> Many will say to Me on that day, "Lord, Lord, did we not prophesy in Your name, and in Your name cast out demons, and in Your name perform many miracles?" And then I will declare to them, "I never knew you; depart from Me, you who practice lawlessness." (Matthew 7:22-23 NASB)

We must exercise carefulness in our yearning to preach the whole counsel of God. Many will quickly sign up to escape Hell, but if they don't sign up to know God, they will one day surely hear, "I never knew you. Depart from me!" (Matthew 7:23 NASB). With this considered, let us proclaim Christ as the prime jewel of salvation; the "treasure hidden in the field" for which our hearer should gladly sacrifice everything (Matthew 13:44 NASB); the "pearl of great value" for which they should happily surrender all (Matthew 13:46 NASB); the very meaning and glory of life! If we do, by God's grace many of our hearers will truly encounter the Savior and follow Him for His own sake, not for selfish ends. If you ask me, that's a recipe for a successful invasion of light.

THE FREENESS OF SALVATION

Finally, we must faithfully and confidently declare the *freeness of salvation.* We must emphasize the blessed reality that salvation can never be bought. Our hearer can never earn God's favor and will certainly never deserve it. Rather, God freely and abundantly offers all the glorious benefits of the gospel to them as gifts from His eternal throne of grace. As Paul declared:

> By grace you have been saved through faith; and that not of yourselves, *it is the gift of God; not as a result of works, so that no one may boast.* For we are His workmanship, created in Christ Jesus for good works, which God prepared beforehand so that we would walk in them. (Ephesians 2:8-10 NASB)

Yes, if our hearer will but surrender to the eternal King, God will give "His glorious grace . . . freely . . . in the One He loves [Jesus]" (Ephesians 1:6), forgiving their sins, reconciling them to Himself, and transforming their life as a free gift. He won't reject them for their prior wickedness; nor will He require them to somehow prove their worthiness. Instead, He requires them to come in an attitude of humility and repentance, openly confessing their *unworthiness,* throwing up their arms and saying, "all have sinned and fall short of the glory of God, being justified as a gift by His grace through the redemption which is in Christ Jesus!" (Romans 3:23-24 NASB).

"IS THIS TOO GOOD TO BE TRUE?"

After hearing this message, our hearer may wonder—is this too good to be true? Would God *really* release me from the need to prove myself worthy of salvation? But we can assure them God established the free way of salvation with infinite wisdom. Realize—if we could earn our salvation by good works, we would receive the worship for our achievement, not God. Eternal life would be a pay-off; a hard-earned reward for our moral brilliance. As a result, we wouldn't consider God's gifts "as a favor, but as what is due" (Romans 4:4 NASB). We would feel no thankfulness in God's eternal kingdom—for how many truly thank their boss for giving a payment they worked to earn?

Since we can't possibly earn our salvation, *God has freely made a way of salvation for us.* And since He alone made a way of salvation, He alone receives the worship for our salvation. Now, the glory goes not to "the one who works," but to "Him who justifies the ungodly"! (Romans 4:4-5 NASB). If we could earn our salvation, we would rejoice in our own goodness—but since through Christ's blood alone we've "obtained access by faith into this grace in which we stand . . . we rejoice in hope of the glory of God"! (Romans 5:2 ESV). Yes, God has established it so on purpose to bring eternal glory and worship to His name, and to birth eternal gratefulness in our hearts. As Paul declared:

God, being rich in mercy, because of His great love with which He loved us, even when we were dead in our transgressions, made us alive together with Christ (by grace you have been saved), and raised us up with Him, and seated us with Him in the heavenly places in Christ Jesus, *so that in the ages to come He might show the surpassing riches of His grace in kindness toward us in Christ Jesus.* (Ephesians 2:4-7 NASB)

With this considered, whenever we invade with light, let us echo the free offer of grace God expressed through the prophet Isaiah:

Ho! Every one who thirsts, come to the waters;
And you who have no money come, buy and eat.
Come, buy wine and milk
Without money and without cost.
Why do you spend money for what is not bread,
And your wages for what does not satisfy?
Listen carefully to Me, and eat what is good,
And delight yourself in abundance.
Incline your ear and come to Me.

Listen, that you may live;
And I will make an everlasting covenant with you,
According to the faithful mercies shown to David. (Isaiah 55:1-3 NASB)

Let us also echo Jesus's invitation in Revelation 22:17:

The Spirit and the bride say, "Come." And let the one who hears say, "Come." And let the one who is thirsty come; let the one who wishes take the water of life without cost. (NASB)

THE PROMISER'S PARADIGM

Now, I would like to shortly consider the *manner* in which you should testify of the promises of salvation to most clearly represent the heart and message of God in your invasion of light.

PROMISE CONFIDENTLY

First, you must declare God's salvation promises confidently. Never let your hearer feel that Christ's message is on trial. Ambassador of Christ, God called you to proclaim the gospel, not propose it. Don't say, "Jesus could really change your life if He's truly the Savior." Say, "Jesus is truly the Savior, and He will change your life if you'll submit to Him!" Obey Jesus's call, and make your hearer feel that no promise is more sure than that of salvation in Jesus Christ. Help them to see God has truly removed every obstacle and provided every need. Open their eyes to see that He now waits to bless them from on high—that He has been waiting to bless them from eternity past, and the only obstacle remaining is their indecision. If they oppose, don't back down from your confidence but only insist on it all the more.

PROMISE PERSONALLY

Second, be sure to declare God's promise *personally*. Many believe Jesus died for *the world's sins*—trouble is they don't believe Jesus died *for their own sins*! Put them in a room with a hundred sinners just like them, and ask—"Did Jesus die for that person's sins? And that one?" Many will answer yes for all ninety-nine; but ask them if Christ died for their own sins, and they'll say, "Well . . . I'm not sure." This type of faith will never obtain salvation. The hearer must understand that *Christ died for him to reconcile him to God, rose again to set him free from the slavery of sin,* and *sat on the throne to welcome him into the blessing of His kingdom.* He must know Christ did all these things *for him*—just as much as if no one else existed in the whole world—and that He did so already knowing all of his difficulties and sins long before He made the sacrifice. Until he understands this, he will never experience the freedom of the gospel, though he might pray a prayer by rote and become quite an active church member.

If your hearer thinks himself too wicked to receive God's grace, remind him of the glorious promise of Romans 5:6: "At just the right time, when we were still powerless, Christ died for the ungodly." You might ask them—"Right now, do you feel powerless to do right? Do you see yourself as too ungodly for His salvation? Well, look at this promise. Christ died for people just like you! He died for the powerless and the ungodly. That certainly includes me apart from Jesus's grace—can you really tell me it doesn't include you?"

PROMISE THOROUGHLY

Third, be sure to promise thoroughly. You can do much damage by declaring part of God's promise at the expense of the other. Let's say you promise God's forgiveness without God's transformation. Your hearer may spend their whole life expecting to go to Heaven, but at the judgment, they'll hear, "Depart from Me, you who practice lawlessness!" (Matthew 7:23 NASB). Or let's say you promise God's transformation without God's forgiveness. They may rightly seek to grow in "the holiness without which no man will see the Lord" (Hebrews 12:14 ESV), but they'll make little progress because they won't have the assurance and love that inspire true holiness.

PROMISE SIMPLY

Fourth, be sure to promise simply. Paul set a wonderful example of evangelistic simplicity in 1 Corinthians 2:1-5:

> When I came to you, I did not come with eloquence or human wisdom as I proclaimed to you the testimony about God. For I resolved to know nothing while I was with you except Jesus Christ and him crucified. I came to you in weakness with great fear and trembling. My message and my preaching were not with wise and persuasive words, but with a demonstration of the Spirit's power, so that your faith might not rest on human wisdom, but on God's power.

The principles *behind* biblical evangelism might seem complex—and we should understand them well to prepare for a variety of cases—but our gospel message should always be as plain and simple as possible. When dealing with the lost, make sure they don't need to pull out a thesaurus to understand you. Avoid heady theological words unless you can explain them in the simplest terms. Avoid tripping up your hearers with excessive human reasoning unless a philosophical approach is appropriate to the audience. Never assume they already truly understand *anything* about the message of salvation—not even basic principles. At all costs, avoid being driven along by your own eloquence. You're not training doctors; you're saving sinners!

Remember, your audience can't even understand the basics of spiritual reality without the Holy Spirit's revelation. As Paul says, "The person without the Spirit does not accept the things that come from the Spirit of God but considers them foolishness, and cannot understand them because they are discerned only through the Spirit" (1 Corinthians 2:14). Please, don't add another level of difficulty by preaching like a walking dictionary! As a guide, I encourage you to adopt the same goal as Evangelist Steve Hill—he sought to preach the gospel so simply that even a three-year-old could understand it.

PROMISE WITH IMMEDIACY

Fifth, be sure to promise *with immediacy*. Do not make your hearer feel that Jesus will forgive, transform, and adopt them *later*. Don't let them feel that He'll renew them *after an hour of seeking His face, after a week of moral rectitude, or after a year of sincere churchgoing*. Help them see that God's will is to save them *now*, for "now is the day of salvation" (2 Corinthians 6:2). Use phrases of immediacy like "*right now*," "*on the spot*," and "*this very moment*." Help them see that Christ's salvation has been waiting in the wings long enough, and He is prepared to release them from their sins *immediately* if they would only come to Him as He's commanded. If it helps, tell them plainly—"You aren't waiting on God—God is waiting on you! Every second you delay to trust His promise, you actually disobey Him!" This promotes practical faith in the Savior and helps the sinner understand just how much the ball is in their court.

PROMISE WITH JOY

Finally, promise with exuberant joy. Remember Isaiah's promises:

> You will go out in joy and be led forth in peace; the mountains and hills will burst into song before you, and all the trees of the field will clap their hands. (Isaiah 55:12)

> How beautiful on the mountains are the feet of those who bring good news, who proclaim peace, who bring good tidings, who proclaim salvation, who say to Zion, "Your God reigns!" (Isaiah 52:7)

Keep ever before you the reality that the glorious God has commissioned you to preach gloriously good news. Therefore, let His glory shine through your face, your tone, and your entire manner. Let your joy itself proclaim God's kindness in Christ, and your exuberant zeal unveil the urgency and passion with which Christ longs to bless the repentant sinner.

Once you've done all this in the power of God's Spirit, and your hearer has come to a genuine understanding, appreciation, and desire of the good news, you can safely proceed to the next crucial phase of your invasion of light—advising in the practicals.

CHAPTER THIRTEEN

P #5: ADVISE IN THE *PRACTICALS* OF CONVERSION

Once the Holy Spirit has convicted of sin and testified of Christ, our hearer must decide if they'll submit to Jesus or continue in rebellion. If they're prepared, we can now advise them in *the practicals of conversion*, helping them immediately "repent and believe in the gospel" (Mark 1:15 NASB). Thank God, we can set upon this work with confidence in God's saving power, for Jesus promised: "I, if I am lifted up from the Earth, will draw all men to Myself" (John 12:32 NASB).

THE QUESTION OF IMMEDIATE OBEDIENCE

Right at this point, many reach a critical question. Every sane Christian knows we should never lead someone to an immediate decision *if they're not prepared to receive Christ.* We'd be fools to take the sickle to an unripe harvest! But what if our invasion of light seems to succeed? What if we see the evidences of Jesus's drawing power—that our hearer is convicted by the Law, blessed by the message of the gospel, and aware of their desperate need of the Savior? Should we normally help them immediately submit to Jesus, or leave them to consider it in their own time?

Perhaps an answer came to mind of which you feel quite sure. That's fine, but I'd ask you to set your prior thoughts aside for a moment and sincerely consider the question afresh. As we reconsider, let's resort to the scriptures rather than our own human reasoning. After all, God has given the Bible as our guide for the invasion of light—we don't have permission to follow any other example! To discern what evangelistic action we should normally take with a God-readied soul, we must answer one crucial question: What did the soul-winners of the New Testament do when they saw a soul ripe for harvest?

THE NEW TESTAMENT EXAMPLE

First, let's consider the Savior's invasion of light. How did Jesus usually deal with His hearers when He saw an opportunity for grace?

Let's analyze the case of Peter and Andrew. Jesus caught these brothers during work hours, "casting a net into the sea; for they were fishermen" (Matthew 4:18 NASB). But did He mind their sense of enterprise? Did He say, "I see you have plenty on your hands, but I have a proposition: I want you to follow me. Would you consider it after work and get back to me when you make a choice?" No way! Rather, He pressed them to an immediate decision—even an immediate change of vocation—urgently calling them: "Follow Me, and I will make you fishers of men!" (Matthew 4:19 NASB). As a result, they "immediately . . . left their nets and followed Him" (Matthew 4:20 NASB).

How about Matthew? Jesus caught him on work hours, too, "sitting in the tax collector's booth" gathering funds for the government (Matthew 9:9 NASB). Did He give Matthew time to "mull over" his decision for Christ? Of course not—Jesus stood before him, looked him in the eye, and said: "Follow Me!" (Matthew 9:9 NASB). As a result, Matthew "got up and followed Him" (Matthew 9:9 NASB)—and he's rejoicing in Heaven this very moment that He did. Jesus took the same approach with John and James (Matthew 4:21), the rich young ruler (Mark 10:17-22), several souls in Luke 9:57-62, and undoubtedly many others the gospels never mention.

Next, let's consider Peter's invasion of light on the day of Pentecost. After preaching the gospel, did Peter send the convicted crowds home to consider their eternal fate? Did He say, "Don't make a hasty decision—go home and consider if you'll follow Jesus Christ"? No way! He lifted up his voice as a herald and cried—"Repent, and each of you be baptized in the name of Jesus Christ for the forgiveness of your sins; and you will receive the gift of the Holy Spirit" (Acts 2:38 NASB). And He didn't wait a single day to baptize those who wanted to follow Jesus. Rather, "those who had received his word were baptized; and that day there were added about three thousand souls" (Acts 2:41 NASB). Such moves of instantaneous salvation occur everywhere in the book of Acts. The gospel had only just premiered, yet "the Lord was adding to their number day by day those who were being saved" (Acts 2:47 NASB), constantly advancing the glorious invasion of light.

Next, let's consider the conversion of Paul. This zealous Pharisee had a radical encounter with Jesus Christ that left him with blind eyes and a bleeding heart (see Acts 9:1-19). Soon, God sent an everyday evangelist, Ananias, to lead him into the Savior's love. When Ananias met Paul, did he encourage him to calmly ponder receiving Christ? No—Ananias pressed Paul to an immediate decision, saying, "Why do you delay? Get up and be baptized, and wash away your sins, calling on His name!" (Acts 22:16 NASB). Paul got up, received water baptism, and very soon flipped the world upside down for Christ.

Finally, let's consider the Ethiopian eunuch. The Holy Spirit led Philip to join the eunuch's chariot and explain the gospel (Acts 8:29). He clearly preached the good news and pressed home its conditions, and the Holy Spirit deeply stirred the eunuch's soul. Soon, the eunuch spotted some water and jumped on his chance.

"Look! Water! What prevents me from being baptized?" (Acts 8:36 NASB)

How did Philip respond? Did he say, "Well, you really should take some time to think about it. You don't want to make a hasty decision." Of course not! Rather:

> Philip said, "If you believe with all your heart, you may." And he answered and said, "I believe that Jesus Christ is the Son of God." And he ordered the chariot to stop; and they both went down into the water, Philip as well as the eunuch, and he baptized him. (Acts 8:37-38 NASB)

The consensus of the New Testament example is clear—"God is *now* declaring to men that all people everywhere should repent" (Acts 17:30 NASB). As Paul declared, "*Now* is 'the acceptable time,' behold, now is 'the day of salvation!'" (2 Corinthians 6:2 NASB). Therefore, whenever we invade with light, we must urge our hearers to surrender to Christ *now*—for no other time is acceptable, and in no other moment does God call all people everywhere to repent!

FACING THE FEAR OF FALSE CONVERSION

I understand why many avoid this urgent call to repentance. In many cases, they want to avoid discomfort. I've felt that way plenty of times. In other cases, they want to avoid creating false converts and leading people into spurious decisions for Christ. I deeply share that sentiment—I've preached about it often! But I've learned by experience that we can't let our fear of *false conversions* stop us from calling people to *immediate true conversion.*

Dear friend, in your quest to avoid making false disciples, don't make the fatal mistake of creating *no disciples at all*! Invade with light, preach the gospel, test the soil, and immediately lead as many to Christ as God grants. The harvest is great if we'll reap it!

If we don't, many will lazily wait for a more convenient time only to eventually slip into Hell. Let's consider the story of a famous evangelist who learned that lesson the hard way.

D.L. MOODY'S GREATEST REGRET

In the blazing autumn of 1871, D.L. Moody held a series of evangelistic meetings in his home city of Chicago. He felt few would naturally come in the Chicago heat, so he asked for God's wisdom about how to reap the greatest possible harvest of souls. After praying, he received an inner-witness that God would send many hearers if he preached on Bible characters.

Obedient to God's voice, Moody began preaching through the lives of the Bible's saints and misfits—first Adam, then Enoch, then Noah, then Abraham. Before long, just as God promised, the meetings filled with massive crowds of earnest listeners ready to hear the Word of God. Finally, Moody set upon the final Bible character in his series—Jesus Himself. He planned to preach the life of Christ for six consecutive Sundays, inviting the crowds to receive Jesus at the final meeting. Tragically, Moody's plans would be cut short by the cruel flames of fate.

On October 8, 1871, Moody stood in the pulpit of Farwell Hall for the fifth Sunday of messages about Jesus. When he looked out at the audience, he must have felt amazed. God had filled the room to greater capacity than ever before! Was the Holy Spirit about to move in tremendous saving power? How many would soon rush into the arms of the Savior? Yearning for souls as always, Moody opened his mouth and declared Christ with passion and clarity.

After the stirring message, Moody decided to announce his plans for the next meeting. He had chosen Matthew 27:22 for his text: "What shall I do then with Jesus which is called Christ?" (KJV). Reflecting on this passage, he asked his hearers to take a week to consider what they would do with Jesus and return the following Sunday to make their final decision. "I wish you would take this text home with you and turn it over in your minds during the week," Moody said, "and next Sabbath we will come to Calvary and the Cross, and we will decide what to do with Jesus of Nazareth.[1]

With that, Moody's music partner Ira Sankey mounted the stage and sang the final benediction:

> "Today the Savior calls;
>   For refuge fly;
> The storm of justice falls,
>   And death is nigh!
> The Spirit calls today;
>   Yield to His pow'r;
> O grieve Him not away,
>   'Tis mercy's hour!"

Tragically, this song would ring in Moody's ears with regret for all his days. Only hours later, the historic Chicago fire rushed through the city, stealing hundreds of lives. In fact, Moody firmly believed that many who attended that very meeting stood before the Throne of God for judgment that night. Many years later, he remarked with tremendous pain:

> I have never seen that congregation since. I have hard work to keep back the tears today. I have looked over this audience, and not a single one is here that I preached to that night. I have a great many old friends and am pretty well acquainted in Chicago, but twenty-two years have passed away, and I have not seen that congregation since, and I never will meet those people again until I meet them in another world.[2]

Yes, that night, Moody made perhaps the greatest mistake of his whole evangelistic career. He failed to give his audience a clear opportunity to receive Christ *on the very night of a historic American tragedy*—and he knew eternal souls were lost because of his negligence.

Yet Moody didn't allow this tremendous failure to go to waste. Instead, he turned to God, and God turned the pain of his missed opportunity into a life lesson that would change his ministry forever. He explained the crucial principle he learned:

> I want to tell you of one lesson I learned that night, which I have never forgotten, and that is, when I preach, to press Christ upon the people then and there, and try to bring them to a decision on the spot. I would rather have that right hand cut off than to give an audience now a week to decide what to do with Jesus. I have often been criticized; people have said: "Moody, you seem to be trying to get people to decide all at once: why do you not give them time to consider?" I have asked God many times to forgive me for telling people that night to take a week to think it over, and if He spares my life, I will never do it again.[3]

Moody never *did* do it again, and that was one great secret of his immensely successful invasion of light. In all of his evangelistic meetings, Moody pled with his audience to *immediately* turn to Christ—so many thousands did receive Christ through his ministry. We do well to apply the same principle whenever God's Spirit has convicted of sin and testified of Christ in a hearer's soul.

Then, how can we discern a soul ready for harvest? Let's consider three vital signs without which we should never lead an individual into a discipleship decision.

THREE SIGNS OF A RIPE HARVEST

Jesus declared, "Do not give what is holy to dogs, and do not throw your pearls before swine, or they will trample them under their feet, and turn and tear you to pieces" (Matthew 7:6 NASB). Here, Jesus forbids us from giving God's precious things to the careless and irreverent—and this principle also applies to evangelism. You see, you can never genuinely lead a soul to Christ if they don't truly value Him. Therefore, we must never lead our hearer into an immediate decision unless they show clear signs of *understanding, concern, and willingness.*

SIGN #1:
UNDERSTANDING

First, we must consider if they *understand the message* and its gravity. Remember, the good soil listener is one who "hears the Word and understands it" (Matthew 13:23 NASB). Before we lead someone to decide for Christ, we should always ask ourselves—do they understand their sin? Do they understand that they deserve God's righteous eternal judgment? Do they understand that Christ died to save them from sin and reconcile them to God? Do they understand that Christ freely offers them forgiveness, freedom, new life, and above all, a relationship with God? Finally, do they understand what they must do to receive salvation? I find it helps to simply ask in review: "What do you understand from our conversation? What did Jesus do to save you? What does He call you to do to receive His salvation?" They might not yet understand some of the minute details of the gospel, but they must grasp the basics before they can genuinely decide for Christ. After all, if they don't understand the gospel, how can they believe it? And if they don't understand how to receive Christ, how can they receive Him?

SIGN #2:
CONCERN

Second, we should test the soil for *concern*. Are they concerned about their eternal fate, or do they feel unbothered by the thought of eternal judgment? Are they concerned about their rebellion against the Holy God, or do they feel fine with how they've lived? If they feel no distress over sin, rest assured that they've yet to experience the true conviction of the Holy Spirit. In that case, you must *not* lead them to an immediate decision. Remember, Jesus *promised* that the Holy Spirit would convict of sin, righteousness, and judgment (John 16:8). If our hearer hasn't experienced genuine conviction, God hasn't yet prepared their soul to truly respond to the gospel. In that case, either continue to reason with them about the Law, give them some convicting literature, plan to talk another time, or leave them in God's hands—but whatever you do, *don't yet lead them to an immediate decision.* If you do, it will surely prove spurious sooner or later.

SIGN #3:
WILLINGNESS

Third, we should test the soil for *willingness*. Are they willing to immediately reject all sin and turn in obedience to Christ? Are they willing to receive Christ and all His gifts by faith? In other words, are they ready to immediately surrender all to Jesus Christ? If not, by all means press them to submit all to Him—faithfully remind them that their delay is denial, that the sands of time are running down, and that the day of judgment creeps closer every moment—but don't lead them to an immediate decision. If you do, it will quickly prove spurious, and they may never listen to the gospel again.

Finally, what if our hearer *does* show all three signs of a ripe harvest? What if they understand the basics of the gospel, feel concerned about their sin, and express a willingness to surrender all to Jesus? If so, the Father has *drawn* your hearer, they've *learned* from His drawing and teaching voice, and now they must *come* to Jesus. As Christ explained:

> No one can come to Me unless the Father who sent Me *draws* him; and I will raise him up on the last day. It is written in the Prophets: 'AND THEY SHALL ALL BE *TAUGHT* OF GOD.' Everyone who has heard *and learned* from the Father, *comes* to Me. (John 6:44-45 NASB, emphasis mine)

Now, you can help them decide for Christ by confidently explaining the biblical conditions of salvation. Paul expresses these clear conditions in Acts 20:21: "I have declared to both Jews and Greeks that they must turn to God in repentance and have faith in our Lord Jesus."

Let's dive deeper into the Bible's teaching about receiving Christ. First, I'll unpack the realities of repentance and faith at length to grant you a well-rounded view of biblical conversion. In doing so, I hope to prepare you for a variety of cases and prevent you from crucial pitfalls. Then, I'll present a simple illustration you can use to shortly and clearly explain the conditions of salvation without confusing your hearer. Let's dig in.

WHAT REPENTANCE IS NOT

First, to receive salvation, our hearer must *repent*. They may have a false concept of repentance, so at times you may need to clarify *what repentance is not*.

First, repentance is *not* merely feeling sorrowful or shameful—even in a violent manner that brings tears. For example, the book of Hebrews speaks of a man who "found no place for repentance, though he sought for it with tears" (Hebrews 12:17 NASB). Though repentance often does produce deep feelings of remorse, repentance itself is not a *feeling*, but a choice of the will.

Second, repentance is *not* merely weeping. Many weep over sin but refuse to turn from it. One thinks painfully upon Judas. He committed suicide out of remorse for his sin—yet he didn't truly repent, for the Bible tells us he was condemned (Matthew 26:24, John 17:12). Repentance often leads to weeping, but tears don't prove repentance. Repentance is a choice of the will, not a wetting of the eyes.

Third, repentance is *not* merely confession of sin. Many confess their sins every day of their lives but never truly repent. While confession is an important aspect of repentance, only "he who confesses and forsakes" his sins "will obtain mercy" (Proverbs 28:13 ESV). Repentance definitely *implies* confession, but confession itself is not repentance. Repentance is a choice of the will, not a word on the tongue. On the same note, repentance is not merely *a prayer of repentance*. I tell you, millions have prayed a prayer of repentance but have never truly repented.

WHAT REPENTANCE IS

Then what is repentance? The Bible uses at least two words for *repent*. The Hebrew word translated "repent" is *shub* (בוש), which means *to return or turn back*.[4] The Greek word translated "repent" is *metanoia* (μετάνοια), which literally means "*a change of mind*" *or heart*.[5] When we combine these meanings, we reach a simple biblical definition: to repent is to turn to God from the heart. It's to *change your mind* about who rules your life, *turn back from sin*, and return to God from the great depths of your being. In even simpler terms, it's to enter a life of obedience to Jesus. This grand return implies four simultaneous choices: confessing sin, denying self, sanctifying Christ as Lord, and therefore abandoning individual sins.[6] Let's unpack these four aspects of true repentance.

THE FOUR CHOICES OF BIBLICAL
REPENTANCE: CHOICE #1 - CONFESS SIN

First, to repent, our hearer must *confess their sins*. God requires the same of us as He required of rebellious Israel:

> Return, O Israel, to the LORD your God, For you have stumbled because of your iniquity. *Take words with you and return to the LORD.* Say to Him, "Take away all iniquity and receive us graciously, that we may present the fruit of our lips." (Hosea 14:1-2 NASB)

Perhaps your hearer once believed they were good enough to earn God's favor. Not anymore. Now, by God's gracious conviction, they know the truth—they've rebelled against God every moment of their lives, grieving the Lord's heart and earning His eternal judgment. Knowing this, before they can receive salvation, they must return to God and plainly confess their wrongs.

This confession must not be tame or permissive. Rather, we should instruct them to exercise brutal honesty, not sparing themselves an inch, but utterly condemning their own sin, and openly admitting they deserve the eternal judgment of God. Though not essential to salvation, it would help them to obey the advice of Charles Finney:

> Take up your individual sins one by one, and look at them. I do not mean that you should just cast a glance at your past life, and see that it has been full of sins, and then go to God and make a sort of general confession, and ask for pardon. That is not the way... Your sins were committed one by one; and as far as you can come to them, they ought to be reviewed and repented of one by one.[7]

If you lead them to Christ on the spot, you may ask them to confess their sins quietly for a moment and make a more thorough confession later when alone. Whatever you do, impress upon them that they must face up to the God they have wronged and tell the hard truth about their choices—otherwise they can never be saved.

CHOICE #2 - DENY SELF

Second, to repent, our hearer must choose to forever *deny themselves*. As our Creator, God has the absolute right to rule our lives. God doesn't want to use this right to hurt us—He longs to lead us with love into "green pastures" of wholeness and purity for His glory (Psalm 23:2). That's one major reason He forbids us from going "our own way" (Isaiah 53:6). Sin destroys—and the essence of sin is self-rule! For this reason, Jesus said, "If anyone wishes to come after Me, he must deny himself, and take up his cross daily and follow Me" (Luke 9:23 NASB), and "whoever does not carry his own cross and come after Me cannot be My disciple"

(Luke 14:27 NASB). Yes, now that our hearer has confessed their rebellion against God, they must utterly renounce the right to rule their own lives. They must echo the desperate cry of Gethsemane: "Not My will, but yours be done!" (Luke 22:42 NASB). If they won't, they can never be saved.

CHOICE #3 - SANCTIFY CHRIST AS LORD

Third, to repent, they must "sanctify Christ as Lord in [their] heart" (1 Peter 3:15 NASB). It's crucial to confess your sinfulness and refuse to rule your own life—but this means nothing unless you also submit to the King who demands your allegiance. Yes, now that our hearer has confessed their sin and denied themselves, they must humbly bow before King Jesus as His loyal servant, surrendering unconditionally to *His rule*. They must place their entire being on God's altar, leaving nothing under their own control. Their thoughts, will, character, time, possessions, and relationships must now be subjected to the rule of Jesus Christ, or else they cannot be His disciple (see Mark 8:34, Luke 9:24, Luke 14:26-27, 33). Remember, Jesus died for them that they would live for His smile above all else—"He died for all, so that they who live might no longer live for themselves, but for Him who died and rose again on their behalf" (2 Corinthians 5:15 NASB). Therefore, all who desire eternal life must obey the Psalmist's exhortation:

> Do homage to the Son, that He not become angry, and you perish in the way,
> For His wrath may soon be kindled. How blessed are all who take refuge in
> Him! (Psalm 2:12 NASB)

CHOICE #4 - REPENT OF INDIVIDUAL SINS

Finally, in light of their *general repentance*, they must *repent of their individual sins*. The Holy Spirit often awakens the human conscience by pinpointing some particular practice that displeases Him. With the rich young ruler, He confronted covetousness (Mark 10:17-27). With another, He confronted the love of comfort (Matthew 8:19-20). With some of John the Baptist's audience, He confronted greed (Luke 3:11), and with others of his audience, theft (Luke 3:13-14). In these cases, God deeply convicted of *one sin in particular*, and He required each moral agent to repent of *that* sin if they wanted forgiveness. God wouldn't let them bargain— He wouldn't trade ninety-nine sins for the one He asked for. No, if they wanted God's merciful friendship, they had to repent of the one sin they held the dearest as well as the ninety-nine others less precious. The same applies to our hearer. God has likely already revealed the obstacle in their conscience, and they must address *that* obstacle, or their repentance means nothing.

Some argue that Jesus abolished this specific call to repentance on the cross. But the New Testament never suggests so. Sure, it was before the resurrection that John the Baptist said, "Bear fruit in keeping with repentance" (Matthew 3:8 NASB). But Paul echoed the same idea after Jesus's sacrifice, proclaiming "that they should repent and turn to God, performing deeds according to repentance"

(Acts 26:20 NASB). In other words, he commanded people not only to generally repent of sin, but to make hard, real choices to cut ties with their specific sins. If our hearer refuses these tough decisions, their repentance is greatly to be questioned. God's call is clear—we must step by faith upon the narrow road to life, or else risk losing our soul in Hell. As Jesus warned:

> If your right hand makes you stumble, cut it off and throw it from you; for it is better for you to lose one of the parts of your body, than for your whole body to go into Hell! (Matthew 5:30 NASB)

Knowing this, when counseling those who want to follow Christ, we do well to kindly ask questions like: "What sins do you practice that you need to abandon?" "What is your idol—what goes first in your life right now?" "When I say 'repent,' a particular sin likely comes to mind louder than any other. What is it? And what choices must you make to flee that practice?" Or at an altar meeting, "What did God speak to your heart during this message that led you to this altar? What is He *really* telling you to do?" If you don't feel comfortable probing that personally, you might simply ask, "Do you know what sins you practice that you need to repent of?" And then, "Are you ready to repent of that sin, and all else that displeases God?" Then they can repent privately before the Lord.

Obviously, you can counsel with more wisdom when your hearer opens up to you. But ultimately, the only person who *really needs to know* what they must repent of is your hearer himself. For that reason, in many cases, you can offer these questions rhetorically, have them decide the answer for themself, and then give them generalized scriptural directions.

WHAT IS
BIBLICAL FAITH?

Now, let's consider the second condition of salvation—*faith in Jesus Christ*. Biblical faith implies three simultaneous choices: renouncing all trust in our own works, believing the gospel message, and personally trusting (or receiving) Jesus Christ as Savior, Liberator, and Lord. Let's consider these aspects of faith in detail.

FAITH-STEPS #1 & 2: RENOUNCE SELF
AND BELIEVE THE GOSPEL MESSAGE

First, to trust in Christ, your hearer must forever renounce all self-reliance in respect to salvation. This implies two things.

First, they must renounce all reliance upon good works as a path to eternal life. Paul warned, "All who rely on the works of the Law are under a curse, as it is written: 'Cursed is everyone who does not continue to do everything written in the Book of the Law'" (Galatians 3:10). When convicted of sin, many try to save themselves by good deeds. They might pray impressive prayers to make up for their former blasphemy. They might tell the truth to make up for their many lies. They may even begin going to church to make a public showing of goodness. By this legalistic scurry they hope to tilt Heaven's scales in their favor and escape God's righteous judgment. Tragically, they're engaging in spiritual bribery—a sin that will condemn them just as badly as any other. Before they can trust in Christ, they must understand that one-hundred-thousand acts of penitence could never erase a single sin—for "whoever keeps the whole law and yet stumbles in one point, he has become guilty of all" (James 2:10 NASB). Knowing this, they must come to God like the penniless sinner they are, crying, "Nothing in my hands I bring, simply to thy cross I cling!"

Second, they must renounce all hope of escaping sin's slavery in their own power. You see, most people see themselves as naturally good. Blinded by this pride, they believe they can fix their moral character on their own. Contrary to this moral myth, Paul declares all unbelievers are "held captive by [Satan] to do his will" (2 Timothy 2:26 NASB), and Jesus declares, "everyone who commits sin is the slave of sin" (John 8:34 NASB). Our hearer is a slave to sin just like we were without Christ, and no one can set them free from their sinful character but the Savior Himself. To receive Christ's freedom, they must realize they have no power to change themselves—then they can fully surrender to the God who promises to set them free. (As a caveat, don't let them think they can't *surrender* unless God makes them. It's true that transformation is God's task, but surrender is man's task. If our hearer has come under conviction and seen the light of the gospel, God has already granted them all the spiritual influence they need to submit to Christ.)

Next, they must *believe the gospel message*—"that Christ died for our sins according to the Scriptures, and that He was buried, and that He was raised on the third day according to the Scriptures" (1 Corinthians 15:3-4 NASB).

FAITH-STEP #3:
RECEIVE CHRIST PERSONALLY

Finally, having believed this glorious message, they must *receive Christ* as their Savior, Liberator, and Lord. As John declares, "As many as received Him, to them He gave the right to become children of God, even to those who believe in His name" (John 1:12 NASB)! Christ offers our hearer the gift of Himself—the perfect Savior, Redeemer, Sanctifier, Lord, Counselor, and friend! He alone is the living stream of salvation, and He calls upon our hearer to be bold and take a drink. As He cried in the book of Revelation: "Let the one who is thirsty come; let the one who wishes take the water of life without cost!" (Revelation 22:17 NASB). By faith, our hearer must believe Jesus's promise, see Jesus standing offering Himself, trust Jesus's heart, approach the living stream, and *drink freely, claiming Him as their own*. Their heart must cry—"Jesus, You are now my Lord! Jesus, You are now my *Savior, Liberator, Counselor, and friend*! You have offered Your grace, and now I freely drink it in! You are mine, mine, mine, by the grace offered at the cross! Thank You for this matchless gift!" *This* is biblical faith—to trust Christ's promises and cling to Him—heart, soul, and very life—knowing He has forever sworn that "the one who comes to Me I will certainly not cast out!" (John 6:37 NASB).

A HELPFUL ILLUSTRATION: EMPTYING OUR
HANDS TO RECEIVE GOD'S FREE GIFT

I often use one clear and unmistakable illustration to help hearers understand how to receive Christ. It concisely explains all the above concepts, demonstrating the true nature of repentance and faith without tempting the hearer to try to earn their salvation.

The illustration follows like this. God stands here before you, offering you an unspeakable gift, neatly and beautifully wrapped—Christ Himself. In Christ are all the glorious gifts of the gospel, including forgiveness of sins, reconciliation to God, a new heart of holiness, the gift of the Holy Spirit, and a promised eternity in God's presence. God has held His hands out to you with this gift all your days,[8] and now He finally has your attention.

But one problem keeps you from receiving this free gift: Your hands are full. You're holding on to your own autonomy, desiring to rule your own life. You're holding on to pet sins you don't want to let go of. You're holding on to excuses and self-justifications—explaining why you haven't surrendered yet, or trying to explain why you don't need the Savior, or trying to convince yourself you can fix it all on your own. God wants to give you the free gift of salvation, but first, you must empty your hands.

Let go of your sins—surrender your life to Christ! Declare the folly of your own excuses; decry the evil of your best deeds and cast them far from you! Empty your hands entirely, submitting perfectly to the will of the saving God, and willing only to hold what He desires for you. Then, trust God's promise, reach out your hands, and take hold of the free gift of Christ and His salvation. Come to God, acknowledge His promise, and claim the gift of Christ as yours!

Turning to Christ really is that simple—you don't need to bribe; you don't need to pay; you don't need to twist God's arm. No, He is the one twisting *your arm*, commanding *you* to repent and receive His favor. Now, believe His promise, empty your hands, and receive Christ's free gift at once! As soon as you receive Him, He will bestow on you the right to be called a child of God (see John 1:12).

WINNING THEM
ON THE SPOT

Once my hearer understands these instructions, I often like to ask a simple question: "Are you ready to surrender all to Jesus Christ *right now* and freely receive His salvation?" If they respond in the negative, I normally ask, "Why not?" Then I reason with them by the Holy Spirit's leading according to their specific case. But if they express readiness to repent and believe in Jesus Christ as I've described, I seek to lead them to Jesus Christ on the spot. How can we lead someone into an immediate discipleship decision? Here, I'll suggest two possible options—one best, and one good, but both with biblical precedent.

First, if possible, we should invite our hearer to receive *immediate water baptism* in the name of the Father, the Son, and the Holy Spirit. A quick study of the New Testament reveals that the apostles *always immediately baptized* those who wanted to receive Christ. Baptism is no mere dead ritual, "but an appeal to God for a good conscience—through the resurrection of Jesus Christ" (1 Peter 3:21 NASB). Through baptism, we call upon the name of the Lord, plunge our old sin and guilt into the water, and rise up as new creatures in the Lord Jesus Christ, "created in Christ Jesus for good works, which God prepared beforehand so that we would walk in them" (Ephesians 2:10 NASB). As Paul explained:

> We have been buried with Him through baptism into death, so that, just as Christ was raised from the dead through the glory of the Father, so we too may walk in newness of life. For if we have become united with Him in the likeness of His death, certainly we shall also be in the likeness of His resurrection, knowing this, that our old self was crucified with Him, in order that our body of sin might be done away with, so that we would no longer be slaves to sin. (Romans 6:4-6 NASB)

When Peter called the masses to appeal to God through baptism, He promised that God would surely respond by sending "the gift of the Holy Spirit" (Acts 2:38 NASB). We should promise the same to our hearer, helping them enter the waters with holy expectancy in God's saving power. They must understand—physical water can never save them, but the Spirit's streams of living water will save them when they express their repentance and faith in baptism!

Second, if baptism is not immediately possible, we should press our hearer to immediately call upon the name of the Lord in a sincere prayer of confession, repentance, absolute surrender, faith, and thanksgiving to God for salvation, for "whoever will call on the name of the Lord will be saved" (Romans 10:13 NASB). When I lead this prayer, first, I like to give a word of warning something like this:

> I want you to know this prayer isn't magical. God will not hear your prayer if you offer it falsely. Don't bother calling on the name of the Lord if you aren't ready to repent of all sin and surrender to Jesus Christ. But if you now call on God in sincere repentance and faith, He'll surely receive and forgive you immediately. That's His promise! Are you sure you want to surrender all to God and receive the gift of Christ?

If they answer positively, I like to kneel and invite my hearer to join me. I may say, "Right now, let's kneel before God, lift our hands in an attitude of total surrender, and offer our lives to the Savior. I'll pray, and you follow along in your own way from the depths of your heart."

LEADING A PRAYER OF SURRENDER

Every surrender prayer will turn out different, and that's beautiful. Only make sure to lead the prayer in a way that voices the hearer's choice to acknowledge their evil ways, immediately die to sin, surrender all to God, and freely receive the gifts of Christ's friendship, forgiveness, and freedom by grace. I often proceed in a prayer somewhat like this:

Dear God, I know I've sinned. I've broken Your law every day of my life and dishonored You over and again. I deserve nothing less than Your righteous eternal judgment and have no right to approach You by my own merit. But I know that You love me and sent Your Son, Jesus Christ, to pay for my sins and reconcile me to You. You've offered me this gift all my life, but I've never been ready to submit until now. Right now, I want to receive Christ as my Lord, Savior, and Liberator.

I recognize that You have an absolute right to govern me, so I surrender my everything to You. I surrender my life. I surrender my autonomy. I surrender my worship. I surrender my relationships. I surrender my possessions. I surrender my fears, hopes, and dreams. I surrender my attitudes and grudges. I surrender my future. I surrender my all! This very moment, I grant You practical control of my entire life! [Here, I like to encourage the hearer to quietly tell the Lord some of the specific issues they now surrender.] In particular, I surrender *these issues.*

I also repent of all my sins. [Here, I like to encourage the hearer to take a moment to confess any specific sins they know they must repent of, or any issue they've decided to surrender to God.] In particular, I repent of *these sins I've practiced.*

I also forgive all whom I've held bitterness towards. [Here, I encourage the hearer to take a moment to specifically forgive those who they've held bitterness toward.] In specific, I forgive *this person for doing this, and this person for doing that.* I release them from their guilt, pray that You bless them, and ask You to forgive my former unforgivingness.

Thank You for sending Jesus to die and rise again to cleanse my evil deeds and grant me total freedom! Right now, by faith, I receive Christ as my Savior. Please send Your promised Holy Spirit to cleanse my heart, reconcile me to You, and teach me to live a life that pleases You with every breath!

Yes, by faith, I receive You now—and I thank You for receiving me back! Thank You so much for freely forgiving my sins! Thank You for this new life You have granted me! Help me to serve You all my days, and please welcome me into Your presence after life's journey ends. In Jesus's name, amen.

ENCOURAGING THE DECIDED
WITH WISDOM AND CAUTION

Once you finish praying, avoid too quickly assuring the hearer that God has received them. Remember, God only receives those who truly turn to Him, and we don't know our hearer's heart. Ultimately, it's the *Holy Spirit* who "testifies with our spirit that we are children of God" (Romans 8:16 NASB). Instead, give them an unshakeable biblical promise: "If you just truly surrendered to God, repented of sin, and received the gift of Christ, the Lord has forgiven your sins, made you new, and received you into His family!" Then collect their contact information, give them a Bible, offer some basic discipleship instruction, exhort them to follow through on their commitments, and plan a baptism as soon as possible.

Now, don't get me wrong—you don't want to discourage them and make them second-guess their decision. How counterproductive! Rather, you should avoid *falsely encouraging them* by stating things that only God knows. By all means encourage them, but do so with the conditional promises of God's Word, and let God Himself testify to their heart that they're children of God.

DON'T FEAR TO PLEAD FOR PENITENCE

Finally, just as you reasoned for revival, co-labored for conviction, and promised for *pistis*, do not fear to *plead for penitence*. Many of us try to keep our evangelism tame to avoid losing favor with others. We must renounce this fear and follow the example of Paul, who said: "We are ambassadors for Christ, as though God were making an appeal through us; *we beg you on behalf of Christ*, be reconciled to God" (2 Corinthians 5:20 NASB). Yes, as you preach, *do not fear to plead with souls*—for God is now pleading with souls, and He has anointed you as His ambassador. Honoring this sacred office, trust God, be bold, and obey the counsel of Charles Spurgeon:

> If sinners be damned, at least let them leap to Hell over our dead bodies. And if they perish, let them perish with our arms wrapped about their knees, imploring them to stay. If Hell must be filled, let it be filled in the teeth of our exertions, and let not one go unwarned and unprayed for.

If you will, God will surely use you as a vessel of His kingdom on Earth. His kingdom will begin to come in your surroundings as in Heaven, winning souls, reviving saints, and transforming lives. And by God's grace, God will record your invasion of light in the annals of His victories!

CHAPTER FOURTEEN

PREVAILING PRAYER: THE AMBASSADOR'S MIGHTIEST WEAPON

"Prayer is the preacher's mightiest weapon. An almighty force in itself, it gives life and force to all." E.M. Bounds

"The man who can get believers to praying would, under God, usher in the greatest revival that the world has ever known."
Leonard Ravenhill, *Why Revival Tarries*

In the past five chapters, we studied how to work wisely toward a great harvest, or successful invasion of light. We discussed how to receive God's power, test the soil of men's hearts, plow hard and rocky soil with God's law, plant the miraculous seed of the gospel, and—once God has done His special work—to reap the harvest by leading men to surrender all to Christ. Now, we'll discuss *prayer*, the crucial condition upon which all our labors hang.

Without prevailing prayer, our invasion of light will always fail. It doesn't matter how perfectly you test the soil, plow, or sow—if you neglect to pray for God's saving hand, you'll never witness the great harvest Jesus promised. Remember, "salvation belongs to the Lord" (Psalm 3:8 NKJV)—true transformation can't be manufactured; only sent from God's throne as His ambassadors advance His cause. As Paul declared, "I planted, Apollos watered, but God gave the growth. So neither he who plants nor he who waters is anything, but only God who gives the growth" (1 Corinthians 3:6-7 ESV).

Knowing this, we witness the great folly of running into spiritual battle without prayer! You might as well try to start a fire without a match, cook a meal without heat, or drive a car without fuel. Prayer is imperative to our battle with Satan's kingdom; all fruitful Kingdom work is born, maintained, and completed in true intercession!

GOD'S ROADMAP OF TRUE PRAYER

Of course, not just any type of prayer will destroy Satan's works, exalt Jesus's name, and welcome God's transforming power in our world. To forge a successful invasion of light, we must follow God's roadmap of true prayer: we must intercede in the name and by the blood of Jesus, in true repentance and humble confession of sin, with a listening spirit, a heart confident in God's promises, a persistent petition, and—when possible—in corporate agreement. Of this type of prayer, E.M. Bounds declared: "Prayer is the preacher's mightiest weapon. An almighty force in itself, it gives life and force to all."[1] "Prayer is the condition by which all foes are to be overcome and all the inheritance is to be possessed!"[2]

I (Brian) learned early in ministry that the prayer closet is where spiritual vision is received and launched. It is where God's vision, burden, and calling are initiated and kept burning. Through true prayer, we hear and receive God's call to do things we could not possibly accomplish in our own power, intellect, and resources. God wants His kingdom to come and will to be done on Earth as it is in Heaven—and to accomplish that, He commands us to pray (see Matthew 6:10)!

Does prayer play an important role in your invasion of light at this time? If not, are you ready to make the change and dedicate yourself to an intercessory life? Are you prepared to leap out of a lazy, lukewarm, and distant relationship with God, and dive into the joy of adventuring with Him? If so, let's press on to better understand the conditions of effective prayer.

KEY #1: PRAY IN JESUS'S NAME
AND BY HIS BLOOD

First, to prevail in prayer, we must pray in Jesus's name and by His blood. Many try to approach God based on their own merit, hoping He'll answer their prayers because of their supposed goodness. Be assured—if you pray that way, you'll receive nothing from God's hands. As James warned us—"God opposes the proud but shows favor to the humble" (James 4:6). We must never proudly approach God on the basis of the filthy rags of our own righteousness (see Isaiah 64:6). Rather, we must pray from total dependence upon the blood of Jesus shed for us on the cross.

Remember, Jesus is the only way to the Father. He boldly declared, "I am the way, the truth, and the life. No one comes to the Father except through Me" (John 14:6 NKJV). This doesn't only mean Jesus is the way to "get to Heaven after we die." Even more importantly, He's the only way we can enter into a relationship with God *today*. The grand purpose of His earthly mission was to reconcile us to the Father, and now He connects us directly to Him through prayer. For this reason, whenever we pray, we can "approach God's throne of grace with confidence, so that we may receive mercy and find grace to help us in our time of need" (Hebrews 4:16).

How can we approach the Father standing on Jesus's sacrifice alone? By praying in Jesus's name. As Jesus declared in John 16:23—"Most assuredly, I say to you, whatever you ask the Father *in My name* He will give you" (NKJV). As He said in John 15:16:

> You did not choose Me, but I chose you and appointed you that you should go and bear fruit, and that your fruit should remain, that *whatever you ask the Father in My name* He may give you. (NKJV)

Finally, as He said in John 16:26-27:

> In that day you will *ask in My name*. I am not saying that I will ask the Father on your behalf. For the Father Himself loves you, because you have loved Me and have believed that I came from God. (NKJV)

Then what is it to pray in Jesus's name? Is it just a phrase we tack onto the end of our prayer? "In Jesus's name, amen!" Not quite. While it's great to end prayers with that formula, what's more important is the attitude of our hearts. As R.A. Torrey said:

> To pray then in the name of Christ is to pray on the ground, not of my credit, but His; to renounce the thought that I have any claims on God whatever, and approach Him on the ground of God's claims. Praying in the name of Christ is not merely adding the phrase "I ask these things in Jesus' name" to my prayer. I may put that phrase in my prayer and really be resting in my own merit all the time. But when I really do approach God, not on the ground of my merit, but on the ground of Christ's merit, not on the ground of my goodness, but on the ground of the atoning blood (Heb. 10:19), God will hear me.[3]

Yes, as our high priest and intercessor, the Lord Jesus "always lives to intercede for" us at the throne of grace (Hebrews 7:25). As Paul declared, "It is Christ who died, and furthermore is also risen, who is even at the right hand of God, who also makes intercession for us" (Romans 8:34 NKJV). Knowing this, humble yourself, trust Jesus's work on the cross, and boldly approach the throne of grace with total dependence on Jesus's sacrifice for your sins. Relinquish all trust in your own works and boldly ask God the Father in Jesus's name. Jesus promised what would happen if you do: "Most assuredly, I say to you, whatever you ask the Father in My name He will give you" (John 16:23 NKJV). What a promise for the invasion of light!

KEY #2: PRAY FROM A CLEAN HEART
(CONFESSION, REPENTANCE, AND SURRENDER)

The next key to prevailing prayer is *a clean heart.* While good deeds never earn us a place in God's presence, unrepentant sin does distance us from God, causing our prayers to "be hindered" (1 Peter 3:7 NKJV). As Isaiah explained:

> Behold, the Lord's hand is not shortened, that it cannot save; nor His ear heavy, that it cannot hear. But your iniquities have separated you from your God; and your sins have hidden His face from you, so that He will not hear. (Isaiah 59:1-2 NKJV)

And as Peter echoed: "The eyes of the Lord are on the righteous and His ears are attentive to their prayer, but the face of the Lord is against those who do evil" (1 Peter 3:12). Unrepentant sin separates us from God and blocks the prayer channels. There's no surer way to hinder an invasion of light!

Of course, every Christian stumbles at times (see James 3:2); and we all must face the battle between the flesh and the Spirit (see Galatians 5:16-26). But that doesn't mean we need to live distant from God. On the cross, Jesus provided the perfect sacrifice for sin so we can live near to God all our days. To walk in that nearness—and to prevail in prayer—we must remain honest with the Lord and continually avail ourselves of Jesus's cleansing blood. As James exhorts us: "Confess your trespasses to one another, and pray for one another, that you may be healed. The effective, fervent prayer of a righteous man avails much" (James 5:16 NKJV).

This verse has long exhorted and encouraged me (Brian) to pour my heart out to God in honest confession. At times it has even led me past the outer courts of confession and prayer and into the inner sanctum of God's holy and gracious presence—that place where we meet with God, and God meets with us. I want to break down this sacred conditional promise to help you experience the same.

THE SNARE OF SECRET SIN;
THE FREEDOM OF CONFESSION

First, let's look at James's command: "Confess your trespasses to one another, and pray for one another, that you may be healed" (James 5:16 NKJV). Have you ever prayed with unconfessed sin in your heart? I have—and those prayers always halted right where I spoke them. After all, I had hidden sin, and "if I regard iniquity in my heart, the Lord will not hear me" (Psalm 66:18 KJV). Perhaps it was unforgivingness, jealousy, rebellion, or a fault I refused to confess to someone. By keeping it in, I was acting in pride—a great evil in God's sight. As a result, I experienced James's grave warning firsthand: "God resists the proud" (James 4:6 NKJV).

You see, to pray in a way that "avails much" (James 5:16 NKJV), we must extinguish pride and willful sin from our lives by the power of the Holy Spirit.

One way to kill sin is to "confess your trespasses to one another, and pray for one another" (James 5:16 NKJV). God often works radical transformation when we establish accountability with caring mentors or disciplers—whether trusted leaders or spiritual family members [of course, that accountability should almost always remain between people of the same gender]. Corporate confession—what we here call accountability—helps keep our spiritual slate clean before God and man.

What will happen when we become honest with God and man, seeking to follow Jesus in total surrender? James tells us: we'll "be healed" (James 5:16 NKJV). "Having our hearts sprinkled from an evil conscience" (Hebrews 10:22 NKJV), we'll finally have access to the promise of James 5:16: "The effective, fervent prayer of a righteous man avails much" (NKJV). God will hear and answer our requests as we pray by the Holy Spirit's leading! Furthermore, the closer we grow toward God in holiness, honesty, and humility, the easier it will be to resist asking for things outside God's will. Let's break down James 5:16 in Greek to gain more perspective.

THE PRAYER THAT
AVAILS MUCH

In James 5:16, the Greek word translated "effectual fervent" comes from *energeō* (ἐνεργέω), which can mean *operative, at work, putting forth power, displaying one's activity,* or *showing oneself operative.*[4] As such, it implies passion and fervency (we derive the English word *energy* from this word). The word translated "prayer" is *deēsis* (δέησις), which refers to *a request or supplication*—to ask God for something.[5] The word translated "righteous" comes from *dikaios* (δίκαιος), which means *righteous, just, virtuous, and obedient to the commands of God.*[6] The word translated "avail" comes from *ischyō* (ἰσχύω), which can mean *able to, can do, is mighty to do, has the strength to do and prevail in doing it.*[7] Finally, the Greek word here translated "much" is *polys* (πολύς), which can mean *much, plenty, great, often,* and *for a long time.*[8]

What do we conclude? God wants our prayers to avail much—to have the spiritual might and strength to make a great impact on the invasion of light for a long time. To avail much in prayer, of course, we must pray with fervent and active faith in God's promises and faithfulness. But even more, we must pray from a righteous life of nearness to the Lord. God wants to transform us by grace, and He promises to answer our prayers in spectacular ways as we walk in His gift of imparted righteousness by the Holy Spirit's power.

In summary: the effectual, fervent, energetic prayer and request for God's will by a righteous, virtuous person seeking to obey God's commands can accomplish mighty and marvelous things often and for a long time in this grand invasion of light. Then we must ask ourselves—are we living unrighteous lives? Are we hiding unconfessed sin in our hearts? Have we refused to surrender some area of our lives to God? If so, our prayers will never avail much, and our invasion of light will never succeed. It's time to get honest with God, receive His cleansing, and start walking in His gift of righteousness.

KEY #3: PRAY WITH A LISTENING EAR

Next, to prevail in prayer, we must pray with a listening ear to God's voice. In John 16:13–15, Jesus promised the Holy Spirit's daily guidance:

> When He, the Spirit of truth, comes, He will guide you into all the truth. He will not speak on His own; He will speak only what He hears, and He will tell you what is yet to come. He will glorify Me because it is from Me that He will receive what He will make known to you. All that belongs to the Father is Mine. That is why I said the Spirit will receive from Me what He will make known to you.

Prayer isn't only talking *to* God—it's also hearing *from* God. Oftentimes God will give us specific guidance about how to pray and what to pray for. This guidance is essential to effective prayer. As John Piper said, prayer is "a wartime walkie-talkie."[9] With it, God's soldiers hear God's vision, receive His burden, and understand His eternal calling on their lives. Without it, we lose communication with our Commander-in-Chief and forfeit the leadership, guidance, and provision God promised the intercessor.

The benefits of listening prayer are many. Through listening prayer, God speaks to us and prepares us for the difficult things ahead. He prunes us of wrong thinking and sets us on His narrow path where we become genuinely fruitful and productive. He affirms our calling and activates our spiritual gifts. How we need the guiding and teaching voice of God in our invasion of light!

Jesus gave the perfect example of listening prayer during His earthly pilgrimage. In the gospel of John, He said:

> Most assuredly, I say to you, the Son can do nothing of Himself, but what He sees the Father do; for whatever He does, the Son also does in like manner . . . For I have not spoken on My own authority; but the Father who sent Me gave Me a command, what I should say and what I should speak. (John 5:19, 12:49 NKJV)

You see, as the model ambassador, Jesus always stayed in contact with Heaven's headquarters. Both in private prayer and throughout the day, Jesus always sought to hear clearly from God the Father. Why? Because He knew His invasion of light could only succeed if He obeyed the Father's plan as revealed to Him by the Holy Spirit. It's no different for us!

We must remember that God's Kingdom makes no lone rangers. We have no right to stop listening to our Supreme Commander in the invasion of light. If you want to become an effective spiritual soldier in God's army, you must hear God's voice, pray God's will, and obey God's leading!

Praise God, through the Holy Spirit, our Heavenly Father offers direct, loving, insightful, and inspirational guidance to His blood-bought children. He leads, directs, and helps us know what to pray for and how. As the Apostle Paul promised: "Likewise the Spirit also helps in our weaknesses. For we do not know what we should pray for as we ought, but the Spirit Himself makes intercession for us with groanings which cannot be uttered" (Romans 8:26 NKJV).

And Spirit-led prayer is unstoppable in God's hands! As Derek Prince said in *Rules of Engagement*:

> Focused prayer, directed by the Holy Spirit, can reach across continents and oceans and strike with unerring accuracy at any target assigned to it. Undoubtedly, it is the most powerful and the most effective of all the weapons in the Christian arsenal.[10]

Then how can we hear God's voice and receive His wisdom in prayer? It all starts by inviting Him to speak into our situation. As James declared, "If any of you lacks wisdom, let him ask of God, who gives to all liberally and without reproach, and it will be given to him. But let him ask in faith, with no doubting, for he who doubts is like a wave of the sea driven and tossed by the wind" (James 1:3-6 NKJV). Once you ask, be on the lookout for God's response. He may speak to you through a scripture (Psalm 119:50), a biblical promise (2 Peter 1:4), a spiritual prompting or inner witness (Luke 2:27), a Spirit-born burden (Matthew 11:29-30, Romans 8:26-27), an inner vision or dream (Acts 2:17), or the inner voice of the Holy Spirit (John 16:13, Acts 8:29). Come to Him in an attitude of obedience, believe He will send the answer, and "prepare your mind for action" (1 Peter 1:13 BSB). Only make sure to always test what you receive against God's Word, for the Holy Spirit will never speak contrary to biblical truth (John 16:13, 1 John 4:1-3).

KEY #4: PRAY FROM TRUST IN GOD'S PROMISES

Next, to prevail in prayer, we must pray from faith in God's promises. Jesus gave many spectacular promises about the power of the prayer of faith. In John 15:7, He promised: "If you abide in Me, and My words abide in you, you will ask what you desire, and it shall be done for you" (NKJV). In Matthew 21:22, He promised: "Whatever things you ask in prayer, believing, you will receive" (NKJV). In Mark 11:24, He promised, "I say to you, whatever things you ask when you pray, believe that you receive them, and you will have them" (NKJV). And in John 14:13, He declared, "Whatever you ask in My name, that I will do, that the Father may be glorified in the Son" (NKJV).

God has given over 7,000 promises in His Word. Then why do many of those promises seem dormant in our lives? James answers with crystal clarity: "You do not have because you do not ask God" (James 4:2). God wants His will to be done in our lives as in Heaven, but first, He calls us to pray for His promised will: "Your kingdom come. Your will be done on Earth as it is in Heaven!" (Matthew 6:10 NKJV). Yes, to receive God's promises, often we must pray for God to bring them to pass.

But dead, faithless prayer won't prevail with God. James points out one crucial mistake many make when praying the promises:

Let him ask in faith, with no doubting, for he who doubts is like a wave of
the sea driven and tossed by the wind. For let not that man suppose that he
will receive anything from the Lord; he is a double-minded man, unstable
in all his ways. (James 1:6-8 NKJV)

Yes, when we pray God's will, we must not doubt, but always ask in faith and
then stand our ground in confidence, knowing the promises of God are yes and
amen in Him (see 2 Corinthians 1:20). As John assures us:

If we ask anything *according to His will*, He hears us. And if we know that
He hears us, whatever we ask, we know that we have the petitions that we
have asked of Him. (1 John 5:14-15 NKJV)

You see, God has magnified His Word above His name (see Psalm 138:2)—so
He'll never fail to fulfill even one of His promises. As God spoke through Balaam,
"God is not human, that He should lie, not a human being, that He should change
His mind. Does He speak and then not act? Does He promise and not fulfill?"
(Numbers 23:19). God's promises are never limited by His power—but they are
often limited by man's doubt![11] Why? Because God commands us to receive them
by faith! Knowing this, we should always pray in absolute confidence that God
will provide what He promises.

WHEN DOUBT
ATTACKS

We all know doubt is a notorious faith-killer. Satan often attacks with doubt to
try to make us double-minded and unstable in our faith. Through doubt, Satan
longs to rob our faith, nullify our prayers, destroy our souls, and halt our invasion
of light! As Jesus warned, "The thief comes only to steal and kill and destroy"
(John 10:10). Yes, doubt is always on the prowl—we must remain ever aware of
this spiritually menacing foe!

But thank the Lord, fear and doubt cannot stand in the brilliant presence of
overcoming faith in God. Just as darkness disappears when light floods a room,
fear and doubt flee when faith in God's Word steps on the scene. Through faith,
we gain access to the sword of the Spirit, which has measureless power to destroy
Satan's works when in the hands of a true disciple.

Just imagine how much we could accomplish for God's glory if we actually believed God would do what He said! What kind of believers would we
become if we truly believed God wants to fulfill His promises—and even waits
for us to ask for them! We would be spiritual powerhouses! Our simple faith
and obedience to God's promises would invite the power of God's Kingdom to
Earth. Ambassador of Christ, revolt against doubt, take hold of God's promises,
and pray—"Your kingdom come. Your will be done on Earth as it is in Heaven!"
(Matthew 6:10 NKJV).

A CRUCIAL KEY:
NEVER ABUSE GOD'S PROMISES

Only one thing—as we pray in faith, we should make sure we are truly praying for God's will. As James explained, many pray in a false faith that seeks its own pleasure: "When you ask, you do not receive, because you ask with wrong motives, that you may spend what you get on your pleasures" (James 4:3). Knowing this pitfall, we must make sure to pray for *God's will, not our whims.*

You see, there is a big difference between faith and presumption. Those who pray in faith know God will answer—either because God's Word promises the request, or because the Holy Spirit reveals it privately. Conversely, those who pray in presumption merely *hope* the Lord will answer—though they never truly seek God's mind about the request. Unfortunately, droves of believers waste their lives this way, constantly asking for things God *never* promised. Then they wonder why God never seems to answer!

Christian, it can be dangerous and ineffective to haphazardly pluck Bible promises out of context and without the Holy Spirit's leading. In doing so, many have opened their eyes to covetousness, their hearts to greed, and their minds to deception. Knowing this threat, always seek to pray for God's will as accurately explained by the Bible and the leading of the Holy Spirit. If you do, there's no limit to what God can do you through your prayers. As William Carey declared, "The future is as bright as the promises of God!"

THE PROMISES TO PRAY

Then what scriptural promises should we pray to forge a successful invasion of light? God has promised so many wonders for His glory and our good! As we invade, we can always pray with confidence for God's wisdom in ministry (James 1:5), God's power to overcome sin (1 John 5:4), a deeper connection with God the Father (John 17:23, 26), a more profound revelation of Jesus (2 Corinthians 4:6, Colossians 1:27), God's leading in our preaching (Matthew 10:19-20), the conviction of the Holy Spirit upon our hearers (John 16:8, Jude 1:15), the revelation of the gospel to the convicted (John 15:26), God's drawing of the lost (John 12:32), the outpouring of the Holy Spirit (Acts 2:17), and so much more.

We can also pray in faith for God to provide whatever we need for the spiritual battle, as Paul promised, "My God will meet all your needs according to the riches of His glory in Christ Jesus" (Philippians 4:19). Initially, for me (Brian), that meant trusting the Lord for small things, like opening doors of local ministry and supplying hundreds of dollars for God's work. Later on, it meant trusting the Lord to open international doors of ministry, trusting Him for thousands in ministry funds, and more. I can attest—and praise God!—that the Lord has provided for my personal call countless times over the last four decades.

Yes, for more than forty years I've seen the reality of the adage: "If it's God's will, it's God's bill." And I'll tell you from experience—God wants to provide all of our needs for the invasion of light, but first, we must learn prayerful dependence upon Jehovah Jireh, the Lord, Our Provider. Then, we often must turn our trust into action, following Jesus in "the obedience of faith" (Romans 1:5 ESV). Yes, as we pray for God's invasion of light, He will often require us to take specific steps of faith, leaps of faith, and even dives of faith. We must fulfill these marching orders out of a simple trust that God will meet every need associated with the vision, burden, and calling He planted in our hearts. As we walk by faith, God will do what seems impossible through our invasion of light! "Through God we will do valiantly, For it is He who shall tread down our enemies!" (Psalm 60:12 NKJV).

KEY #5: PRAY IN FERVENCY AND HOLY PASSION

The next key to prevailing prayer is fervency, or holy passion. As James declared, "The effective, *fervent* prayer of a righteous man avails much" (James 5:16 NKJV).

Now, fervency is not an air we put on when we pray, nor a passionate accent we use to twist God's arm in prayer. Rather, fervency is a natural fruit of the revived life (something we discuss further in Part 3, "How to Walk in the Light: The Ambassador's Character and Crown"). The revived Christian sees and feels the urgency of God's will. He knows God's honor matters more than anything else. He also knows the alternative to God's reign is the reign of sin and death; that destruction and damnation reign wherever Jesus is dishonored. Seeing these stark realities, he yearns with all his being that God's kingdom would come and His will be done on Earth as in Heaven. Having this desire, he cannot help but pray—and that with unbridled passion and urgency. How else would he intercede, seeing his glorious Savior dishonored, his God's will neglected, and his peers racing boldly towards eternal judgment?

You see, many professing believers treat God's will, promises, and glory like a luxury rather than a desperate need. They don't much care if God's kingdom comes, nor if His will is done. Self-satisfied by worldly distractions, they don't see or feel how desperately they need God's promises, nor how urgently their neighbors need Jesus's salvation. This cavalier attitude reveals itself in their prayers. Their prayers have no fervency; no urgency; no burden; no stretching forth towards God's perfect will. They could pray in all the faith they want, but unless they learn to pray like God's will matters, they'll never receive God's promises through prayer, nor will they win great victories in the invasion of light. As E.M. Bounds explained:

Fervourless prayer has no heart in it; it is an empty thing, an unfit vessel . . . Prayers must be red hot. It is the fervent prayer that is effectual and that availeth. Coldness of spirit hinders praying; prayer cannot live in a wintry atmosphere. Chilly surroundings freeze out petitioning; and dry up the springs of supplication . . . Heaven is a mighty poor market for ice . . . To be absorbed in God's will, to be so greatly in earnest about doing it that our whole being takes fire, is the qualifying condition of the man who would engage in effectual prayer.[12]

Yes, prevailing prayer must often come from a desperate yearning for God's will, glory, and promises. As John Henry Jowett exhorts us:

> The ministers of Calvary must supplicate in bloody sweat, and their intercession must often touch the point of agony. If we pray in cold blood we are no longer the ministers of the Cross. True intercession is a sacrifice, a bleeding sacrifice, a perpetuation of Calvary, a "filling up" of the sufferings of Christ . . . Do our prayers bleed? Have we felt the painful fellowship of the pierced hand? . . . As soon as we cease to bleed we cease to bless.[13]

What a challenge! And Jowett's call to pray in "bloody sweat" is no mere artistic flourish of expression. He's calling us to emulate the spirit of Jesus's prayer in Gethsemane, where "being in anguish, He prayed more earnestly, and His sweat was like drops of blood falling to the ground" (Luke 22:44). Oh, to pray with that type of burden for God's will and honor! To model ourselves on the example of Jesus, who, "during the days of [His] life on Earth . . . offered up prayers and petitions *with fervent cries and tears* to the one who could save Him from death, and . . . was heard because of His reverent submission" (Hebrews 5:7). Fervent cries! Tears! Reverent submission! Yet confidence in God's saving power! Do our prayers imbibe these crucial keys of Jesus's prevailing prayer? Do we share in "the fellowship of His sufferings" through prayer (Philippians 3:10 NKJV)? When was the last time Heaven heard genuine *fervent cries and tears* from us?

Truly, sometimes prevailing prayer must become too fervent for words to express. In these moments of intense intercession, our words are replaced by the very pain and groaning of the Holy Spirit for the completion of God's will, the salvation of souls, and the coming of God's kingdom. As Paul explains:

> We do not know what we should pray for as we ought, but the Spirit Himself makes intercession for us with groanings which cannot be uttered. Now He who searches the hearts knows what the mind of the Spirit is, because He makes intercession for the saints according to the will of God. (Romans 8:26-27 NKJV).

Yes, the most intense form of prayer steps into God's very heart, feels the burning intensity of His will, emotions, and love, and speaks [or groans] those divine burnings back to God, saying "Your kingdom come, Your will be done, on Earth as in Heaven!"

FROM GROANING TO GLORY:
A STORY OF REVIVAL PRAYER

Revivalist Charles G. Finney recounts a story that unveils the radical impact of fervent prayer upon the invasion of light—even when coming from the weakest of saints. He records in his *Memoirs*:

A pious man in the Western part of this State was sick with consumption. He was a poor man, and sick for years . . . This poor man lingered in this way for several years, and died. After his death, I visited the place, and his widow put into my hands his diary . . . She told me that he was so exercised in prayer during his sickness that she often feared he would pray himself to death . . . .

Among other things, he says in his diary: "I am acquainted with about thirty ministers and churches." He then goes on to set apart certain hours in the day and week to pray for each of these ministers and churches, and also certain seasons for praying for the different missionary stations. Then followed, under different dates, such facts as these: "To-day," naming the date, "I have been enabled to offer what I call the prayer of faith for the outpouring of the Spirit on _____ church, and I trust in God there will soon be a revival there." . . . Thus he had gone over a great number of churches, recording the fact that he had prayed for them in faith that a revival might soon prevail among them . . . .

Not long after noticing these facts in his diary, the revival commenced, and went over the region of country, nearly, I believe, if not quite, in the order in which they had been mentioned in his diary . . . The revival was exceedingly great and powerful in all the region . . . Thus this man, too feeble in his body to go out of his house, was yet more useful to the world and the church of God than all the heartless professors of the country. Standing between God and the desolations of Zion, and pouring out his heart in believing prayer, as a prince he had power with God, and prevailed.[14]

Praise God, this feeble man offered himself as a channel for God's fervent passion for souls, and God sent the glory in response. Being deathly sick, he couldn't preach to the masses—but He could pray to the God who loved them. Moved with extreme burden for the lost, this righteous man prayed fervent prayers for revival with loud cries and tears. The rest was history: his prayer availed much (see James 5:16); he "was heard because of his reverent submission" (Hebrews 5:7), and Heaven is fuller today for it. Glory to God! Let us follow his example as we invade our world with light.

KEY #6: PRAY WITH PERSISTENCE

The next key to prevailing prayer is persistence. Sometimes the path of prayer stretches long, testing our patience, disquieting our faith, and tempting us to give up. For a while, we fulfill the first conditions of prevailing prayer—we pray in Jesus's name, from a clean heart, with a listening ear, in faith for God's promises, and with great urgency and fervency. Reminded of God's call to persist, we may even push through the first few levels of satanic opposition. But soon enough, Satan's whispers grow more persuasive. "God isn't listening," he hisses. "The answer will never come. Your prayers are useless!" Sometimes he even cloaks his lies in religious garb, saying, "God doesn't will to fulfill that promise you're praying for. You're fighting against God's plan, kicking against the goads. You need to submit to His perfect will—and this isn't part of it!" Oh friend, what dangerous lies—yet often so convincing!

You see, Satan can more easily trick our generation into quitting on God's promises than any other generation in history. Why? Because we're the first generation of Christians who never has to wait for anything. We are the generation of fast food, LTE, and two-day shipping. We always rush to the shortest line in the supermarket. We complain if our internet lags for five seconds above average. We choose one product over another because it promises to ship one day earlier. For so many of us, it's high-speed or nothing! And if it doesn't come fast, something's wrong with management.

Many call this light-speed life an advancement—but from Heaven's view, it's regression. The truth is, our now-or-never mindset has deeply damaged the cause of true prayer. We may not like it, but prayer doesn't always work like Amazon Prime's two-day shipping guarantee. Oftentimes, God calls us to pray long in the face of terrible odds; like Abraham, to believe "against all hope" (Romans 4:18), knowing "He who promised is faithful" (Hebrews 10:23). Addicted to outrage, we're used to angrily calling customer support to demand an immediate fix to our consumer catastrophes—but God's kingdom is not a company, we aren't customers, God isn't a support representative, and the Bible never claims "the intercessor is always right." God is our Creator and Lord, and we are His loyal subjects. As such, we never demand the timeline of answered prayer. God's standard is simple: either wait for the answer in God's time or forfeit it altogether. Oh, how we need persistence!

Jesus knew many of His followers would struggle to pray until the answer came. Knowing this, "Jesus told His disciples a parable to show them that they should always pray and not give up" (Luke 18:1). In Luke 18:2-8, he tells the story:

> In a certain town there was a judge who neither feared God nor cared what people thought. And there was a widow in that town who kept coming to him with the plea, "Grant me justice against my adversary."

> For some time he refused. But finally he said to himself, "Even though I don't fear God or care what people think, yet because this widow keeps bothering me, I will see that she gets justice, so that she won't eventually come and attack me!"

> And the Lord said, "Listen to what the unjust judge says. And will not God bring about justice for His chosen ones, who cry out to Him day and night? Will He keep putting them off? I tell you, He will see that they get justice, and quickly. However, when the Son of Man comes, will He find faith on the Earth?"

How relevant for the everyday Christian! Sometimes, we feel like God doesn't hear us. Just like the widow, "we keep coming to [God] with [our] plea," "crying out to Him day and night" (Luke 18:3, 7). We pray, fast, wait, believe, pray, fast, wait, believe and repeat—but soon, doubt interrupts the cycle. We try to pray, but suddenly God's promise seems hard to believe anymore. After a long and valiant fight, we succumb to discouragement, conclude God won't hear us, and hang up God's promises for later. What a tragedy!

Most saints understand the temptation to quit crying out for God's promises. But we need not lose heart! The truth is, God is listening with infinite love, working out the answer as He bottles our tears of intercession (see Psalm 56:8, Revelation 5:8). He cares about our yearnings for His will, and promises "He will see that [we] get justice, and quickly!" (Luke 18:8). Yes, God will eventually fulfill every genuine promise we take to Him in prevailing prayer. Only one question stands—when the time for the answer comes, "will He find faith" in our hearts (Luke 18:8), or will we have already thrown in the towel? What will we believe in more—our problem, or God's promise?

THE TEST OF
PERSISTENCE

You see, the path of persistent prayer often tests our hearts. It's not that way by accident—God has designed prayer with infinite wisdom to purify our motives, increase our surrender, strengthen our spiritual resolve, and bind our hearts to the God who promised. If we persist, the process will purge us; if we forge ahead, the fight will strengthen our faith! God *will* answer our cry for His will—especially His will to save souls! But first, He sometimes chooses to strengthen us through the waiting. As Jim Cymbala explained in *Breakthrough Prayer*:

> This is how God's Word refines all of us. We act on his promise, and the testing begins. Things turn worse instead of better. Opposition springs up against us. God doesn't seem to hear our prayers. Discouragement leaves us susceptible to temptation. This purging process rids us of self-dependence so that our faith can remain solely in God. It refines us of self-indulgence so we can walk in holiness. It deepens our surrender to God's will in preference to other more convenient options. And the experience reminds us that God's grace is sufficient as we wait for the fulfillment of his word.

Yes, keep interceding, ambassador of Christ—God is working an answer to your cries for His promises, and conforming you to the image of Jesus in the meantime! Oh, what a joy to receive the answer after long tarrying—and to know you grew closer to God in the waiting!

HOW TO PERSIST IN PRAYER

Then how can we practice persistence in prayer as we invade the world with light? Revivalist R.A. Torrey shares a method he used with great fruitfulness until his dying day. First, he suggests we ask God to show us who or what to pray for. Then, he challenges us to persist praying for it until God's light invades:

When you have selected a man to win for Christ, you should pursue him by prayer day and night, day after day, week after week, and if need be, year after year. In order to be definite make a prayer list. Write on a sheet of paper, "God helping me, I promise to pray earnestly and work persistently for the salvation of the following persons," then kneel down and ask God to tell you whom to put on that list. Do not make it too long. When you have made it keep your promise. One by one as they accept Christ you can take their names off the list and add others. Everywhere we have gone around the world we have had people make such prayer lists as this, and people are constantly coming to us and telling us, "Another one gone off my prayer list." One of the leading business men of Belfast, an active Christian worker, made such a prayer list when we were in that city. He came to me toward the close of the mission and said, "The last one has gone off my prayer list today. They have all been saved."[15]

Praise the Lord! You might not choose to make a physical prayer list. That's fine—but be sure to ask the Lord to give you a burden for some person or issue in specific, then pray faithfully until God sends the answer. If you will, you'll soon watch God fulfill His promise: "I tell you, He will see that [you] get justice, and quickly!" (Luke 18:8). We've included a prayer list in the back of the book if you'd like to use one.

KEY #7: PRAY IN AGREEMENT
WITH OTHER BELIEVERS

Finally, to prevail in prayer, we must pray in profound agreement with other faithful disciples of Jesus. As Jesus promised, "Truly I tell you that if two of you on Earth agree about anything they ask for, it will be done for them by My Father in Heaven. For where two or three gather in My name, there am I with them" (Matthew 18:19-20).

We've seen that God wants to move through *our* prayers. If we persistently cling to Jesus's blood, obey God's will, hear God's voice, and confidently pray God's promises, God will work incredible miracles in and through our lives. Then how much more gloriously would God move if we prevailed in prayer *together*? No doubt, the results would look like the move of God in Acts:

They devoted themselves to the apostles' teaching and to fellowship, to the breaking of bread and to prayer. Everyone was filled with awe at the many wonders and signs performed by the apostles. And the Lord added to their number daily those who were being saved. (Acts 2:42-43, 47).

As revivalist Charles Finney declared: "When Christians are united, and praying as they ought, God opens the windows of Heaven, and pours out His blessings till there is not room to receive them!"[16]

CORPORATE PRAYER: THE ENGINE OF THE INVASION

E.M. Bounds once wrote:

> When the Church is in the condition of prayer God's cause always flourishes
> and His kingdom on Earth always triumphs. When the Church fails to pray,
> God's cause decays and evil of every kind prevails. In other words, God
> works through the prayers of His people, and when they fail Him at this
> point, decline and deadness ensue.[17]

Indeed, God wants to move in unspeakable power through our invasion of
light. But tragically, much of modern Christendom looks more like the lukewarm Church of Laodicea (Revelation 3:7-13) than the fiery church of Pentecost.
How have we fallen so low? We fault one multi-generational failure above all
else: we've neglected God's call to prayer! As Leonard Ravenhill warned in his
classic repentance manifesto *Why Revival Tarries*:

> The Cinderella of the church of today is the prayer meeting. This handmaid
> of the Lord is unloved and unwooed because she is not dripping with the
> pearls of intellectualism, nor glamorous with the silks of philosophy; neither
> is she enchanting with the tiara of psychology. She wears the homespuns of
> sincerity and humility and so is not afraid to kneel![18]

And again:

> The ugly fact is that altar fires are either out or burning very low. The prayer
> meeting is dead or dying. By our attitude to prayer we tell God that what
> was begun in the Spirit we can finish in the flesh. What church ever asks its
> candidating ministers what time they spend in prayer? Yet ministers who do
> not spend two hours a day in prayer are not worth a dime a dozen, degrees
> or no degrees.[19]

Ravenhill wrote these chilling rebukes in 1959—then how much more
should his words convict today's sleeping church? Modern Christendom has
lost the art of corporate prayer as the ancient church knew it. How often do
you hear of radical disciples waiting together in the presence of the Lord in
passionate, God-hungry prayer? How often does God hear *our spiritual communities* beseeching the throne of grace in humble, trusting, Spirit-inspired prayer?
That is the only kind of prayer God answers. It is the only kind of prayer that
moves mountains, calms seas of doubt, and welcomes God's peace as a perennial
mainstay. Is that kind of corporate prayer rising to Heaven from your spiritual
community? If not, why not?

Think about it: when was the last time your church, ministry, or spiritual
community held a meeting dedicated to prayer? Mind me—not a meeting with
a sermon and a little prayer; nor a meeting with 45 minutes of worship and 15

minutes of cries to the throne. Just focused prayer! If recently, then praise God, and keep on! But if you can't remember, there's a reason for deep concern. Your ministry will never successfully invade with light until it learns to lean into God's power through fiery corporate intercession.

DISTRACTED BY THE NATURAL

The truth is, many Christian leaders spend more time discussing the natural than the spiritual. They're more concerned about buildings, sounds systems, greeters, publications, social media, web presence, and the pastoral wardrobe than the burden of the Lord. They squeeze in a short prayer at staff and board meetings but focus most of their time on topics of little eternal importance. This will never do. God's will never will be done on Earth as in Heaven until Jesus's ambassadors learn to ram Heaven's headquarters with fervent prayer.

The tragic result of our prayerlessness is a weak and powerless church. Our meetings may sound thunderous with pristine audio, brilliant lights, state-of-the-art cameras, hypnotic smoke machines, and unquestionable style—but without true prayer, one great thing will always lack. We won't have God's true *shekinah* glory—a heavy price for our neglect indeed. It's high time to ask ourselves—"Is my spiritual community united in intercession, thus producing fruit that remains; or are we neglecting prayer and thus mass-producing fruit that rots?"

PRAYER MOVEMENTS:
A HAPPY EXCEPTION

Perhaps you'd say—"Brian, not to worry—a great prayer movement is growing in the world today." Sure, there are significant pockets of prayer sprinkled throughout the modern church. I praise God for those dedicated, passionate prayer warriors, and for those churches that have refused to settle for cheap substitutes for the presence of God! If you belong to that honored spiritual air force, God is using you to keep the church afloat and propel God's invasion of light forward. Stay on the path—keep crying out to the Lord of the Harvest!

Unfortunately, these prayer movements represent the exception, not the norm. The fact is that true prayer is not at the forefront of most churches in the West. As a result, much of the church's decision-making occurs in the board room instead of the prayer room. But if we genuinely want to fulfill God's call as the church triumphant, every significant church decision should first be brought to the Lord in prayer. If not affirmed in the prayer room, it shouldn't even land on the docket in the board room!

MAKING TIME FOR PRAYER

Now that we've unveiled the conditions of prevailing prayer, we need to tackle a common objection. Perhaps this very objection rings in your mind as you read. When faced with the call to pray, many simply cry, "I just don't have time!"

All I can say is—really? You don't have the time?

Don't we all have the same 24 hours each day?

Didn't God Himself give you those 24 hours?

And when God admonished you to pray, didn't He know He had given you those 24 hours?

Let's face it; lack of time is nothing but an excuse. As my missionary friend Jim Randall often echoes—"If you're looking for an excuse, any excuse will do." And as the American proverb states: "Excuses are merely nails used to build a house of failure." As for myself, I don't want any excuse to do—and I certainly don't want to build a spiritual house of failure. How about you?

WE ALL HAVE TIME

The fact is, we all have time for prayer. God commands us to pray, and "His commands are not burdensome" (1 John 5:3). That means He never asks us to do anything we can't do with the Holy Spirit's help. Then the truth is obvious: we don't have a time problem; we have a time-management problem. We're not "making the most of every opportunity, because the days are evil" (Ephesians 5:16).

We could try to justify our prayerlessness all we want. We could offer God our best excuses: I have to work, I have to care for the children, I have to fix the car, I can't neglect to study for that test—the list goes on. Those excuses might even convince our own conscience, or our lukewarm friends—but can excuses trick the omniscient God? Never. He sees right through the mirage and exclaims, "Nothing but excuses!"

Yet His loving offer still stands: "He is a rewarder of those who diligently seek Him" (Hebrews 11:6 NKJV). If we want to experience the reward, we must make the choice and seek Him diligently. No excuses will do. The day for spiritual laziness has long passed. We have to ask ourselves—do we truly want God's heavenly rewards, which transform the world and benefit our spirit, soul, and body? Or will we remain self-satisfied with the temporary gratification of social media, Netflix, sports, news, video games, and other entertainments? The choice is truly ours.

HOW TIME SLIPS AWAY

You see, time slips away at phantom speeds for those who prioritize pleasure over prayer. Such people seem to have time for everything else. They find plenty of time to keep up with the Joneses on social media. They find time to watch their favorite shows, listen to their favorite podcasts, and even gather with friends from time to time. Somehow the only things they can't find time for are the crucial spiritual disciplines of intercession, worship, Bible reading, and witnessing. Do you see the problem here? One interest has replaced the other; entertainment has replaced nearness to God.

Don't get me wrong, I have social media accounts and enjoy news, movies, and sports. But I never want to enjoy those at the expense of my quiet times with the Lord. I've experienced the grave spiritual loss that comes from neglecting prayer, and I've learned to count the cost and pay the price of intercession.

And that's the fact—true ambassadors know by experience that they can never accomplish anything in their own strength. These now fiery warriors of light once failed over and again in the arm of the flesh, and have since learned to bow their knees, open their hearts, and receive marching orders from Heaven's Commander-in-Chief. If we truly want to be God's ambassadors of light, we must acknowledge the failure of our prayerless efforts, reprioritize prayer, and dedicate ourselves to discipline in God's call.

HOW JESUS FOUND TIME FOR PRAYER

Then how can we find time to pray? Jesus gives us the ultimate example. He had an extremely busy schedule of travel and ministry, but He never let it stop Him from praying to His Father in Heaven. Instead, *He made time for prayer.*

He made time for prayer in the mornings:

> In the morning, having risen a long while before daylight, He went out and departed to a solitary place; and there He prayed. (Mark 1:35 NKJV)

He made time for prayer overnight:

> He went out to the mountain to pray, and continued all night in prayer to God. (Luke 6:12 NKJV)

He made time to pray alone while with His disciples:

> Jesus came with them to a place called Gethsemane, and said to the disciples, "Sit here while I go and pray over there." (Matthew 26:36 NKJV)

> And he withdrew from them about a stone's throw, and knelt down and prayed. (Luke 22:41 ESV)

He made time to pray corporately with His disciples:

> He took Peter, John, and James and went up on the mountain to pray. (Luke 9:28 NKJV)

On top of it all, He "often withdrew into the wilderness and prayed" (Luke 5:16 NKJV). Jesus made His whole life a prayer!

Now I'll remind you, I'm talking about Jesus Christ—God the Son! Jesus didn't have to come to Earth as a frail human being. He could have chosen to display all His power—and in that case, He wouldn't need to depend upon the Holy Spirit through prayer. But rather than take the easy way, He chose the frailty of humanity so He could establish a prayer pattern for us to follow. He set the bar high—and then sent us the Holy Spirit so we could reach it! Praise God! This means the life of radical prayer isn't a pipe dream; it's a spiritual reality to be believed in, attempted, attained, and sustained by the power of the Holy Spirit. One great way to sustain that life of prayer is to "pray without ceasing" (1 Thessalonians 5:17 NKJV).

PRAYING WITHOUT CEASING

Some time ago, I (Brian) visited my missionary friend Jim Randall in the 10/40 Window for a scouting trip. One day on that trip, he said something that shocked me:

"Brian, you want to know something? I only pray once a day."

Honestly, I didn't know what to say. Once a day? How could it be? Jim is a fruitful missionary to many unreached nations, has led many to Jesus, and has helped many missionaries excel in God's call. How could he succeed by talking to God only once a day? Not sure how to respond, I asked, "Really?"

Thank God, Jim meant something miles from what I thought. He explained:

"Yep—only once a day. But here's the thing—it's all day."

Phew—that was a relief! Jim wasn't saying he only spoke to the Lord once a day. He meant that he sought to pray without ceasing; to pray all day, lifting up concerns to Heaven as the Holy Spirit showed Him others' needs. That's a form of prayer we all can follow.

You see, passing prayers are a crucial key to our invasion of light. Passing prayers are requests spoken to God throughout the day as we pass between places and tasks. If you're in ministry, you might offer passing prayers between and during ministry appointments. If you're in the labor force, you might pray during or between work tasks. If you're a stay-at-home parent, you might pray during or in between household tasks. In this way, every ambassador can maintain constant communication with Heaven's command center at God's throne of grace. What an excellent way to obey God's call to "pray without ceasing" (1 Thessalonians 5:17 NKJV)!

One great reason to pray without ceasing is to avoid missing divine appointments—the opportunities God provides us to share Jesus with the lost and hurting. For example, when you enter a store, you might ask God, "Do You want me to talk to someone in this store? If so, please set up a divine appointment." Or as you board your flight, you might pray, "Please bless the person next to me. If You want me to talk with them about You, please prepare their heart and mine." You'd be surprised how this simple practice can revolutionize your invasion of light. Ministry doesn't always happen from a pulpit or platform; much of God's work must take place in between everyday tasks in everyday settings.

JESUS'S CEASELESS PRAYER

Jesus modeled ceaseless prayer wonderfully. As we discussed, Jesus started and ended His day in dedicated times of prayer—but then, throughout the day He stayed in constant communication with the Father. As He did, the Holy Spirit gave Him divine directions where to go, who to speak to, and what to say. Through this basic practice, Jesus saved, healed, delivered, and restored countless souls during His earthly invasion of light. Jesus kept His ears open, His prayer lifted up, and His will submitted to the Father's voice—and as a result, God's kingdom came and His will was done almost wherever He went. What a brilliant example to follow as we invade the world with light!

A REFLECTION
FROM E.M. BOUNDS

I want to end this chapter with several powerful reflections from E.M. Bounds, considered by many as the apostle of prayer. Breathe in these inspiring and challenging words from God's heart:

Prayer is a privilege, a sacred, princely privilege. Prayer is a duty, an obligation most binding, and most imperative, which should hold us to it. But prayer is more than a privilege, more than a duty. It is a means, an instrument, a condition. Not to pray is to lose much more than to fail in the exercise and enjoyment of a high or sweet privilege. Not to pray is to fail among lines far more important than even the violation of an obligation. Prayer is the appointed condition of getting God's aid. This aid is as manifold and illimitable as God's ability, and as varied and exhaustless is this aid as man's need. Prayer is the avenue through which God supplies man's wants. Prayer is the channel through which all good flows from God to man and all good from men to men.[20]

Again:

Prayer is the child's request, not to the winds, nor to the world, but to the Father. Prayer is the outstretched arms of the child for the Father's help. Prayer is the child's cry calling to the Father's ear, the Father's heart, and to the Father's ability, which the Father is to hear, the Father is to feel, and which the Father is to relieve. Prayer is the seeking of God's great and greatest good, which will not come if we do not pray.[21]

Finally:

Prayer lifts men out of the earthliness and links them with the heavenlies. Men are never nearer Heaven, nearer God, never more God-like, never in deeper sympathy and truer partnership with Jesus Christ, than when praying. Love, philanthropy, holy affiances—all of them helpful and tender for men—are born and perfected by prayer.[22]

Truly, genuine prayer is empowering, enlightening, and enthralling. It serves as a preemptive strike to the problems always pending in life. Every eternally fruitful endeavor launches from the inner sanctum of the prayer closet.

Conversely, not to pray is to claim we're strong enough to handle life independently of God. It's to dismiss God's greatness and rely instead upon our own intelligence, experience, wisdom, and insights. That, my friends, is a very grave mistake.

So let's "devote [ourselves] to prayer" (Colossians 4:2). You won't be disappointed, and God will be pleased! He's been waiting to hear your urgent cries. He wants to answer—and therein, to use you to invade our world with the light of Jesus Christ. He has a plan for your life, and He'll bring it to pass as you connect with God through prayer. "For we are His workmanship, created in Christ Jesus for good works, which God prepared beforehand that we should walk in them" (Ephesians 2:10 NKJV). Amen!

CHAPTER FIFTEEN

SUIT UP! THE INVASION
REQUIRES ARMOR

After over four decades as a Christian, I (Brian) have heard fellow believers say it all. "The struggle is too hard!" "I'm tired of fighting." "I need a break from this battle." And there's one piercing question many ask. "When will things get easier?"

You may ask the same question at times, too. Without a doubt, this spiritual war can become gruesome and difficult—especially when you openly clash with Satan's kingdom. That's why we have to be painfully realistic about the battle.

Ambassador, you left "the easy life" behind when you trusted Jesus. Now, you live camped in a spiritual warzone. This battle offers no breaks—our clashing Kingdoms will never agree to an armistice. Our demonic enemy never rests—remember, these foul spiritual beings keep fighting even in our sleep. Knowing this, you must stand firm, never surrendering, but forever holding your ground against Satan's assaults upon you, your family, your church community, the lost, and society as a whole. No other path guarantees victory in the invasion of light.

You see, I've often heard Christians pray for God to fight the Kingdom of Darkness *for them*. "God, will You fight the devil and give me victory?" "Will You resist the devil and make Him flee?" This sounds noble—and sometimes may even prove necessary—but it's not entirely consistent with our ambassadorial call. The fact is, Jesus has already done His part to triumph over Satan: "Having disarmed principalities and powers, He made a public spectacle of them, triumphing over them in it" (Colossians 2:15 NKJV). Now, He wants to lead *us* in triumph in Christ. As Paul declared, God "always leads us in triumph in Christ, and through us diffuses the fragrance of His knowledge in every place" (2 Corinthians 2:14 NKJV). How can we walk in Jesus's triumph over evil? Without delay, we must stand up, suit up, and "resist the devil, and he will flee from you" (James 4:7 NKJV).

Yes, thank God, Jesus has granted us the spiritual armor we need to stand victorious through all of life's skirmishes, temptations, and trials. With these spiritual weapons in hand, we can destroy the works of Satan, defeat the Kingdom of Darkness, and forge many successful invasions of light. As Jesus promised, "Behold, I give you the authority to trample on serpents and scorpions, and over all the power of the enemy, and nothing shall by any means hurt you" (Luke 10:19 NKJV). "The gates of Hades shall not prevail against" us when we suit up in God's supernatural armor (Matthew 16:18 NKJV)! Instead, by His grace we'll experience the spiritual triumph Paul promised every Christian: "In all these things we are more than conquerors through Him who loved us" (Romans 8:37)! We can win the battle for souls—it's our inheritance as ambassadors of God's kingdom!

RISING UP, OR RUSTING OUT?

Too many believers neglect to appropriate this mighty heavenly provision. Instead of suiting up for battle, most leave their heavenly armor hanging in their closets, guarded only by spiritual mothballs until they face what they consider "a real battle." Then, suddenly awakened to their need, they rush to the back of the closet to take it out, dust it off, and put it on once more. What a recipe for failure!

Does that sound like you and me? Are you using your spiritual armor, or storing it for later? Do you put it on daily, or is it rusting in your closet?

I'll tell you plainly—if we neglect the armor of God, we'll suffer every day of our lives for it. Remember, the enemy of our souls never tires of stealing, killing, and destroying those God loves. He especially loves to taunt Jesus's blood-bought disciples whom God has set apart as agents of restoration. That's why we so desperately need the armor God has provided. Without it, we'll never win the spiritual battles before us—we'll only experience a seemingly endless string of needless defeats. And when the battle's done, I believe we'll also face serious regret at the Judgment Seat of Christ.[1] Though we may still enter Heaven, we'll finally identify our tactical downfall: we failed in battle because we neglected to wield God's weapons against Satan. Ah, we could have plunged the sword of the Spirit into Satan's dark works, but instead, we kept God's Word sheathed! We could have extinguished the fiery darts of the enemy, but we neglected to guard ourselves with the shield of faith!

SUIT UP, SAINT

None of us want regrets on the day we meet Jesus face to face, finally realizing we could have served Him with greater purity, power, and effectiveness. With this in mind, we need to suit up in our spiritual armor every single day. If we will, we can live protected and armed spiritually, physically, morally, and mentally, 24 hours a day, 365 days a year. Saint of God, don't stand down. Suit up, stand up, and fight for God's glory and the world's salvation!

In this chapter, we want to study our spiritual weapons, the extent of their power, and how to use them to place the spiritual forces of darkness in chains. We'll do this by conducting a word study on Paul's exhortation to the Ephesians:

Be strong in the Lord and the power of His might. For our struggle is not against flesh and blood, but against the rulers, against the authorities, against the powers of this dark world and against the spiritual forces of evil in the heavenly realms. Therefore put on the full armor of God, so that when the day of evil comes, you may be able to stand your ground, and after you have done everything, to stand. (Ephesians 6:10, 12-13)

Let's dig in.

BE STRONG IN THE LORD

In Ephesians 6:10, Paul writes, "Be strong in the Lord and the power of His might." The Greek word here translated "strong" is *endynamoō* (ἐνδυναμόω), which means *to empower or to increase in strength;*[2] the word translated "power" is *kratos* (κράτος) which means *dominion, might, and strength;*[3] and the word translated "might" is *ischys* (ἰσχύς), which means *ability, might, power, and strength.*[4]

These words paint a glorious picture of our calling as Christians. Paul commands us to be strong, to be empowered, to increase in strength, and stand in God's power, dominion, might, ability, and strength, no matter what darkness we face. Yes, as Paul declared, we must live as "more than conquerors through Him who loved us" (Romans 8:37 NKJV). No demonic power can weaken us if God is our strength—for when the Holy Spirit strengthens us, "When I am weak, then I am strong"! (2 Corinthians 12:10).

Next, Paul instructs us why we must grow strong in the Lord—"that you may be able to stand against the wiles of the devil" (Ephesians 6:11 NKJV). The Greek word here translated "wiles" is *methodeia* (μεθοδεία)—from which we derive the English word method—which here means *trickery or deceit.*[5] You see, Satan is the master of deception and spiritual slight. He and his cohorts have spent millennia forging diabolical methods to steal, kill, and destroy (a topic we discussed at length in Chapter Five, "The Enemy of Our Invasion: the Kingdom of Darkness"). To quench these fiery darts of Satan, we must make sure we're truly standing strong in God's power. As Paul warned the Corinthians, "Let him who thinks he stands take heed lest he fall" (1 Corinthians 10:12 NKJV).

THE ARMOR OF GOD: THE PATH TO SPIRITUAL STRENGTH

Then how can we "be strong in the Lord and the power of His might" (Ephesians 6:10 NKJV) so we can successfully battle our satanic enemy? Paul tells us one verse later—we must "put on the whole armor of God, that [we] may be able to stand against the wiles of the devil" (NKJV). In other words, we can only be strong in the Lord and the power of His might if we rightly use the armor He gave us in Jesus Christ. Think of it this way. Would you run into battle in a T-shirt, flip-flops, shorts, and no weapon but your bare fists? Much less should we invade with light without heavily armoring up by God's grace.

Paul went to great lengths to emphasize our need of this protective battle gear. He commands us to suit up again only two verses after Ephesians 6:10, only this time he uses a different imperative: "Therefore *take up* the whole armor of God, that you may be able to withstand in the evil day, and having done all, to stand" (Ephesians 6:13 NKJV). The word here translated *take up* comes from *analambanō* (ἀναλαμβάνω), which can also mean *to receive*.[6] You see, the armor of God will never protect us unless we do two things—*receive it and take it up*. First, we must receive it: we must realize God has provided the resources we need for victory, acknowledge that He offers them as gifts, and *accept those gifts as our own*. Second, we must *take it up*—we must take action to put on each article of armor so we can boldly stand for Jesus.

If we receive and take up the armor of God, Paul promises we'll "be able to withstand in the evil day, and having done all, to stand" (Ephesians 6:13 NKJV). This section of the verse also features interesting Greek words that can add perspective. The Greek word here translated "be able" comes from *dynamai* (δύναμαι), which means to have the necessary *power and might*.[7] The word translated "withstand" comes from *anthistēmi* (ἀνθίστημι), which means *to oppose, resist, and withstand*;[8] and the word translated "evil" comes from *ponēros* (πονηρός), which means *bad, evil, grievous, harm, lewd, malicious*, or *wicked*.[9] Finally, the word here translated "stand" comes from *histēmi* (ἵστημι), which means *to abide, appoint, continue, establish, hold up, stand by, stand forth, stand still, or stand up*.[10]

Here's my loose amplified paraphrase of Ephesians 6:12-13 based on our Greek breakdown so far. I don't mean to offer a literal translation, but an inspirational application of the words we reviewed:

> Therefore, since you must make your stand against the evil attacks of the devil and his demons—and because you're in a spiritual war against principalities, powers, the rulers of this dark age, and spiritual hosts of wickedness in the heavenly places—I urge you to clothe yourselves with heavenly armor, which is the whole armor of God. To do that, you must receive, accept, and take it by faith. [Put it on as the Heaven-sent ambassador that you are.] With it, you are guaranteed the power and might you need to stand against and overcome all of the enemy's onslaughts. You now have the power and ability to oppose, resist, and withstand any attack of these diabolical demonic entities and their evil grievous, harmful, lewd, malicious, and wicked ways. Yes, you soldier of God under God's victorious command can and must stand! Through Jesus Christ, you will stand up, hold up, continue, and abide in God's appointed victory!

I don't know about you, but these divine realities make my heart leap. God promises to give us the power and might we need to withstand all of the enemy's onslaughts! When we suit up in God's armor we'll "be able to stand against the wiles of the devil" (Ephesians 6:11 NKJV)—no force of evil can defeat the power of Christ in us! By God's mighty power surging within, we don't have to run in intimidation from demonic attacks. No, we can *stand* and overcome! And by God's grace, Satan's arrows don't have to throw us to the ground—they can bounce off our armor and fall to the ground! On with the invasion!

CHAPTER SIXTEEN

THE AMBASSADOR'S WEAPONS OF WARFARE: THE ARMOR OF GOD

In this chapter, we'll unveil the spiritual armor God has given us for our battle against the Kingdom of Darkness. But before we examine the armor of God, I (Brian) want to make two crucial points about its tactical design.

THE TACTICAL DESIGN OF GOD'S ARMOR

First, it's important to remember the armor of God is *designed for spiritual conquest.* God didn't give us spiritual armor only to protect us *when under attack.* He gives us armor to protect us *as we surge forward* on the offense against Satan's kingdom, seeking to gain spiritual ground and win victories for the Kingdom of God. The excellent news for the disciple is that Jesus already secured our victory on the cross. Now, we only must learn to apply that victory and overcome the devil's lies. As God's Word declares, "They overcame him by the blood of the Lamb and by the word of their testimony, and they did not love their lives to the death" (Revelation 12:11 NKJV).

Second, the armor of God is *spiritual,* and thus only operates by *spiritual power.* We must always remember God's heavenly armor doesn't work by sheer human willpower. To effectively leverage the armor of God, we must walk in the power of the Holy Spirit; that is, we must "walk by faith, not by sight" (2 Corinthians 5:7 NKJV). Like any gift from God, we have to believe it, study it, seek to understand it, embrace it, and use it—for no tool in God's arsenal does any good without action. It's great to have arrows in your quiver if you plan to shoot them. Otherwise, you're just carrying useless weight.

Now, let's seek a deeper understanding of the armor of God described in Ephesians 6:14-17. When Paul wrote this passage, he was imprisoned in Rome and likely chained to a Roman soldier.[1] As he studied the soldier's armor, it seems God taught him many parallels between physical and spiritual warfare. Those revelations have become a timeless guide for God's warriors against Satan. Let's consider what Paul saw.

THE BELT OF TRUTH

In Ephesians 6:14, Paul exhorts us, "Stand therefore, having fastened on *the belt of truth*" (ESV). The belt of truth is the central piece of our spiritual armor. In Paul's day, Roman soldiers tied their entire uniform together with a belt called a *balteus*.[2] Made of metal and thick, strong leather, this belt seemed unbreakable. The Roman soldier needed it for two main reasons: to hold together the rest of his armor, and to holster his sword.[3] No soldier could confidently run into battle without his belt fastened securely.

Similarly, in the spiritual battle, the truth of God's Word is what holds our armor together. If a Christian ever lets go of God's absolute truth—even in small ways—their spiritual armor will loosen, and they'll begin to stumble in their faith. Before you know, they'll start losing battles with Hell's demonic forces—and even with their own carnal mind, which is "hostile to God" (Romans 8:7).

Knowing this danger, we must gird ourselves with the belt of God's truth to protect ourselves from the constant lies of the world, the flesh, and the devil. One way to strap on the belt of truth is to take time to memorize God's Word. Then, as prepared soldiers of God, we can pull out the sword of the Spirit from the belt of truth and proclaim God's Word right from the heart.

RESISTING SATAN'S SURPRISE ATTACKS

Satan loves to surprise attack. For that reason, we must be prepared to resist at any moment. When he strikes, we may not have time to open the Bible and look up the truths that can put our enemy to flight. Therefore, to prepare ourselves for battle, we must hide God's Word in our hearts and keep it on the tip of our tongues.

Sometimes I picture myself carrying varying pouches of scripture on my belt of truth. One pouch has healing verses, another has verses to ward off fear and doubt, another to cast out demons, and another to invoke courage and build my faith in Jesus. In this way, we can experience the same freedom of which the Psalmist testified: "I have hidden Your word in my heart that I might not sin against You" (Psalm 119:11).

To keep your belt of truth fastened, you must spend time daily in God's Word. I encourage you to start early in the morning while all is utterly still. In that quietness, study verses that can help your greatest areas of weakness. Do you struggle with fear? Memorize verses about courage and God's faithfulness. Do you struggle with anxiety? Memorize verses about trusting the Lord. Do you struggle with immoral thoughts or unbelief? Memorize verses about your freedom in Christ, His call to holiness, and Jesus's perfect provision for your every spiritual need. Whatever your area of struggle, bury the truth of God's Word in your heart in a steady flow. As Paul commanded:

> Do not conform to the pattern of this world, but be transformed by the renewing of your mind. Then you will be able to test and approve what God's will is—His good, pleasing and perfect will. (Romans 12:2)

THE BREASTPLATE OF RIGHTEOUSNESS

Our next article of armor is "*the breastplate of righteousness*" (Ephesians 6:14 ESV). Every Roman soldier wore a breastplate of leather and metal[4] or chainmail[5] to protect his vital organs. This way, the soldier always remained protected against enemy attacks—even if he couldn't lift his shield or sword in time.

The protective breastplate God has granted us is *righteousness*. God's will is that we walk protected by two kinds of righteousness: imputed righteousness, which protects us from Satan's accusations, and imparted righteousness, which protects us from temptation. It's by the breastplate of righteousness that we obey Solomon's counsel: "Above all else, guard your heart, for everything you do flows from it" (Proverbs 4:23). Let's consider exactly how we can guard our hearts through this crucial article of armor.

THE PROTECTION OF IMPUTED RIGHTEOUSNESS

We obtain our principal protection from Satan's blows by knowing and understanding the imputed righteousness (i.e., right standing with God) given to us by our Savior, Jesus Christ. Whenever we run into spiritual battle, we must cover ourselves with this truth—"God made Him who had no sin to be sin for us, so that in Him we might become the righteousness of God" (2 Corinthians 5:21). By the spotless sacrifice of Jesus, we have been declared the righteousness of God! We must never "take off" this heavenly reality, opening our hearts to Satan's fiery arrows of accusation. At all times, let us obey the counsel of Hebrews:

> Let us draw near with a true heart in full assurance of faith, with our hearts sprinkled clean from an evil conscience and our bodies washed with pure water. Let us hold fast the confession of our hope without wavering, for He who promised is faithful. (Hebrews 10:22-23 ESV)

God's Word declares that Satan "accuses [us] before our God day and night" (Revelation 12:10). Believe us—if you invade the world with light, Satan will try to throw as much mud on your conscience as he can, even if you're walking right with God. He'll do whatever possible to convince you God has abandoned you—all in hopes that you'll abandon your invasion of light. Knowing this, you must run into every battle with bold confidence in God's grace toward you. Whether you war for your spiritual well-being, for a prodigal's return, or to rescue perishing souls, never forget that God freely saved you and set you apart for Jesus's glory and honor. The breastplate of righteousness reminds us that God's love and righteousness never fail—even if we do. Even if we fail to lift up our shield, God's grace protects the true disciple of Jesus who longs to walk in His ways!

THE PROTECTION OF IMPARTED RIGHTEOUSNESS

Another aspect of the breastplate of righteousness is *imparted or practical righteousness*. The fact is that no one can live in willful sin and remain strong in the Lord and the power of His might. If we choose sin over obedience, we'd better be careful not to act like spiritual conquerors. When demons see that, they laugh at our masquerade. "Look at that measly Christian, running into battle without his breastplate of righteousness! He just gift-wrapped us a chance to steal, kill, and destroy! Fire your arrows of temptation! Let's make him our slave!" Frankly, discipleship is serious business; it's not a game! Sin not only spiritually cripples us—it quenches the Holy Spirit's power in our lives (see 1 Thessalonians 5:19). Willful sin cracks open our breastplate, giving the devil a foothold (see Ephesians 4:27). Tragically, many who experience God's transforming power gradually begin to neglect the breastplate of righteousness and soon become "entangled and overcome by [sin] again" (2 Peter 2:20 BSB). Of such people, Peter warns:

> They are worse off at the end than they were at the beginning. It would have been better for them not to have known the way of righteousness, than to have known it and then to turn their backs on the sacred command that was passed on to them. Of them the proverbs are true: "A dog returns to its vomit," and, "A sow that is washed returns to her wallowing in the mud." (2 Peter 2:20-22)

FASTENING THE BREASTPLATE

Then, what can we do to keep this precious breastplate of righteousness fastened in place? Two things.

First, thank God daily for the imputed righteousness He gave you through the loving sacrifice of Jesus. That is our anchor; our firm foundation. "For by grace you have been saved through faith, and that not of yourselves; it is the gift of God" (Ephesians 2:8 NKJV). Thank God for His matchless grace!

Next, reject the wisdom of the world, and cling to the wisdom of God. To do this, daily read God's Word and allow the Holy Spirit to test your heart for sinful attitudes and practices. God's Word alone can teach us the difference between right and wrong, as well as how to properly confess and repent of evil. When we ask for God's help, the Holy Spirit will remind us of God's Word, convict us of sin, and lead us to repentance and restoration (see John 14:26).

THE SHOES OF THE GOSPEL OF PEACE

Next, Paul commands us to use another article of spiritual armor—"as shoes for your feet . . . put on the readiness given by the gospel of peace" (Ephesians 6:15 ESV).

Shoes can make or break a warrior. Roman soldiers wore strong sandals called *caligae* to protect their feet during long days on foot for battle or patrol. Made with three layers of ox or cow leather, caligae wrapped around the ankles to protect soldiers from blisters and strapped over the feet to permit ventilation and easy adjustment.[6] Many caligae also featured metal spikes on the bottom, which improved traction and arch support.[7]

Though strong when new, Roman caligae were notorious for wearing out quickly.[8] Thankfully, the spiritual shoes God provides hold strong even in life's harshest battles. These God shoes (as I like to call them) grant us the stability and stamina we need to walk in victory over the world, the flesh, and the devil every day of our lives. With our God shoes, we can forge great spiritual conquests for the gospel of peace. Without them, we can only stumble through life, stubbing our toes on spiritual, mental, and moral distractions.

THREE FUNCTIONS OF
THE GOSPEL OF PEACE

Then what do the shoes of the gospel of peace represent? At least three spiritual realities. First, they represent the comfort of the Gospel of peace. For all our days, may we seek to live, move, and have our being in the glorious message of God's grace towards us. With every step you take—even in the harshest battle!—may the gospel be the comfort beneath your feet. Through the grace of the cross, Jesus saved you, forgave your sins, wrote your name in the book of life, reconciled you to God, and so much more! Dwell often on these truths and you'll find rest for your heart, stability for your emotions, and great motivation for obedience.

Second, these shoes represent the moral power God grants us through the gospel of peace. Without Jesus's salvation, we couldn't walk righteously for five steps. Before Christ, we were "taken captive by [Satan] to do his will" (2 Timothy 2:26 NKJV). We "belong[ed] to [our] father, the devil, and . . . want[ed] to carry out [our] father's desires" (John 8:44). But now, by the new birth, we've "been set free from sin, and [have] become slaves of God" (Romans 6:22 NKJV). As a result, we no longer have any obligation to fulfill the evil desires of the flesh (see Romans 8:12). Yes, God has given you the shoes you need to "walk in the light, as he is in the light" (1 John 1:7)! By His grace, you're absolutely free to live in loving obedience to God! How should you respond to this excellent provision? Put on the shoes and start walking in them. As Paul commanded:

Count yourselves dead to sin but alive to God in Christ Jesus. Therefore do not let sin reign in your mortal body so that you obey its evil desires. Do not offer any part of yourself to sin as an instrument of wickedness, but rather offer yourselves to God as those who have been brought from death to life; and offer every part of yourself to Him as an instrument of righteousness. For sin shall no longer be your master, because you are not under the Law, but under grace. (Romans 6:11-14)

Third—and of vital importance—the shoes represent our calling to carry the gospel of peace. Remember, Paul commanded, "as shoes for your feet . . . put on *the readiness* given by the gospel of peace" (Ephesians 6:15 ESV). Readiness for what? I believe Peter gives part of the answer in 1 Peter 3:15: "*Always be ready to give a defense* to everyone who asks you a reason for the hope that is in you" (NKJV). Put on your gospel shoes, ambassador—we must always remain ready to share the soul-saving gospel of Jesus Christ.

A great way to cultivate evangelistic readiness is to memorize and meditate upon verses about your evangelistic calling. The Bible abounds with these gems, such as 1 Peter 3:15, Romans 10:14-15, Ephesians 2:8-10, Acts 20:24, John 3:16-18, Matthew 4:23, and many more. Many of these verses have helped me immensely as I've ministered at home and abroad. I encourage you to memorize some of these to strengthen yourself in the Lord. It's so important to remain prepared to share Jesus at any moment.

Which leads to my final observation about the shoes of the gospel of peace. To put on these shoes, you need to know the gospel and how to share it. It's impossible to receive comfort from a message you don't know, to receive moral power from a message you don't believe, and to be ready to share a message you've never grasped. Also, it's terribly disappointing to want to share the good news but not know how. It breaks God's heart and ours! But you don't need to live unprepared—God's Word provides a wealth of insight about effective evangelism. We sought to encapsulate those principles in the chapters about The Five Ps of Biblical Evangelism. Those chapters can help you strap on your *caligae* and "put on the readiness given by the gospel of peace" (Ephesians 6:15 ESV). We encourage you to memorize those five Ps and put them into practice as God provides opportunity.

THE SHIELD OF FAITH

The next article of spiritual armor Paul describes is *the shield of faith*. Paul admonishes us, "In addition to all this, take up the shield of faith, with which you can extinguish all the flaming arrows of the evil one" (Ephesians 6:16).

In Paul's time, Roman soldiers used a fortified shield called a *scutum* as their primary defensive weapon. About four feet tall and two-and-a-half feet wide, this shield weighed about twenty-two pounds and could defend the fit soldier's entire body from enemy blows.[9] To make these shields, artisans glued together two or three layers of wood, covered the body with linen and calfskin, and bound the edges with iron.[10] Then many soldiers decorated them with colors and designs from their military units. To go into battle without the scutum was a fool's mission! It's no different for God's soldiers in the spiritual battle against the Kingdom of Darkness.

UNDERSTANDING THE SHIELD

Before we discuss how to use the shield of faith, let's seek to better understand it. We'll do this by conducting a Greek word study on Ephesians 6:16: ". . . taking the shield of faith with which you will be able to quench all the fiery darts of the wicked one" (Ephesians 6:16 NKJV).

First, let's consider the commanding verb Paul uses: "taking" (Ephesians 6:16 NKJV). This command comes from the Greek word *analambanō* (ἀναλαμβάνω), which means *to receive up, take up, lift up, and to raise up*, and denotes a definite picking up.[11] You see, the shield of faith doesn't work when sitting on the shelf, nor when merely hanging over our shoulders. It's not a good-luck charm—it's a spiritual weapon against Satan's kingdom! We need to *choose to take it up*, or we'll never be prepared for spiritual battle.

Next, let's consider what Paul means by "the shield of *faith*" (Ephesians 6:16 NKJV). The Greek word here translated "faith" comes from *pistis* (πίστις), which also means trust, assurance, and belief.[12] Faith is belief in God's message, trust in God's promises, confidence in His faithfulness, and assurance that He'll do what He says. To take up the shield of faith, then, is to choose to trust and live by God's promises, faithfulness, Word, and character, no matter what the battle throws at us.

Next, let's consider what we can do with the shield of faith—we "will be able to quench all the fiery darts of the wicked one" (Ephesians 6:16 NKJV). As we mentioned in the previous chapter, the word here translated "be able" means *can do, could do, may do, and will have the power and might to do*. What in particular will we have the power and might to do? "To quench all the fiery darts of the wicked one" (Ephesians 6:16 NKJV). There's nothing we can't overcome if we walk in trust toward God!

Finally, let's consider the spiritual projectiles the shield of faith can quench—"all the fiery darts of the wicked one" (Ephesians 6:16 NKJV). It's crucial to realize Paul isn't talking about a small play dart you might throw at a target in your office, as Rome's military darts looked more like arrows than like the modern toy.[13] Furthermore, the Greek word here translated "dart" is *belos* (βέλος), which can also mean *a javelin or arrow*.[14] In summary, with the shield of faith, we have the power and might to extinguish all the flaming darts, javelins, and arrows of Satan! I don't know about you, but this promise of God lifts my faith to the sky! This glorious promise should make us most eager to start using the shield of faith in our daily battles with the world, the flesh, and the devil.

STRENGTHENING OUR ARMS TO HOLD THE SHIELD

There is one problem. Many aren't yet spiritually strong enough to easily hold the shield of faith. They automatically picture themselves flinging this glorious weapon like conquerors, spinning it to the left, and then to the right, quenching every fiery arrow of Satan like second-nature. While this is God's will for us, such a skillful defense doesn't always come easily. Often shields can be very heavy—for example, the Roman *scutum* weighed about twenty-two pounds. It took strength to hold it up hour after hour, maneuvering it with one arm while lunging a sword in the other. Likewise, to hold up the shield of faith, we must lean into the Holy Spirit's strength—we must "be strong in the Lord and in the strength of His might!" (Ephesians 6:10 ESV). How? To strengthen our arms for spiritual battle, we must increase in submission to the Holy Spirit, obedience to God, and practical understanding of God's Word, for God "gives the Holy Spirit to those who obey Him" (Acts 5:32).

Thank God, it's not complex to start strengthening your arms for battle. In fact, the spiritual exercise regimen is very simple. All it requires is a measure of faith, a simple understanding of God's Word, and the dedication to follow God's instructions through obedience. Whether you're a silver saint or a baby believer, there's no reason you can't begin this process right now. Let's step into God's weight room and consider how to strengthen our grasp on the shield of faith.

GOD'S WEIGHT ROOM

First, to strengthen our grasp on the shield of faith, we must read and memorize God's Word. David declared, "Your word I have hidden in my heart, That I might not sin against You" (Psalm 119:11 NKJV). We must do the same, for "faith comes by hearing, and hearing by the word of God" (Romans 10:17 NKJV). God promises to give the faith you need for the battles ahead—but you can't expect to conquer Satan's kingdom if you go AWOL from training. Make sure to study God's Word every day to strengthen your faith in His character and promises.

Next, begin to practice proclaiming God's Word aloud in response to the day's trials and temptations. Remember, the shield of faith is a defensive weapon, and God and His Word are your defense. As David proclaimed, "[God] only is my rock and my salvation; *He is my defense*; I shall not be moved!" (Psalm 62:6 NKJV). Knowing this, we must never grow tired or embarrassed of proclaiming God's Word. It puts out the devil's fiery darts like a water cannon! You often won't see the results with your natural eyes, but you will sense God's power flowing through you when you proclaim His Word by the Holy Spirit's leading.

Next, remember to recount God's past victories in your life—especially those most pertinent to your current battle. Remember what scriptures, promises, and truths helped you gain the victory, and wield them in spiritual warfare once again.

Finally, be sure to remain in world-changing fellowship with other believers. You see, the Roman army knew the importance of fighting together. One of their greatest secrets of victory was the *testudo* formation, in which soldiers marched shoulder to shoulder and shield to shield, providing near-perfect protection from head to knees, forming one gigantic and impenetrable barrier. It's high time for us to adapt the testudo formation in our war against Satan's kingdom. As Paul commanded, let us "stand fast in one spirit, with one mind striving together for the faith of the gospel" (Philippians 1:27 NKJV)! How many victories would the church see if we only marched by faith, shoulder to shoulder, knit tightly with God and each other?

THE HELMET OF SALVATION

The next article of armor Paul mentions is "the helmet of salvation" (Ephesians 6:17 NKJV). The helmet of salvation plays a crucial role in protecting our thoughts from Satan's onslaughts.

In Paul's day, Roman helmets were stronger than any other. Forged of tough metals, these helmets couldn't break except by axes and hammers,[15] and securely guarded the forehead, cheeks, and even the neck, leaving nothing but the eyes, nose, and mouth exposed. Paul may have even seen some soldiers cover the whole face with a metal mask![16] Surely, no one dared to wage war with his hair flying in the wind. Neither should we enter spiritual battle without the helmet of salvation.

The reality is that many Christians underestimate the value of the helmet of salvation. Realize—as a physical helmet protects the head, the helmet of salvation guards the mind. That benefit seems even more crucial when we realize the function of the mind—it controls the whole body. If the mind tells the arm to move, it moves. If the mind tells the legs to walk, they walk. But when the mind stops working, everything else stops working. How important to protect our minds!

You see, many believers live as wounded warriors. Why? Precisely because they don't protect their minds with the helmet of salvation. Every day, Satan seeks to issue fierce blows to our worldview, thought life, and mental stability. God has provided us perfect protection against these blows—but if we don't use that protection, Satan will leave us wounded on the battlefield time and again. Let's shortly consider how he often attacks.

SATAN'S BATTLE FOR YOUR MIND

Satan is in a battle for your mind, and his mental attacks come in many forms. For some, they come from a spirit of fear (see 2 Timothy 1:8). For others, they come as thoughts of temptation, condemnation, worry, and more. Satan attacks every mind differently—but he always attacks with the same goal: he wants to leave us feeling spiritually paralyzed, like we can't advance in gospel victory. He knows that if we lose strength of mind, we'll no longer find strength of will. He knows that if we succumb to his mental attacks, we'll find it harder than ever to lift our arms, grab our sword and shield, and boldly destroy the works of Satan all around us. And he knows that if he paralyzes Heaven's ambassadors, the world will never hear the message of reconciliation.

Praise God, you don't have to live handicapped by Satan's attacks of temptation, condemnation, doubt, and fear. In the helmet of salvation, God has provided the spiritual protection you need to advance in faith and courage! If you'll only put on "the mind of Christ" (1 Corinthians 2:16 ESV), being "transformed by the renewing of your mind" (Romans 12:2), you'll finally have the power to make the right decisions with your body. You'll no longer lay crying on the battlefield—instead, moved by God's grace, you'll scale the mountain of Jesus's hope with power and ease.

THE HELMET IN PAUL'S WORDS

Paul often taught about protecting our minds through the helmet of salvation. He exhorted the Romans: "Do not conform to the pattern of this world, but *be transformed by the renewing of your mind. Then you will be able to test and approve what God's will is—His good, pleasing and perfect will*" (Romans 12:2 NKJV). He exhorted the Ephesians: "*Be renewed in the spirit of your minds*; and . . . put on the new self, created to be like God in true righteousness and holiness" (Ephesians 4:21-24 NKJV). He reminded the Corinthians that "we have the mind of Christ" (1 Corinthians 2:16 NKJV). And—perhaps most instructively—he commanded the Thessalonians to put on "as a helmet the hope of salvation" (1 Thessalonians 5:8 NKJV).

That last verse should cause the lights to come on in our minds. What is the true meaning of the helmet? It's the "helmet [of] the hope of salvation" (1 Thessalonians 5:8 NKJV). The hope of salvation is the cornerstone of our faith-walk. Without this hope, our minds break down, and our spiritual strength and motivation tumble with it. That's why the enemy of our souls constantly tries to eradicate our hope. Without God's heavenly assurance, we can only crash under the thundering waves of doubt and unbelief. Surely most Christians have experienced that at some moment or other.

WEARING THE HELMET OF SALVATION

Then, what is it to wear the helmet of salvation? It's to walk in constant confidence in Jesus's mercy, grace, and faithfulness promised once for all upon the cross. It's to live happily convinced that God has "magnified [His] word above all [His] name" (Psalm 138:2 NKJV); therefore, God's promise of salvation is as sure and steadfast as God Himself. It's to live anchored by Jesus to the absolute truth of God's promises, being "no longer . . . infants, tossed back and forth by the waves, and blown here and there by every wind of teaching" (Ephesians 4:14).

I can testify to the power of this helmet of hope. From the day I was baptized in water and the Holy Spirit on March 15, 1975, I've never doubted my salvation. I've never struggled with plaguing thoughts of uncertainty regarding whether I will go to Heaven one day. Why? Because the Holy Spirit has made salvation real to me—and with His help, I constantly remind myself of God's salvation promises.

And that's how you put on the helmet of salvation. You learn and remember God's promises of hope to all who believe in Him. Then, you allow that hope to propel you forward as a conquering soldier in this unending battle for souls. Through the Spirit's revelation, God's Word bestows strength and confidence in our loving Lord and Savior, Jesus Christ. And that confidence makes all the difference as we invade with light.

Are you struggling with assurance of salvation? First, make sure you've repented of your sins and trusted Jesus as Master and Savior. Then, dwell on salvation promises like these:

For God so loved the world that He gave His only begotten Son, that whoever believes in Him should not perish but have everlasting life. (John 3:16 NKJV)

Jesus said to her, "I am the resurrection and the life. He who believes in Me, though he may die, he shall live. (John 11:25 NKJV)

For He made Him who knew no sin to be sin for us, that we might become the righteousness of God in Him. (2 Corinthians 5:21 NKJV)

For by grace you have been saved through faith, and that not of yourselves; it is the gift of God. (Ephesians 2:8 NKJV)

If you confess with your mouth the Lord Jesus and believe in your heart that God has raised Him from the dead, you will be saved. (Romans 10:9 NKJV)

For you were bought at a price; therefore glorify God in your body and in your spirit, which are God's. (1 Corinthians 6:20 NKJV)

These are just a few verses that assure me of God's great hope of salvation.

If you haven't already, begin putting on the helmet of salvation today. Daily put on the mind of Christ by meditating on these "exceedingly great and precious promises, that through these you may be partakers of the divine nature" (2 Peter 1:4 NKJV). Then go forth to invade with light as a battle-ready, triumphing soldier of God Almighty. As Paul commanded, "Do not conform to the pattern of this world, but be transformed by the renewing of your mind. Then you will be able to test and approve what God's will is—His good, pleasing and perfect will" (Romans 12:2). On with the invasion!

THE SWORD OF THE SPIRIT

Now, let's consider the final spiritual weapon Paul mentions: "the sword of the Spirit, which is the word of God" (Ephesians 6:17 ESV).

The Word of God is our primary offensive weapon in spiritual battle. Without it, we can't leave any damage on the Kingdom of Darkness. With it, we can destroy Satan's works and win remarkable victories through Jesus Christ our Lord. To better understand this crucial spiritual weapon, let's consider the Roman sword that likely inspired it.

THE SWORD PAUL KNEW

As a Roman and Israeli citizen, Paul saw the Roman sword—*the gladius*—almost everywhere he went. This is quite likely the sword that filled his imagination when he pictured the sword of the Spirit. But many believers envision a sword vastly different from the one Paul knew. How do you picture the sword of the Spirit?

Let's see. Do you imagine swinging a six-foot sword with both hands, lunging from side to side to destroy demons and their dark works? Do you see yourself running invincible into battle, sending devils to their deaths with a slash of the enormous blade? If so, I can't blame you—it's surely an attractive picture. But I do have to ask one thing. What happened to your shield? No one can carry a six-foot sword and a four-foot shield at the same time!

You see, the Roman *gladius* wasn't designed to work alone. It was created for use in conjunction with the shield! Only two or three feet long and less than four pounds, this sword could be easily maneuvered with a single hand—and soldiers sheathed it next to the shield to assure they never lost a moment's protection. Perhaps most surprising of all, Roman soldiers didn't charge into battle with swords stretching forward. Instead, they held their shield up at all times, only lunging the blade forward and back when necessary.[17] In the same way, as we invade the world with light, we must walk shield first and sword second. In other words, we must always "walk by faith" (2 Corinthians 5:7 NKJV), but keep the sword of the Spirit in hand, "ready to give a defense to everyone who asks you a reason for the hope that is in you" whenever God provides opportunity (1 Peter 3:15 NKJV).

To effectively wield "the sword of the Spirit, which is the word of God" (Ephesians 6:17 NKJV), we must understand its true purpose and function. What is the sword of the Spirit, and how do we use it to send Satan's armies to flight? To find those answers, we must start with a smaller question—what does Paul mean by "the Word of God" (Ephesians 6:17 NKJV)?

THE SWORD OF LOGOS AND RHEMA

The Bible often uses two Greek words for "word"—*logos* (λóγος) and *rhēma* (ῥῆμα). These two words are usually used interchangeably, but in different contexts may reflect a slight difference in meaning. Specifically, in the New Testament, *logos* more often represents the whole body of God's truth, especially represented in Jesus Christ, and now expressed in the written scriptures (see 2 Timothy 2:15, 1 Peter 1:23, John 1:1, etc.).[18] Meanwhile, *rhēma* typically refers especially to a spoken word.[19] For illustration's sake, here I'll refer to *rhēma* and *logos* by these occasional differences.

The New Testament refers to the sword of God's Word as both *rhēma* and logos. In our main text, Paul declares that "the sword of the Spirit . . . is the *rhēma* of God" (see Ephesians 6:17 NKJV). But in Hebrews, the author declares: "The *logos* of God is living and powerful, and sharper than any two-edged sword, piercing even to the division of soul and spirit, and of joints and marrow, and is a discerner of the thoughts and intents of the heart" (see Hebrews 4:12 NKJV).

What does this mean? I look at it this way. God's general truth—what's identified in Hebrews 4:12 as His logos—is a sharp double-edged sword in itself. But to win spiritual victories, we must unsheathe the logos and lunge it forward as a spoken word—what's identified in Ephesians 6:17 as His rhēma. In simpler terms, we must speak the Word aloud—whether by sharing the truth with the lost, exhorting our fellow Christians, refuting the lies of Satan against us, enforcing Jesus's authority in spiritual warfare, or encouraging ourselves in the Lord. When we do this, God's Word will discern between "soul and spirit," acting as "a discerner of the thoughts and intents of the heart" (Hebrews 4:12 NKJV)—for both us and others. Then, by God's grace, we and our hearers won't be fooled by Satan's devices.

To effectively lunge forth a rhēma, we must follow three crucial steps: receive the sword, sheathe the sword, and finally remove and lunge the sword. First, we must receive it—we must believe God's logos recorded in the Bible, accept our calling to declare it, and study it humbly, inviting the Holy Spirit to "guide [us] into all the truth" (John 16:13) and train our "hands for war, [and our] fingers for battle" (Psalm 144:1). Second, we must sheathe the sword—through memorization, we must store God's logos in our hearts so we can easily access it in the heat of the invasion. Third, we must remove and lunge the sword—by the leading of the Holy Spirit, we must speak aloud the rhēma of the realities, promises, commands, and warnings of scripture. Above all, Jesus demonstrated how to do this.

THE SPIRIT-LED SWORDSMAN

Jesus declared that He always obeyed the Father's direction when using the sword of the Spirit. In John 12:49, he declared—"I have not spoken on My own authority; but the Father who sent Me gave Me a command, what I should say and what I should speak" (John 12:49 NKJV). He later echoed, "The words that I speak to you I do not speak on My own authority; but the Father who dwells in Me does the works" (John 14:10 NKJV). In other words, Jesus only spoke what He heard His Father speaking. In the same way, the Holy Spirit wants to constantly show us the best use of the sword of God's Word.

How can we receive that direction? By opening our hearts to the Spirit's holy reminders. When we open our hearts to the Spirit's guidance, He'll remind us of the scriptures we need at just the right time. As Jesus promised, "The Helper, the Holy Spirit, whom the Father will send in My name . . . will teach you all things, and bring to your remembrance all things that I said to you" (John 14:26 NKJV). What a promise for our invasion of light!

Are you surrounded on all sides? Do you have no clue what to say, or what promise to pray? Dwell on the Word, allow the Spirit to remind you of the needed scripture, then thrust the sword of the Spirit into Satan's chest by proclaiming that scripture out loud! Apart from prayer, God's "word in season" (Proverbs 15:23 ESV) is your greatest weapon against the hordes of Hell.

I try to apply this principle whenever confusion descends on me. For example, when the enemy attacks with fear, I might say, "God has not given [me] a spirit of fear, but of power and of love and of a sound mind!" (2 Timothy 1:7 NKJV). If the enemy attacks with anxiety and restlessness, I might remind myself of Jesus's promise—"Peace I leave with you, My peace I give to you; not as the world gives do I give to you. Let not your heart be troubled, neither let it be afraid" (John 14:27 NKJV). If attacked with worry about God's provision, I might declare, "My God shall supply all [my] need according to His riches in glory by Christ Jesus!" (Philippians 4:19 NKJV). And if doubts race through my mind about my ability to fulfill God's call, I might proclaim, "I can do all things through Christ who strengthens me!" (Philippians 4:13 NKJV).

Finally, in many cases, I'll simply proclaim—"Jesus Christ is Lord!" After all, demons run for cover when a true disciple boldly proclaims Jesus's lordship. "Demons are subject to us in [Jesus's] name!" (Luke 10:17 NKJV). Yes, right where you are, Jesus has granted you heavenly authority to enforce God's Word and command demonic forces to leave a person or place. Use your authority; thrust forth the sword of the Spirit in the name of Jesus Christ!

TIME TO SHARPEN YOUR SWORD

Want to begin sharpening your sword now? I advise you to memorize at least ten strategic Bible verses in the next thirty days. Take one verse every three days and speak it over and again until it's sealed in your memory for battle. (We invite you to record your verses in the worksheet "My Ten Sword-Sharpening Scriptures" in the back of the book.) With each new memory verse, continue speaking the previous ones aloud. This practice will help activate the logos and rhēma in your life, leaving you spiritually protected and able to set captives free from Satan's dominion of darkness. Remember, Jesus wants to move in greater ways than you've ever imagined! As He promised, "Most assuredly, I say to you, he who believes in Me, the works that I do he will do also; and greater works than these he will do . . ." (John 14:12 NKJV). Suit up, ambassador of Christ. It's no time for retreat—God's calling us to invade with light!

CHAPTER SEVENTEEN

RECOVERING JESUS'S ORIGINAL
INVASION STRATEGY

Many years ago, a church in the United States planned to build a new fellowship hall. Everyone knew the pastor wasn't a handyman, but the sincere servant of Christ begged to help construct. The construction team tried to let the pastor down easily, but he wouldn't seem to take "no" for an answer. Soon enough, the crew finally conceded with a pastor-proof job.

"Pastor, here's the deal. We need to build roof trusses. You can help by cutting these wood boards at twenty-three feet in length. Watch closely now—we're going to show you how. You shouldn't have any problems if you do what we show you."

They pulled out the tape measure, drew a line at twenty-three feet, and showed the grinning pastor how to use the saw.

"Could you do that?" they asked.

"Of course!" the pastor replied.

Satisfied he couldn't mess up, the workers walked away in peace and left the pastor to work.

Joy overflowed from the pastor's heart as the workers walked away. He got right to work, following the workers' example for three or four boards, using the tape measure, drawing a line at twenty-three feet, and sawing off the side of the wood boards. But suddenly, his eyes widened with the light of revelation.

"Why should I keep using this tape measure?" he thought.

"I'll just measure from the previous board!"

The pastor threw the tape measure to the ground and began measuring by each previous board, grinning wildly. He cut and measured, cut and measured for all the remaining boards needed to construct the fellowship hall roof. Soon the construction workers returned to make sure the pastor hadn't gotten into any trouble.

"Hey Pastor, how's the job coming along? Did you do it how we showed you?"

The pastor's face sparked a smile: "Well, yeah—I did it your way first. But then I had a better idea! Here, come close—I'm going to show you guys something that'll revolutionize your workflow!"

The pastor basked in his brilliance as he demonstrated his new method, measuring a new board by the previous cut. But the construction workers didn't seem as excited as he. In fact, they seemed more and more agitated every moment. Soon, their frustration boiled over and spilled out:

"Ugh . . . Pastor! Look at the last board you cut! It's two inches longer than the first one!"

The pastor had abandoned the perfect metrics of the tape measure, and the boards had grown longer with each fresh cut. His "new revelation" had actually delayed the church's construction!

HOW DO WE MEASURE UP?

I (Brian) think we've done something similar today. Jesus gave us a perfect measurement when He established the New Testament model of Christian life and ministry. God designed that model Himself to forge successful invasions of light and bring His kingdom to bear on society. But since the first century, every new generation has invented new and unbiblical approaches to ministry, thinking, "We can do better than that!" These "new revelations" have often gained immediate fame, but eventually radically stunted the church's growth. Now, though we may have fancy buildings and flashy worship bands, the modern church looks little like the pure, victorious church we find in the book of Acts.

If we want God's kingdom to come through our influence, we must return to King Jesus's original paradigm for the invasion of light. If we don't, we'll only fall farther from God's perfect standard, and the Kingdom of Darkness will continue expanding its evil invasion undeterred.

JESUS'S INVASION STRATEGY

Then, we must ask—when Jesus Christ walked the Earth, how did He daily labor to extend the influence of God's kingdom? How did He invade His surroundings with light, touching lives with His forgiveness, freedom, healing, and hope? Matthew summarizes Jesus's invasion strategy in Matthew 9:35: "Jesus went through all the towns and villages, teaching in their synagogues, proclaiming the good news of the Kingdom and healing every disease and sickness." This verse unveils three crucial aspects of Jesus's missionary approach.

First, He ministered wherever He could. Second, wherever He ministered, He preached the gospel of the Kingdom. Third, wherever He preached the gospel of the Kingdom, He healed every disease and sickness. Let's study these practices one by one to clearly understand the New Testament example we must follow.

JESUS MINISTERED EVERYWHERE HE COULD

Matthew 9:35 tells us Jesus ministered "through all the towns and villages" of Israel. As God's great missionary, Jesus ministered everywhere He could to preach the gospel to all who would hear. In fact, in His journeys, Jesus went to many small and despised villages that meant little to His contemporaries. He based His invasion of light out of Capernaum, a small town of simpleton farmers and fishers. He traveled to Samaria to preach good news to an adulterous woman whom no other religious Jew would have approached (John 4:4-27). He announced His kingdom in Nazareth, a place that many saw as good-for-nothing (John 1:46). When we consider this, we realize Jesus considered no person or place insignificant. Jesus loved each person with an everlasting love, and He forged His invasion of light in such a way that *no one in Israel would fail to hear the good news.*

Likewise, to successfully invade with light, we must bring the gospel to each and every person on Earth. Jesus commanded us to "preach the gospel to every creature" (Mark 16:15 NKJV), and approximately 3.2 billion people alive today have still never heard of Him.[1] That's 41.6% of the world's population! As ambassadors of Christ, we need to speed up the work. God calls us to share Jesus with everyone—the young and the old, the rich and the poor, the "significant" and the "insignificant," and especially those who have never heard before. We can't pick and choose; only obey or disobey!

If we would follow Jesus's invasion strategy, we must also bring the gospel to every town—every geographical location. This planet is home to about 17,000 people groups, and approximately 7,000 of them have little or no exposure to the gospel (see Chapter Nineteen, "The Epicenter of the Invasion: The 10/40 Window").[2] Those are a lot of towns that need visits from God's people! None of us can reach all those places, but we need to play our part. It's time to put away our excuses and begin to reach those who have never heard of Jesus Christ!

Unfortunately, too many Christians focus their evangelistic attention on one nation, group, or person and leave everyone else to suffer in the clutches of Satan's kingdom. What about you? Are you obeying God's call to preach the gospel to every creature, or disobeying it? Do you avoid sharing Jesus with certain types of people? Do you feel satisfied merely sharing Jesus with your friends, community, or local church? When you hear of foreign mission work, do you open up in desire, or tighten up in fear or resentment? Don't get me wrong; God may never call you to go to every nation—but He has already called you to go to every creature. Your calling is clear. Will you obey it or not?

JESUS PREACHED THE GOSPEL OF THE KINGDOM

Now, let's consider the second aspect of Jesus's daily invasion of light: He preached the gospel of the Kingdom wherever He went. Matthew 9:35 tells us, "Jesus went through all the towns and villages, teaching in their synagogues, *proclaiming the good news of the Kingdom.*"

Many modern Christians preach a paper-thin gospel that only reveals "how to get to Heaven when you die"—but Jesus preached the full message of the Kingdom of God. In fact, His first sermon was simply, "Repent, for the Kingdom of Heaven has come near" (Matthew 4:17)!

What is the gospel of the Kingdom, then? As we discussed, The Kingdom of God is the rule, reign, realm, and royalty of God. Jesus continually preached that God's gracious rule and reign had come, and all people now needed to submit to Him as King. As Jesus's disciples would later say, "The times of ignorance God overlooked, but now He commands all people everywhere to repent, because He has fixed a day on which He will judge the world in righteousness" (Acts 17:30-31 ESV). Now, if we submit to Jesus as King, we'll receive His royal blessing; but if we rebel against Him, we'll receive His royal judgment. After Jesus's death and resurrection, the apostles preached this message in its mature form: Jesus Christ is the King, He died for the sins of the world, and those who submit to Him can freely receive the grace of His kingdom now and forever.

THE SCOPE OF THE KINGDOM GOSPEL

The gospel of the Kingdom affects not only our eternal destiny, but our whole being—spirit, soul, and body. In fact, one New Testament Greek word used of salvation is *sózó* (σῴζω), which means *to be saved, healed, and delivered.*[3] When a good king takes over a broken region, the whole area is transformed: the economy grows, security strengthens, hope arises, and dirty places are made clean. In the same way, when the Kingdom of God comes near, whole lives are transformed and restored by God's power—sinners receive forgiveness and freedom, the demonized receive deliverance, and the sick receive healing! King Jesus brings the transforming power of the gospel to our spirits, souls, and bodies, and makes us whole again by His grace, power, and love.

Obviously, we should prioritize the gospel of salvation by grace, never preaching God's healing without God's salvation or God's deliverance without the call to repentance and faith. But God does long to bring healing from sickness and deliverance from demonic oppression—and He longs to do it through you and me! Which brings us to the next part of Jesus's invasion strategy.

JESUS HEALED EVERY SICKNESS AND DISEASE

Wherever Jesus went, He healed every sickness and disease and cast out demons. As Matthew 4:23-24 says:

> And Jesus went about all Galilee . . . healing all kinds of sickness and all kinds
> of disease among the people . . . and they brought to Him all sick people who
> are afflicted with various diseases and torments, and those who are demon
> possessed, epileptics, and paralytics, and He healed them. (NKJV)

And as Matthew 9:35 says:

> Then Jesus went about all the cities and villages . . . healing every sickness
> and every disease among the people. (NKJV)

These verses show us that no power of Hell could withstand the royal authority of Jesus Christ. He healed people with acute and constant pain. He cast out tormenting demons, many of whom had imparted sickness (see Luke 13:11-13). He healed seizures, leprosy, paralysis, fevers, bleeding disorders, blindness, muteness, deafness, and so much more! (Matthew 4:24, 8:1-4, 8:5-13, 8:14-15, 9:20-22, 9:21-31, Mark 7:31-37). He even raised the dead (see John 11:1-44). The ancient world didn't have medicine for many of these problems, but Jesus came to Earth with divine authority to heal the sick and set the captives free (see Isaiah 61:1-3). Fulfilling His heavenly mission, He fully preached the gospel of the Kingdom and confirmed it visibly by demonstrating the healing power of His reign.

We see the glorious results of Jesus's healing and deliverance ministry in Matthew 4:24-25:

> Then His fame went throughout all Syria; and they brought to Him all sick
> people who were afflicted with various diseases and torments, and those who
> were demon-possessed, epileptics, and paralytics; and He healed them. Great
> multitudes followed Him—from Galilee, and from Decapolis, Jerusalem,
> Judea, and beyond the Jordan. (NKJV)

Praise the Lord! Jesus preached the gospel, healed the sick, and cast out demons—and as a result, the gospel of the Kingdom spread everywhere. The masses were shocked to hear about Jesus's healing and delivering power, so before long, thousands flocked to Him—not just for salvation, but for freedom from disease and demons. He cured all who came to Him, gloriously advancing the Kingdom invasion—and this granted Him the opportunity to preach the salvation of God's kingdom to thousands more! *That* is a model we must not neglect in our day! In fact, Jesus sends us out to do exactly the same: "Heal the sick, raise the dead, cleanse those who have leprosy, drive out demons. Freely you have received; freely give!" (Matthew 10:8).

MIRACULOUS MINISTRY TODAY

I want to say something controversial but undeniable—our generation needs Jesus's miracle-working power just as much as first-century Israel did. In fact, it probably needs it much more!

Think about it. Right now, billions of lost souls desperately need a supernatural touch from Jesus. Even many believers still need freedom from demonic oppression or health problems that God would quickly heal. Despite all our preaching and counsel, they can't seem to break free from some struggle that has chained them for years. But the gospel of the Kingdom declares that Jesus wants to set these oppressed souls free! How does He grant that freedom? Often it must come through the ministry of healing and deliverance—two crucial mandates the modern church has neglected to obey.

You see, Jesus commands us to minister God's power the same ways He did. This miraculous call is crucial to the gospel of the Kingdom. As Jesus commanded in Mark 16:15-18:

> Go into all the world and preach the gospel to every creature. He who believes and is baptized will be saved; but he who does not believe will be condemned. And these signs will follow those who believe: In My name they will cast out demons; they will speak with new tongues; they will take up serpents; and if they drink anything deadly, it will by no means hurt them; they will lay hands on the sick, and they will recover. (NKJV)

Yes, as Jesus promised, "Most assuredly, I say to you, he who believes in Me, the works that I do he will do also; and greater works than these he will do, because I go to My Father" (John 14:12 NKJV). God longs to do much more through us than the modern church has welcomed Him to do. He wants to use us as channels of His supernatural power as a testimony to the message of reconciliation!

When I think of this, I can't help but wonder—how many would God heal and deliver if we stopped relying on earthly methods, received the Holy Spirit's power, and started preaching the whole gospel of the Kingdom? I have nothing against medical attention or Christian counseling, but today these have utterly replaced the essential ministries of healing and deliverance. We must learn to seek God's power first and foremost!

Now, this is where some become discouraged, overthinking their lack of faith to minister healing and deliverance. JJ and I have both battled that kind of thinking before—but we must fight through it and stretch towards God's promise: "These signs will follow those who believe: In My name they will cast out demons; . . . they will lay hands on the sick, and they will recover" (Mark 16:17-18 NKJV). God has called us to proclaim the whole gospel of the Kingdom and demonstrate its power—and to do that, we must walk by faith, not by sight.

Unfortunately, many base their understanding of God's will on their experience instead of God's promises. Some don't believe God wants to heal because they've had little success praying for the sick. The enemy accused them of faithlessness, and instead of renewing their minds, they surrendered the battle and quit praying for healing. Others think to themselves [I've done this too], "Let someone with more faith pray—it rarely works for me." In this way, we forfeit the Kingdom power Jesus called us to walk in. What a tragedy! We must get past our overthinking and urgently recover this critical aspect of Jesus's invasion strategy.

WALKING CLOSE TO THE MIRACLE-WORKER

Then how do we begin to walk in God's miraculous power? Here, we'll discuss the process rather than the practicals.[4]

First and foremost, we must follow Jesus's example and walk close to the miracle-worker. Yes, to walk in God's "greater works" (John 14:12 NKJV), we must live as Jesus did—keeping close communion with the Father through prayer, devotion, Bible study, and obedience.

Remember, Jesus said:

> Most assuredly, I say to you, the Son can do nothing of Himself, but what He sees the Father do; for whatever He does, the Son also does in like manner. For the Father loves the Son, and shows Him all things that He Himself does; and He will show Him greater works than these, that you may marvel. (John 5:19-20 NKJV).

Yes, to forge a truly miraculous invasion of light, we must walk close to God and receive His strategy. As we walk closely to Him, He'll reveal His plan by providing us with clear opportunities to preach the gospel, pray for the sick, and minister deliverance. Remember this—God is not obligated to do what we request, only what He commands! If He commands it through the Holy Spirit, He will do it through the Holy Spirit.

As you walk close to the Lord, make sure to cling to Jesus's promises about miraculous ministry and pray for God to activate them in your life—no matter how long it takes. Then, be sure to obey Jesus's command: "Heal the sick, cleanse the lepers, raise the dead, cast out demons" (Matthew 10:8 NKJV). In other words, step out on a limb whenever He gives an opportunity to minister His power. You may or may not see many results at first; don't get discouraged—it's all part of the journey. Just move on—keep praying and practicing! Soon enough God's kingdom will begin to break through you, healing bodies, delivering the oppressed, and saving souls.

Finally, prepare for pushback. Many Christians will not be happy about your attempt to minister Jesus's power. Don't let the naysaying and faithless discourage you from growing in healing and deliverance under God's protective guidance. Just be kind, remember your call, and keep up the invasion!

JESUS'S HEART AS AN AMBASSADOR

Now, let's consider Jesus's heart as an ambassador. You see, many closely follow Jesus's invasion strategy but don't share His heart of love, compassion, and radical obedience. They preach the gospel of God's reign, heal the sick, and cast out demons—but at the end of the day, they don't genuinely love those they minister to. Such Christians can never wage truly effective invasions of light. Paul says to such people, "If I have the gift of prophecy and can fathom all mysteries and all knowledge, and if I have a faith that can move mountains, but do not have love, *I am nothing*" (1 Corinthians 13:2). If we want to succeed as ambassadors of God's kingdom, we must not only adopt Jesus's ministry practices, but "be conformed to [His] image" (Romans 8:29)! Here, we'll study three attributes of Jesus's heart we must adopt—His radical compassion, His perfect obedience, and His dependence on God the Father.

JESUS'S RADICAL COMPASSION

One of the most striking features of Jesus's original paradigm is His radical compassion. We see this compassion clearly revealed in Matthew 9:36-38.

One day, Jesus and His disciples walked near a multitude of souls. They saw people of all sorts: short, tall, young, old, male, female, rich, poor, affluent, and despised. But one feature of this crowd pierced Jesus's heart like an arrow, stirring Him to holy compassion. Matthew tells us, "when [Jesus] saw the crowds, He had compassion on them, because they were harassed and helpless, like sheep without a shepherd" (Matthew 9:36). The multitudes were cast down, needing a leader, and lost, needing a Savior. Jesus knew only He could save them.

Matthew had observed Jesus's heart and attitude towards others throughout His ministry, but this instance stuck out to him in a special way. On this day, it seems God granted Matthew to see Jesus's love and compassion for others like never before. By a mere look in Jesus's eyes, Matthew could tell Jesus deeply loved each and every person. At a simple glance, Matthew could discern Jesus's motive for ministry: He loved people and wanted to draw them to the Father.

In the midst of this, Jesus turned to His disciples and said something that couldn't wait until later. Looking out over the crowds of hopeless people, He said to His disciples: "The harvest is plentiful but the workers are few. Ask the Lord of the harvest, therefore, to send out workers into His harvest field" (Luke 10:2).

You see, the Great Commission was forged in the fires of Jesus's holy compassion. Jesus sent laborers into the field because He could not stand to see sheep without a shepherd. In our invasion of light, we must cling to Jesus's holy compassion; we must let it burn in us as it did in Him, for only His holy compassion will stir us to action. Only if we see and feel the needs of the spiritually lost will we fulfill our evangelistic calling. Yes, Christians typically avoid God's call when they *lose God's heart*!

As ambassadors of Jesus, many of us have lost the pure compassion of Jesus. We've become fixated on our felt needs and have forgotten that the spiritually lost have needs much greater than ours. Remember, they are "sheep without a shepherd" (Matthew 9:36), wandering through life without true hope or direction, plunging towards Hell with no other hope of escape. How can we look at hurting and lost people without a tinge of holy sympathy or desire for their salvation? How far from God's heart must we be to feel no pain when we think of souls going to Hell?

Only God's compassion will drive us to carry Jesus's light to this lost world. We have God's Great Commission to obey; and we need God's great compassion to break our selfishness and thrust us out to obey it. With that considered, it's time to start asking ourselves the hard questions. Does my heart break for the lost? Do I love others like Jesus did? Can I really stand to see the world die and go to Hell? Do I weep in prayer for their souls, or give my time and money that they might know Jesus? If we answered honestly, many of us would realize how unlike Jesus we still are. Then, we might finally cry out to Jesus for an impartation of His holy compassion for the lost.

DOWN ON THE TRACKS: MY STORY OF GOD'S BURDEN

I (Brian) remember one crucial moment when the Lord allowed me to experience His burden for lost and hurting souls. I was on my first foreign mission trip, visiting an extremely poor area of Guatemala called the tracks. A major earthquake hit not long before my visit, and many families fled to the railroad tracks to seek refuge in makeshift shacks of tin, wood, and plastic. It was the worst poverty I had seen up to that point in my life! We did what we could to share God's hope, singing Spanish songs of salvation, reading Spanish Bible verses in broken accents, and praying as our Spanish-speaking partners shared the gospel with clarity. Many received Christ that day, and we returned to the mission base to talk about our experience, pray together, and get to bed.

But something life-changing happened to me that night. As I lay down in my top bunk, I suddenly became overwhelmed by all I had seen. My eyes welled up with tears, and soon I began to weep uncontrollably. I covered my face with a pillow so the five other men in the room wouldn't hear me—but what could I do to stop it? As the tears flowed, I did the only thing I could—pray.

Through my sobs I pleaded with God—"Lord, what is happening to me?" Immediately the Holy Spirit responded with something that would change my life forever. His still-small voice rang out crystal clear:

"I have given you just a small taste of my burden for the lost and hurting people of the world. If I gave you any more your heart would not be able to contain it. I want you to treasure this as a gift. Hide it in your heart and hold onto it. This burden will propel you to the lost and hurting people around the world."

I have never forgotten that moment. That was when God strengthened my burden for missions beyond anything I thought possible. Jesus had given me a piece of His heart—He had allowed me to taste His immense love for the lost and hurting, and painfully uncovered how much He longed to save them. I knew at that moment that He was looking for compassionate messengers—ambassadors of His love who would go on His behalf to tell the lost how much He cares.

God is calling us all to receive that heavenly burden—the burden of the Lord. His love for souls would be a heavy burden in itself—but as we carry that burden by the Holy Spirit's power and direction, we find that His "burden is light" and fits just right (Matthew 11:30). Tragically, many Christians spend so much time trying to lighten their own load that they forget about the masses of lost souls devoid of hope. We need to open our eyes and look on the fields. It's time to look in the eyes of the lost and hurting masses, and then look to God to say, "Here I am, Lord, send me!"

JESUS LIVED FOR GOD'S WILL

Another crucial feature of Jesus's original ministry paradigm is His hunger and dedication to complete the Father's will.

In John 4:34, Jesus said, "My food . . . is to do the will of Him who sent Me and to finish His work" (John 4:34). Jesus hungered for God's will, and satisfied that hunger by doing God's work. Many complain about the ministry opportunities God has given them, but Jesus lived to hear the Father say well done (see Matthew 3:17). The pleasure of God satisfied His heart and propelled His actions as He invaded the world with light.

Because Jesus found His ultimate satisfaction in the Father's will, He always immediately obeyed the commands God gave Him; that is, He obeyed without delay. Unlike many of us, He never shrank back from His original obedience. Instead, He continued to obey until He had completed God's will. Why did Jesus obey the Father's will no matter the cost—even until He breathed His last on the cross? Our verse answers: "My food . . . is to do the will of Him who sent Me and finish His work" (John 4:34). Jesus could never be satisfied unless He completed the mission God had given Him. For this reason, He perfectly obeyed God for His whole earthly life until He could finally cry, "It is finished."

HOW WELL DO WE FOLLOW JESUS'S EXAMPLE?

I wonder how we measure up to Jesus. Do we offer instant obedience as Jesus did? When God calls, do we answer without delay? Christians too often tell God, "I'm busy right now . . . I'll do it later." Maybe you've never spoken those words—but what do your *actions* say?

As students of Jesus, we must answer God's call *immediately when we hear* and *never* hesitate. If I hesitate when God speaks, I am *considering disobedience*. Can you truly bear the thought of saying no to God? Can you bear to go your own way when Jesus paid the ultimate price to win you to His way? If so, your priorities are out of line with God's. You must return to the model of Jesus. Recover the vision of God's will and act on it joyfully and without delay!

THE TEST OF LORDSHIP

In Luke 6:46, Jesus asked, "Why do you call me, 'Lord, Lord,' and do not do what I say?" The Greek word here translated "Lord" comes from *kurios* (κύριος), which means *supreme in authority*.[5] Jesus is only my Lord if He is my supreme authority—that is, if I always seek to do what He says. He is not my Lord if I'm not His obedient servant. As servants of the Lord Jesus, we must obey God's will as soon as He reveals it, and stick to it until we finish His work. I certainly don't want to hear the Lord ask me, *"Why do you call me, 'Lord, Lord,' and do not do what I say?"* (Luke 6:46).

The truth is, sometimes we believers live life like a roller coaster. We go up high in the Lord, then swoop down into darkness, then suddenly speed up into God's calling, then slow down to our own dreams and desires. Like Jesus, we need to learn to stay steady in God's will. When the Holy Spirit leads us to run, we must run; when He leads us to be still, we must be still; when He leads us to leap, step, or dive in faith, we must leap, step, or dive. Until we learn to live for God's will, we'll always miss Jesus's ambassadorial paradigm, and we'll never be very useful to God's invasion of light. And if we live in true rebellion against God, perhaps we'll never even see the Kingdom of God:

> Or do you not know that wrongdoers will not inherit the Kingdom of God? Do not be deceived: Neither the sexually immoral nor idolaters nor adulterers nor men who have sex with men nor thieves nor the greedy nor drunkards nor slanderers nor swindlers will inherit the Kingdom of God. (1 Corinthians 6:9-10)

THE TEST OF COMPLETION

Finally, we need to ask ourselves—do we complete the work God has given us like Jesus did? Many have come to me throughout the years with great ideas, claiming God gave them a vision to complete for the invasion of light. But too many left those "God-given-ideas" untried or unfinished. Some never took the steps of faith necessary to start the task God gave them. Others started the work but never brought it to completion. Now, don't get me wrong, dreams and visions are great—but God intends for them to leave dream-stage, enter start-stage, and end in finish-stage. God is a finisher! As Paul declared, "He who began a good work in you will carry it on to completion until the day of Christ Jesus" (Philippians 1:6).

People with great ideas don't impress me very much at all. I've seen so many wonderful ideas rust away in the back of people's minds. Some people are great visionaries but terrible missionaries. They talk big but walk small. God is not impressed with our talk. He sees deep in our hearts where our thoughts and motives fester. He knows what we're really doing with His call. That is an awesome reality we all need to think about.

I'll tell you what kind of people do impress me (and, more importantly, God)—those who truly seek to glorify God by fulfilling His call on their lives. Many precious Christians are risking everything to bring the gospel to as many as they can. Many sacrifice their lives to feed the poor and care for orphans and widows. Many hear God's voice, answer His call, and keep working until they finish the job. Such people truly model what it means to be an ambassador of Jesus. Is this you I'm describing? If so, I urge you to keep your hand to the plow and continue to "press on toward the goal to win the prize for which God has called me heavenward in Christ Jesus" (Philippians 3:14). You are truly a rarity.

Yes, if you're reaching people with the true gospel, God takes notice. Whether you're ministering to children, a small group of adults, a teenager, a group of youth, or even one neighbor, it is precious and important in God's eyes. Don't ever belittle your labors if you're seeking to glorify God through wholehearted service! Don't ever rust out and retire from God's work! In John 5:17, Jesus said, "My Father is always at His work to this very day, and I too am working." We'll have plenty of time to rest when we're in His heavenly kingdom. For now, let's finish the job and continue the invasion of light!

CHAPTER EIGHTEEN

FINDING YOUR ROLE IN
THE INVASION OF LIGHT

Now, let's ask a crucial question. "What should *I do* to advance the Great Commission and fulfill my role in the invasion of light? How do I find the specific tasks God has called me to perform? Where do I start?" I (Brian) want to help you discern God's *personal battle plan for you* as an ambassador. Here we'll learn four ways to find our place as ambassadors and grow into mature messengers of God's kingdom. They are as follows:

1. Believe God has already prepared a valuable role for you in His kingdom.

2. Take note of the gifts God has given you—these will likely point towards part of your role as an ambassador.

3. Start to live out your role as an ambassador in "your Jerusalem"—your daily sphere of influence.

4. Seek opportunities to live as an ambassador in other locations and nations.

Let's dive in.

STEP #1: BELIEVE GOD HAS PREPARED YOUR ROLE

First, you must realize God has *already* prepared you a valuable role in His invasion of light. Many Christians fail to see their calling because they don't believe God values them or wants to use them. Defeated by discouragement, they slump down and ask, "How could God use someone like me?" But we don't need to succumb to such discouragement. God has lovingly prepared a unique role for every one of His ambassadors. In Ephesians 2:10, Paul says, "We are God's handiwork, created in Christ Jesus to do good works, which God prepared in advance for us to do."

You see, Satan loves to lie to God's ambassadors and tell them they'll never succeed in God's invasion of light. We must not heed his lies but align ourselves with the truth of God's kingdom. If you feel like a failure in life, God wants you to know He has created you to walk in spiritual success. What is spiritual success? Obedience to the King's orders! Our failures will become victories when we adjust our lives to fit into God's Word.

Ambassador of Heaven, don't listen to the lying taunts of the enemy! When you look at yourself in the mirror, learn to believe: "I am God's workmanship, created for good works which God has prepared for me to do." By God's grace, your mission is set, and your destiny as an ambassador is already prepared. Now, you only have to discover that mission and walk it out.

STEP #2: OBSERVE WHAT GOD HAS WORKED INTO YOU

Next, you must take note of the gifts and strengths God has worked into you, for these will likely point you to your calling. Ephesians 2:10 says, "We are God's handiwork, created in Christ Jesus to do good works, which God prepared in advance for us to do." In other words, God has already begun to shape and form you to do specific works for His kingdom. Do you want to know what good works God has called you to do? Well, what has He been working into you? What gifts and strengths has He given you? Also, what talents has He given you? We can generally trust that His work in us will match the work He wants to do through us—our calling will match our gifting.

You see, the invasion of light best succeeds when Christians simply *use their gifts as a springboard for the gospel*, all to the glory of God alone. His kingdom doesn't only depend upon Christian clergy—pastors, teachers, evangelists, church planters, and prophetic voices. He also wants to make a radical difference through Christian waiters, writers, firefighters, filmmakers, schoolteachers, sound engineers, artists, accountants, mothers, musicians, and more. Plain and simple—God wants to use your skills to open doors for the gospel wherever He has placed you—no matter how great or small it seems to you.

Many languish because they think the Lord wants them to minister outside of their giftings. I'll give you an example. I have ministered to youth since the 1990s, and if I've learned anything in that time, it's that youth ministry requires much patience. Youth workers must realize the flock under their care are in adolescence—a tough season full of questions and changes. Once when I was a youth pastor, a very impatient person asked me if they could help with the youth, and without much consideration, I let them lend a hand. I very quickly discovered my mistake. This person often took their short temper out on the teenagers, so the youth didn't want to be around them. In fact, this person's short fuse started to cause problems. They certainly weren't advancing the invasion of light! Soon it became clear to me God hadn't led them into youth ministry. How could I tell? Simply because they didn't have the necessary skills to minister to youth. They would have saved a lot of sweat if they realized that at the outset.

Here's a funnier example. For eight years, I traveled around the country doing full-time music ministry. From time to time, people would come up and tell me about their "calling." It would go something like this:

"Hey Brian. You know, God has called me into a music ministry too. I'd like to sing a song for you."

I'd respond, "Awesome! Let me hear it."

What followed would sound something like the horrible auditions from *American Idol.* Certainly a joyful noise . . . but not a beautiful one! How was I supposed to respond to that? They had no musical ability—yet they thought the Lord had called them into music ministry! Tragically, they had failed to discern their God-given gifts, and thus had utterly confused their role in the invasion of light.

This is why we have pastoral leadership. A loving pastor can gently redirect a person who has confused their calling. An involved, Spirit-led pastor can point out strengths and appreciate what God is working into a person to point them in the right direction. How we need that pastoral guidance!

Now, don't get me wrong—I'm not saying the Lord won't call you to do something past your ability. I can guarantee you He will! I'm simply saying you can usually discern *the good works God has prepared* by the way *God has created you in Christ Jesus* (see Ephesians 2:10). "You are God's handiwork . . ." (Ephesians 2:10); what strengths and talents has He worked in you? That's a great place to start your invasion of light.

STEP #3: BEGIN AS AN AMBASSADOR
IN YOUR JERUSALEM

Next, start living as an ambassador in your Jerusalem—right where you are. When Jesus gave the Great Commission, He commanded the disciples to preach the gospel "in Jerusalem, and in all Judea and Samaria, and to the ends of the Earth" (Acts 1:8). He wanted them to preach the gospel to all nations, but first they had to invade with light nearby.

Ambassador of Christ, don't wait till you can travel to the ends of the Earth to live out your calling. First, begin to respond to the needs you see around you every day. If you've discerned your God-given gifts and talents, use them for God's kingdom when you see opportunities. If you don't see opportunities, pray for them to come. Meanwhile, begin to live as a kingdom ambassador to your peers, neighbors, family, and children through evangelism, prayer, encouragement, practical help, and generosity. How? I like to encourage people to start their invasion of light with one person. Who do you know personally that needs Jesus? Is it a person from work? A neighbor? A family member, child, or close friend? Ask God to lay the person on your heart and start right there.

You may never have realized it, but opportunities to share God's hope pass by you every day. Perhaps you sit down on a crowded bus, and a tired mother with her newborn baby can't find a seat. Maybe you're driving down the road, and you see a young man's car needs a jump. Perhaps you're taking care of your kids—and they're really testing your patience today. These everyday frustrations provide us opportunities to represent the Kingdom of God by giving help, practicing compassion, showing genuine care, and soon speaking of Jesus.

Ambassadors don't *always* practice cold-evangelism: "What's your name? Do you know Jesus Christ?" Rather, many evangelism opportunities come as we live out our calling as the light of the world and the salt of the Earth. Yes, when we display the love, hope, care, and joy of God, we'll often find opportunities to preach the gospel of God. As we take these opportunities, we'll mature as ambassadors; then we'll minister more effectively if and when God calls us to minister in another culture.

STEP #4: FIND WAYS TO SERVE IN SAMARIA AND THE ENDS OF THE EARTH

Once we've begun to invade with light locally, we soon should begin to look for opportunities outside our immediate community. You might travel around the world as a missionary, or simply to another county to minister in a prison or special outreach. Perhaps you can't go to other nations; that's all right, but be sure to send a substitute by praying and offering your finances. No matter what you do, be sure to spread your wings past your hometown. Remember, God wants His kingdom to come all over the Earth.

Do you desire to gain a worldwide vision for God's kingdom? I suggest you browse a map of the world and see if God gives you a burden for any particular area. God may call you to go there as a missionary, to visit on a missions trip, to support a native worker, or simply to pray for the region. Whatever he calls, this spiritual exercise will help you begin to develop a burden for worldwide evangelism. As missions pioneer William Carey said, "To know the will of God, you need an open Bible and an open map."

HOW I BEGAN TO LIVE AS AN AMBASSADOR

Perhaps you're afraid of walking out your calling to invade with God's light as an ambassador of Christ. The thought of sharing Jesus makes your knees shake and your voice tremble. You know God has placed a call on your life, but you don't know how you could ever muster up the courage to dive in obedience to God's will. You're not alone—I (Brian) remember when I first started to live out my calling as an ambassador of God's kingdom.

Before I met Jesus, my friends and I often went to Clearwater Beach to hang out and get high. A year after I got saved (at the age of nineteen), the Holy Spirit urged me to go back and share the gospel on that beach. My body trembled at the thought. How would I gain the courage? Would I soon stand before my old friends and share the love of Jesus? Was God really leading me to talk to complete strangers on the street? My fears stood like a mountain before me, but I knew God was calling me to act.

My mind teetered between fear and love; between the fear of preaching to strangers and a loving burden for the lost. In those dreadful moments, the Holy Spirit reminded me of something: in my four years of high school, no one had ever approached me with the message of Jesus. I had been invited to drug parties, witch coven meetings, and more, but I had never been invited to a Christian church. Until my brother Bruce got saved, I never had the opportunity to truly hear about Jesus, let alone receive Him. How many other people had never truly heard either? What if I were still one of those lost in the world?

One Friday night, I mustered up the courage to go to that beach and witness, as nervous as I was. I asked some of my new Christian friends if they would like to go with me, hoping for some backup and emotional support. They declined my invitation, but I knew I needed to go whether or not others would join.

I jumped in my 1963 Ford Fairlane 500 and blasted Christian music on the radio all the way there. When I pulled into the beach parking lot, I didn't only feel nervous—I felt downright terrified! After driving for thirty minutes, I found myself gripped by terrible fear. Arriving at the beach was step one, but now I needed to progress to step two: I had to actually get out of the car and begin sharing with someone.

I sat in my car and cowered in fear for about ten minutes. My thoughts raced with great intensity. All of my worries now stood before me in plain sight. In this place of fear, a song came on the radio that gave me great courage. In the song, Larry Norman sang about the one way to Heaven, and exhorted Christians to follow Jesus, free and forgiven.

As I listened to Larry Norman's challenging lyrics, the Holy Spirit's power began to surge through me. I could feel Him. I knew God was specifically talking to me through the song. He was calling me to action and granting me the courage to go. I faced my fears, prepared my heart to declare the one way to Heaven, and placed my hand on the door handle to leave the car. In that very moment, the Lord spoke very clearly to me, saying something that has propelled me all of these years: "Their need to hear is greater than your fear to share."

That settled it. There was no doubt I was in the right place, and about to do exactly what God wanted. I got out of the car and shared the love of Jesus with people on the beach. That's the moment my personal invasion of light began! That divine moment continues to inspire me decades later to share the gospel with as many as I can.

Just like in my story, many of us have heard God's call but are still hiding in the car. Right outside, we see lost souls and a harvest greater than anything we can imagine—but inside, we have little more than timidity, fear, and worry. Friend, let these words guide you to grab the car door handle and step out into your calling: "Their need to hear is greater than your fear to share." As an ambassador of God's kingdom, God has given you a message the lost need to hear. Take a step of faith today to reach the lost right where you are. Reach out to the people around you, and invade with God's light, life, love, and truth. You'll never regret it.

CHAPTER NINETEEN

THE EPICENTER OF THE INVASION: THE 10/40 WINDOW

Next, we want to tackle a crucial question for our worldwide invasion of light: Where are Christ's ambassadors most urgently needed? *Where in the world* should the Christian church focus its invasion strategy? In this chapter, I (JJ) want to answer loud and clear. One region of the world needs our invasion of light more than any other. God may not call you to go there physically, but He has certainly called you to contribute to its invasion of light through prayer, advocacy, and giving. That region is called the 10/40 Window.

Today, 3.2 billion people have never heard of Jesus Christ. 97% of these live in a region called the 10/40 Window.[1] Yet the modern church sends only 0.5% of its offerings and 3.3% of its missionaries to reach these unreached masses.[2] I think you'd agree—this must change now. We must prioritize the 10/40 Window, making it the first priority of our invasion of light. In this chapter, I want to consider four reasons why.

MOST UNREACHED REGION OF THE WORLD

First, we must prioritize the 10/40 Window because it's the most unreached region in the world.

Think about it. Jesus called us to disciple all nations (Matthew 28:19). He left us one all-consuming mission—to reach "every nation, tribe, people and language" (Revelation 7:9), leaving no people group untouched by the invasion of light. Yet the church still hasn't completed this crucial mission: to this day, many nations and people groups remain undiscipled. Then, where lies the clear path of obedience? To obey Jesus's command, we must complete the heavenly task He gave us in the beginning—we must focus on discipling the undiscipled until we've truly made disciples of all nations. Anything less is disobedience to God's will! Can we bear to re-reach the reached while the unreached have never heard?

Perhaps the statistics seem far-fetched. "You're telling me to believe billions have never heard the gospel?" I understand if you're surprised, and I'm certainly not judging the unaware. We live in such a gospel-saturated culture. We have no radar for the idea of "unreached people groups." The gospel is everywhere, right? Well, not quite.

Actually, almost half of the world's population has never clearly heard the gospel. Approximately 3.2 billion people alive today (41.6% of all) live in what we call unreached people groups (UPGs).[3] UPGs are ethnic groups with very few evangelical Christians (2% or less). Many living in UPGs have never even heard Jesus's name. Most have never clearly heard the gospel. 97% of them—3.1 billion people—live in the 10/40 Window.[4] What are the ramifications? If Jesus returned today, 41.6% of the world's population would likely go to Hell unwarned.

Does this concern you? It ought to. Before ascending to Heaven, Jesus gave us one final command: "Go and make disciples of all nations" (Matthew 28:19). Two thousand years later, this vital mission remains uncompleted. In this crucial hour of history, we must begin to question our obedience! If Jesus said, "Go into all the world," why have we excluded half of it? If Jesus commanded us to disciple all people groups, why have we focused on 9,929 and excluded 7,165 (41.6% of the world's population)?

LEAST FUNDED AND MANNED MISSION FIELD

Second, we must prioritize the 10/40 Window because it's the least funded and manned mission field in the world. Where better to place fresh focus?

Few realize it, but many modern ministries have a completely backward spending philosophy. First, most financial offerings don't leave the four walls of the church at all. 85% fund internal operations like salaries, rent, electric, water, air conditioning, and technological upgrades.[5] 4.5% fund "local missions" in Christian-majority nations.[6] And how much goes to the unreached, where we ought to focus our finances? A tragic 0.5%.[7] Can you believe it?

These statistics force us to ask—how did we get here? Church history tells the sad tale. Two thousand years ago, God called us to go into all the world, invading everywhere with the light of the gospel. About 300 years ago, we started this mission afresh. We labored hard. Men and women sacrificed their lives as martyrs for the cause of world evangelism. We preached the gospel, made disciples, planted churches, and transformed cultures. We looked into the regions beyond where Christ had still never been named, seeking to win the world to Jesus.

Then at some point, we looked back.

Rather than reach the unreached, we decided to re-reach the already reached. As a result, only 3.3% of modern missionaries work in the 10/40 Window.[8] Yes, the unreached world has only 1 Christian missionary for every 216,300 people.[9] We're feeding the full while half the world starves! How we've missed God's mission and misdirected our efforts against the Kingdom of Darkness!

Now, realize—I don't write this to make you feel guilty, but to impart the *burden and vision* for unreached people groups. Paul said, "It has always been my ambition to preach the gospel where Christ was not known" (Romans 15:20). It's high time for each of us to share that ambition and engage in this crucial invasion of light. Don't you think?

POOREST REGION IN THE WORLD

Third, we must prioritize the 10/40 Window because it's the most impoverished region in the world.

Keep in mind—God calls us to "remember the poor" (Galatians 2:10). It's great to help the poor locally, but we must remember *God sees the needs of the whole world*. And where in the world does He see the greatest needs? In the 10/40 Window. In fact, Over 80% of the poorest of the poor live in the 10/40 Window, surviving on less than $1 a day.[10] Yet only 3.3% of Christian missionaries work among them.[11] 80% of the world's poor receive only 3.3% of the world's Christian missionaries? How hard to believe! We've failed to offer aid to those who need it most!

Maybe it's easy to stomach the numbers, but not the stories. In the 10/40 Window, billions live without simple needs like clean water, secure homes, and medical care. Children grow up in garbage dumps, running around barefoot and naked in puddles of contaminated water (we witnessed this in Cambodia's Steung Meanchey slum). Desperate for income, many parents even sell their own children into the sex trade for financial gain. Poverty leads to desperation, which leads to unbelievable immorality. And countless souls have been lost in the crosshairs of this spiritual calamity.

But we must not let that moral darkness dissuade us from invading with Jesus's light. The poor should matter to us because they matter to Him. Don't forget, Jesus came "to proclaim good news to the poor" (Luke 4:17-19). He instructed His disciples: "Sell your possessions and give to the poor" (Luke 12:33). In the Sermon on the Mount, Jesus says, "*when* you give to the needy," not *if* (Matthew 6:2).

The New Testament authors saw the poor as a vital part of their mission, too. Before the apostles officially commissioned Paul, they gave clear instructions—"that we should continue to remember the poor, the very thing I had been eager to do all along" (Galatians 2:10). Do we share the same eagerness as Paul—to remember the poor? To "defend the cause of the poor and needy . . . what it means to know [God]" (Jeremiah 22:16)?

You see, any mission that neglects the poor is incomplete. And we've neglected 80% of the world's poorest. Therefore, we've radically missed God's missions standard. Jesus commands us to care, and it's high time we start! If 80% of Earth's poorest live in the 10/40 Window, where better to place fresh focus?

A WORLD CAPITAL OF DEMONIC OPPRESSION

Finally, we must prioritize the 10/40 Window because it's a world capital of demonic oppression. Remember, Jesus is anointed "to set the oppressed free" (Luke 4:18). He has given us "authority to trample on snakes and scorpions and to overcome all the power of the enemy" (Luke 10:19). What a crucial aspect of our invasion of light! And no region needs Jesus's liberating power more than the 10/40 Window. Can we bear to hold back the help they need?

You see, most in the 10/40 Window live in deep fear of evil spirits (a few atheistic nations excepted). They offer daily sacrifices to appease their ancestors, avoid retribution, and seek blessing. Statues of demons and spirits adorn almost every street. Reports of ghost encounters abound. Many cultures regularly seek out witch doctors, psychics, spiritists, blessings, spells, and potions, and fear curses and omens. The Kingdom of Darkness has established a fortuitous stronghold of false religion, idolatry, and occultism there, leaving many people groups cowering in fear.

And the 10/40 Window's demonic fears aren't baseless. Inhabitants of the 10/40 Window fear evil spirits because they've lived under Satan's vicious taunt. Demonic forces work out in the open there, spreading torment, confusion, rage, and addiction. Our partners regularly tell us stories of the most shocking demonic attacks.

I'll give one example.

A 19-year-old Burmese man lived under severe demonization since age 15. Demonic illness, madness, and rage constantly plagued him and often drove him running into the jungle. He soon became so violent that his teachers had to remove him from school, and his own parents locked him in his room and chained him to his bed. They sought every cure possible, but neither medicine nor monks nor mysticism could turn the tide. Soon, the parents met our partner, Pastor J, and asked him to pray for their son.

What happened next should blow us away. Our partner prayed for the young man in the name of Jesus, and the tormenting spirit left immediately. Our partner invaded with light, and in a matter of seconds, Jesus had delivered the young man from an insanity that four years of Asia's best cures could not heal! Can you imagine the joy and relief his family experienced? He soon received Christ, and today he would rather die than reject Jesus.

LOOK AT THE FIELDS

Our ministry partners tell us similar testimonies regularly. Jesus is invading the 10/40 Window with His light every day, setting the masses free, person by person, soul by soul. He longs to liberate every unreached captive, for He is "not willing that any should perish but that all should come to repentance" (2 Peter 3:9 NKJV). What keeps this great deliverance from the pages of history? "The harvest truly is great, but the laborers are few" (Luke 10:2 NKJV). In light of this sober reality, Jesus commands us: "Lift up your eyes and look at the fields, for they are already white for harvest!" (John 4:35 NKJV). Have you neglected the 10/40 Window? Jesus calls you to lift up your eyes and see the harvest of souls waiting in the fields. I want to echo His call. It's time to lift up our eyes.

Let's lift up our eyes and see 3 billion souls who have never heard of Jesus Christ.

Let's lift up our eyes and see billions ensnared in poverty.

Let's lift up our eyes and see a generation taunted by demons.

Yes, let us look into those dark fields and realize how few workers are laboring there to shine Jesus's light.

But don't just look. Do something. Invade with light—somehow, some way! Begin to pray. Advocate for the unreached to your friends, family, spiritual leaders, and mentees. Support missionaries to the 10/40 Window. If you're a pastor, radically reshape your missions program. If God calls, go to reach the unreached in person. As Keith Green said, "This generation of Christians is responsible for this generation of souls on Earth." We each have only one life to offer in obedience to Jesus's Great Commission. It's time to invade the 10/40 Window with the glorious light of Jesus Christ while the flames of our lives still burn! Let our driving motto become—"My generation for Christ!"

Part 3.

How to Walk in the Light
(The Ambassador's
Character and Crown)

CHAPTER TWENTY

THREE REVIVAL VITALS:
RIGHTEOUSNESS, PEACE, AND JOY

In previous chapters, we discussed how to invade *the world* with the light of Jesus, living out our calling as ambassadors for Christ. In the following three chapters, I (Brian) want to help you to *walk in the light of Jesus for yourself*, experiencing the revived life God offers you as an ambassador. I'll do this by revealing three signs of the inner life of the Kingdom—three kingdom vitals, if you will. If we truly submit to King Jesus, we'll experience three inner blessings—righteousness, peace, and joy. When we keep these vitals strong, we can cause serious damage to the Kingdom of Darkness. As Jesus promised, the lost will "see [our] good deeds and glorify [our] Father in Heaven" (Matthew 5:16). This is our inheritance as Christ's ambassadors! But if we don't walk out this revived life, few will believe our message, and we won't cause much damage to Satan's reign at all.

As you read the next three chapters, I want you to examine your life. Perhaps you'll see you only regularly experience one or two of these signs of personal revival. That's okay—we're all works in progress. But by the end of these chapters, you'll know what needs adjustment.

I want to point out that I need this section of the book as much as you. I'm not pointing fingers. Whatever I teach you, the Lord had to teach me first—and He's still teaching me!

LIVING IN THE SHALLOWS

Recently at a pastor's retreat in Peru, I decided to jump in the pool. I went by the ladder and put my foot in—but it was cold. I mean *freezing cold*. I wanted to refresh myself in the crystal-clear pool, but the frigid water held me back. Trying to stoke my bravery, I went to the shallow end of the pool and walked in ankle-deep. Soon I came to the cliff of the shallow end and peered over the deep end. The pool water looked so relaxing—but the thought of the cold overwhelmed me. Finally, I counted the cost and made my choice. Determined to enjoy the pool, I counted down. "One . . . two . . . three . . . *Geronimo!*"

When I think back on that experience, I can't help but draw a parallel. Some of us are walking in the shallow end of God's kingdom. We know God has much more to give, but we're holding back instead of diving into the deeps of revival.

Some reading this book want their pastors to keep holding their hands. Perhaps you should be teaching others already, but instead you clasp Reverend Doe's hand like a spiritual three-year-old. You can't seem to defeat the invasion of darkness in your own life, let alone lead dying souls to victory. Maybe you don't have righteousness, peace, or joy—but you can. "God is no respecter of persons" (Acts 10:34 KJV) but "a rewarder of them that diligently seek him" (Hebrews 11:6 KJV). God gave us all the same promises for personal revival. What will we do with them? What will *you* do with them?

I believe when we cross into eternity, many of us will feel shocked at what we could have experienced. "That was for me? I could have had the same joy as him? Or the same peace as her? I could have lived that clean? I could have won that many souls? I could have forged *that kind of* invasion of light?" Yes, you could have—and you still can. But will you jump into the Kingdom of God, or not? It's really that simple.

As you read the next three chapters, I want you to realize something: All of God's revival promises and commands are for you. But if you don't seek those promises, you won't find them. If you don't knock for them, the door will never open. If you don't ask, you won't receive. The Kingdom of God is no respecter of persons—but God's promises are unlocked by our obedience to His commands! We'll never become effective ambassadors of light until we begin to "walk in the light" ourselves (1 John 1:7 NKJV).

In Romans 14:17, Paul says, "The Kingdom of God is not eating and drinking, but righteousness and peace and joy in the Holy Spirit" (Romans 14:17 NKJV). This verse clearly describes the revived life we'll experience if we walk in the Kingdom of God. We must keep these vitals strong to live as ambassadors and welcome God's kingdom to Earth. Let's examine our lives by God's Word.

CHAPTER TWENTY-ONE

VITAL #1: RIGHTEOUSNESS
IN THE HOLY SPIRIT

To effectively invade the world with light, we first need to live under Jesus's lordship by the Holy Spirit's power—what Paul calls the Kingdom of God. The first sign that we walk in this revived life is that we have *righteousness*. In Romans 14:17, Paul says, "The Kingdom of God is not eating and drinking, but righteousness and peace and joy in the Holy Spirit" (NKJV). The New Testament teaches two types of righteousness—imputed and imparted.

Imputed righteousness is the gift of God's forgiveness and acceptance by grace through faith in Jesus Christ. Paul describes imputed righteousness in Ephesians 2:8-9: "By grace you have been saved through faith, and that not of yourselves; it is the gift of God, not of works, lest anyone should boast" (NKJV). How did we receive this gift of righteousness? By the sacrifice of Jesus Christ: "For He made Him who knew no sin to be sin for us, that we might become the righteousness of God in Him (2 Corinthians 5:21 NKJV). Without this righteousness, no one can be saved or even begin the Christian life.

Romans 14:17, however, speaks of *imparted righteousness*—God's gracious gift of practical holiness and new life through the Holy Spirit. John describes imparted righteousness this way: "If you know that He is righteous, you know that everyone who practices righteousness is born of Him" (1 John 2:29 NKJV). John emphasizes that our only proof of imputed righteousness is that we've experienced imparted righteousness: "Little children, let no one deceive you. Whoever practices righteousness is righteous, as He is righteous" (1 John 3:7 ESV). I (Brian) believe with John Wesley that imparted righteousness works hand-in-hand with God's gift of imputed righteousness. God imputes righteousness to us once as a free gift, and imparts practical righteousness to us throughout our lives by God's grace and the power of the Holy Spirit. That's the only way we can ever walk in true holiness.

In Romans 14:17, the Greek word translated "righteousness" is *dikaiosuné* (δικαιοσύνη), which essentially means *integrity, virtue, and purity of life*.[1] It also means *correct thinking and correct actions*. Effective ambassadors seek to live in spiritual integrity, virtue, and purity of life through correct actions and thoughts. They seek to do right before God in everything—what they think, say, do, watch, listen to, and more. Out of love to God and others, they refuse to steal, lie, cheat, burst out in anger, speak behind other people's backs, gossip, or slander. They seek integrity in their private lives by conquering private sins by the Holy Spirit, and when tempted, they overcome the tempter by the Word of God and often by the help of other Christians.

As a result, their lives testify of King Jesus's righteousness and power to transform sinful people. Their lives "shine before men," and when others "see [their] good works [they] glorify [our] Father in Heaven" (Matthew 5:16 NKJV). By King Jesus's grace, they are "blameless and innocent, children of God without blemish in the midst of a crooked and twisted generation, among whom [they] shine as lights in the world" (Philippians 2:15 ESV). And by God's grace, that light of righteousness pushes back the Dark Kingdom's power in the world. This is the glorious fruit of the revived life!

By that standard, do you currently live under the rule of God's kingdom? If not, you can start right now. Let's open the scriptures to learn how to experience the righteousness of God's kingdom through the Holy Spirit.

LOVE SLAVES TO RIGHTEOUSNESS

In Romans 6:18, Paul reveals an amazing truth: all true believers have "been set free from sin and . . . become slaves to righteousness." Before Jesus, we all shared the same experience: we were "slaves to impurity and to ever increasing wickedness" (Romans 6:19). I certainly was. Before Jesus saved me, I was a good sinner. I rarely drank one bottle of wine at a time; I drank *two or three*. I didn't only smoke ten cigarettes a day; I smoked two or three packs. I didn't only smoke marijuana; I took hard drugs. Maybe you've never touched those things, but inward sin still enslaves you—selfishness, pride, envy, unforgivingness, lust, or some other work of the flesh. Without a doubt, apart from Christ we are slaves to the merciless master of unrighteousness. But when we bow the knee to Jesus Christ, God declares a new reality over our lives: "You have been set free from sin and . . . become slaves to righteousness" (Romans 6:18)!

In this verse, the phrase "have become slaves" comes from the Greek verb *douloó* (δουλόω), which means *to become a bondslave*.[2] We could explain this word from many angles—but here, I want to reflect on its connection to an Old Testament pattern. You see, God's law required slaves to serve their masters for seven years before they could return to freedom (Exodus 21:2-4). After this, if a slave loved his master's family, he could devote his life to his master as a *volunteer love slave*. Then the master would pierce the love slave's ear, marking him for service and accepting him into the family's future (see Exodus 21:5-6). That loving submission is part of what *dulóo* reflects here.

If you've received Jesus as your master, you've been set free from the cruel master of sin and have become a slave of righteousness! Just as good masters accepted love slaves by piercing the ear, God has accepted you by sending the Holy Spirit to live within you! (Ephesians 1:13, Galatians 4:6). Now, we should want to put a smile on our Heavenly Father's face every day.

OFFERING OURSELVES AS LOVE SLAVES

Do you want to experience holiness of life? In Romans 6:19, Paul tells us how: "Just as you used to offer yourselves as slaves to impurity and to ever-increasing wickedness, *so now offer yourselves as slaves to righteousness leading to holiness*" (Romans 6:19). If you follow God as a slave of righteousness, you'll experience a special connection with your Heavenly Father, and you'll know you're in right standing with Him. As Jesus said, "He who has My commandments and keeps them, it is he who loves Me. And he who loves Me will be loved by My Father, and I will love him and manifest Myself to him" (John 14:21 NKJV). Yes, to the obedient disciple, Jesus promises: "We will come to him and make Our home with him" (John 14:23 NKJV).

Paul also expresses our need to offer ourselves as slaves of righteousness in 2 Timothy 2:22: "Flee the evil desires of youth and pursue righteousness, faith, love and peace, along with those who call on the Lord out of a pure heart." The Greek word here translated "flee" is *pheugó* (φεύγω), which means *escape*.[3] The temptations of the world are like chains—and God calls us to escape them by pursuing righteousness and offering ourselves to the King as bondslaves! Only then can we become truly effective in God's invasion of light!

You see, it doesn't mean much to claim the title "slaves of righteousness" if we don't live it out. In the United States, I often hear of Christian leaders caught in addictions to alcohol, sexual sin, pornography, and more. Sometimes I won-der—how did this happen after God brought freedom from sin? For many, they stopped offering themselves as slaves of righteousness, and instead became slaves to unrighteousness. At one point in my Christian life, I had to go through a time of restoration because I, too, had yielded my freedom in Christ to sin.

With this considered, we must remember that God never promises to bless the rebellious. If you live in willful sin—secret or public—you'll experience destruction, and so will your invasion of light. As Paul warned: "Do not be deceived: God cannot be mocked. A man reaps what he sows. Whoever sows to please their flesh, from the flesh will reap destruction; whoever sows to please the Spirit, from the Spirit will reap eternal life" (Galatians 6:7-8). Do you want to set others free? You must get free yourself—and the only way to do that is by becoming God's slave.

HEALED OF UNRIGHTEOUSNESS

Every true Christian sometimes feels wounded by their failures. But Jesus died on the cross to heal us of those wounds and restore us to righteousness. Peter expressed this truth wonderfully in 1 Peter 2:24: "'He Himself bore our sins' in His body on the cross, so that we might die to sins and live for righteousness; 'by His wounds you have been healed.'" Yes, when you and I offer ourselves as slaves to righteousness, God heals us of the effects of sin in our lives. He binds up the wounds of our disobedience, then uses us to achieve the same in others' lives. This is God's amazing grace!

Growing up Catholic, my childhood priests taught me to pick the wounds of my guilt for quite a while if I sinned (they called it penance). I would go to confession every Saturday to try to get rid of my shame—but nothing healed my wounded conscience. I'm glad to say I discovered something that does heal the soul—the love of Jesus. Not only has He forgiven me of sin; He also has bound up my sores and caused me to grow in righteousness by His love. I am eternally thankful to Him for it.

Have you experienced Jesus's healing from unrighteousness? Do you need to experience it afresh? In John 12:35 Jesus said, "Whoever walks in the dark does not know where they are going." Some readers are experiencing that right now. You're living as a slave to unrighteousness, chained by temptations and sins. The farther you go, the more you feel like you're living in a dark house with no lights. But there is freedom and light for you in Jesus! Offer yourself to Him as a love slave—He'll heal you of unrighteousness and make you a slave of righteousness, leading to holiness. Then He can use you as an instrument of healing in others' lives as you invade our world with light!

Now, I want to discuss two ways the Holy Spirit trains us to live righteous lives—through scripture and discipline.

HOW GOD TRAINS US FOR RIGHTEOUSNESS:
#1 - THROUGH SCRIPTURE

First, let's discuss the role of scripture in our training for righteousness. In 2 Timothy 3:16-17, Paul says, "All scripture is God-breathed and is useful for teaching, rebuking, correcting and *training in righteousness* so that the servant of God may be thoroughly equipped for every good work." I want to point out two crucial truths we find in this verse.

First, God only promises to train us in righteousness *through the Word of God*. If we don't spend time reading the scriptures, we'll never receive our training in righteousness. Hebrews 4:12 tells us: "The Word of God is alive **and** active. Sharper than any double-edged sword, it penetrates even to dividing soul and spirit, joints and marrow; it judges the thoughts and attitudes of the heart." God's Word has supernatural power to reveal things that destroy our relationship with the Lord, and then to show us the way to fruitful Christian obedience. If we want to benefit from this promise, we must spend time listening to God through the Bible.

Second, the Holy Spirit provides this spiritual training *to equip us thoroughly for the Christian life*. If we listen to Him, we'll receive the equipping we need for life—but if we ignore Him, we won't. It's that simple. In John 14:26, Jesus promises that the Holy Spirit "will teach you all things and will remind you of everything I have said to you." The Holy Spirit teaches us all things by helping us understand the Bible, then reminds us of what God's Word teaches by speaking to our conscience.

Which leads me to a question. Has the Holy Spirit revealed an area of disobedience to God's Word in your life? Has He revealed a promise that He wants you to take hold of? If you reject or neglect that portion of God's Word, you'll never be thoroughly equipped to fulfill your role in the invasion of light. He wants to train you in righteousness through His Word, but you need to follow Him.

The truth is, sometimes our spiritual pipes get clogged, and God has to graciously clear them out. The Holy Spirit doesn't convict us of sin so we'll feel bad. He convicts us to restore us; He breaks us to bind us up. Conviction should lead to repentance, repentance leads to restoration, and restoration leads to revival and a renewed relationship with our Heavenly Father through Jesus Christ. Then, God can use our testimony of renewal to win souls and transform lives. We all need God's loving conviction!

#2: THROUGH DISCIPLINE

Next, let's consider another way God trains us for righteousness—through loving discipline. Hebrews 12:11 says, "No discipline seems pleasant at the time, but painful. Later on, however, *it produces a harvest of righteousness* and peace for those who have been trained by it" (Hebrews 12:11). You see, if we sin, the Holy Spirit will first address our wrong thinking and actions through conviction; but if we then rebel against His conviction, He'll discipline us so we know not to continue in the wrong way.

As Proverbs 3:12 says, "The LORD disciplines those He loves, as a father the son he delights in." Just as fathers don't enjoy disciplining their sons, God grieves when He has to discipline us—but He'll do it if we refuse to learn any other way.

The theme of God's discipline reminds me of an incident from when my Grandson Noah was only two years old. I loved Noah, and he knew me as the *fun Grandpa*. I always played and laughed with him, and for a good while, I never had to tell him "no" about *anything*. I definitely never had to *discipline* him! But to my disappointment, very soon, that would change.

One day, I sat next to Noah as he ate lunch, and we were smiling, laughing, and having a good time. He would give me a piece of his cut-up strawberries to eat, and then he would eat one. But all of a sudden, Noah decided it would be fun to throw fruit across the table to get attention. I knew I had to tell him "No;" but I also knew this would instantly change our relationship. It hurt to say it, but I had to tell him for his well-being. When I did, he looked at me with astonishment. His face seemed to say, "But Grandpa—it's fun to throw fruit across the table!" Soon he did it again and waited to see my response. I gently took his hand, looked him right in the eyes, and said, "No, Noah." He knew I meant it and stopped (this Grandpa was thankful the situation didn't escalate).

Our Heavenly Father is like that. With gentleness He warns us: "No. If you do that you'll regret it." He doesn't enjoy disciplining His children, but He knows the results discipline will bring: "No discipline seems pleasant at the time but painful, but *later on* however, it produces *a harvest of righteousness and peace* for those who have been trained by it" (Hebrews 12:11). Yes, when we respond to God's fatherly discipline, we begin to experience a harvest of righteousness in our own lives. Perhaps even more importantly, we'll begin to see a harvest of salvation in *others' lives*, as God will empower our invasion of light for victory!

Let's welcome God's discipline so we can have a harvest of righteousness. I want righteousness to grow out of me like a garden, inspiring others to cry out to God for the same! But we can never reach that place in God without enduring God's loving discipline. And without a harvest of righteousness, we'll leave little damage on the dark invasion—though we might seriously damage God's invasion of light.

CHAPTER TWENTY-TWO

The second sign that we're walking in the light of God's Kingdom is that God has filled us with peace. Romans 14:17 says, "The Kingdom of God is not eating and drinking, but righteousness and *peace* and joy in the Holy Spirit" (NKJV). The Greek word here translated "peace" is *eiréné* (εἰρήνη), which can mean *prosperity of peace and quietness.*[1] In other words, the Kingdom of God will give you so much peace *that you can give it away to others.* The effective ambassador experiences an abundance of peace and quietness inside, and this peace affects every area of their life. God's peace transforms their inner life: they've learned not to give in to worry, pity, and anxiety. God's peace transforms their devotional life: they know God loves them as His child, and they seek to serve Him out of love rather than from strivings for acceptance. God's peace also transforms their social life: they usually keep a cool head instead of overreacting, rarely get angry, and don't hold unforgivingness or jealousy in their heart. As a result, these fruitful ambassadors often *transmit peace to others.* People don't feel anxious, criticized, or wrongfully hurried in their presence. They don't feel like they have to walk on pins and needles to stay in our favor. Yes, when we walk in God's peace, the lost often experience it second-hand and long to understand how to walk in the same. What a crucial key to our invasion of light! Are you walking in it? If not, you aren't yet walking in your inheritance as an heir of God's kingdom—but by God's grace, you can. You need God's peace to fulfill your role in God's invasion of light.

"MY PEACE I GIVE TO YOU"

Are you tossed by the winds and waves of life? Jesus promises to give you supernatural peace. In John 14:27, Jesus said, "Peace I leave with you; My peace I give you. I do not give to you as the world gives." Jesus doesn't want to give you worldly peace, but the very peace He had on Earth—unshakeable peace in the face of trouble.

Think about it. On the road to the cross, Jesus faced the taunts, mockery, and torture of many He loved with all of His heart. Even His beloved disciples abandoned Him to save their own lives. As God the Son, He could have called fire from Heaven on His murderers and retreated to the worldly peace of physical comfort with a snap of His fingers. Instead, He chose the painful cross, looked at His crucifiers with a heart of mercy and eyes of love, and said, "Father, forgive them, for they do not know what they are doing" (Luke 23:34). His body was racked with pain, but He had peace in trouble.

UNSHAKEABLE PEACE IN A TROUBLED WORLD

Many seem to define peace as personal comfort and physical ease, but Jesus never defined it that way. In fact, in John 16:33, He promised: "In this world you will have trouble." That's a promise—especially if you want to fulfill your role in the invasion of light. The truth is, if you're not facing any resistance, you're probably not following Jesus very closely. Jesus never told us we wouldn't have trouble or tribulation—instead, He promised to give us peace to get through the trouble. As He said in John 16:33, "I have told you these things, so that in Me you may have peace. In this world you will have trouble. But take heart! I have overcome the world." Yes, trouble isn't as troublesome when we have God's peace to walk us through.

You see, Jesus wants to give you His own peace—a heavenly peace beyond comprehension (John 14:27, Philippians 4:7). His peace is "not as the world gives" (John 14:27 NKJV)—we can't receive it by earning or lose it by shaking. Like a flood it washes away anxiety, worry, and fear. It's always there; constantly available. And we desperately need Jesus's peace to work effectively in God's invasion of light. Why? Because God's peace doesn't only help us feel well—it helps us fight well! Let's discuss a few ways God's peace prepares us for spiritual battle.

GOD'S PEACE: OUR PROTECTION FROM OVERREACTION

When I was a kid, I loved to watch movies about cowboys and Indians. Whenever I watched, I always felt amazed by something I'll call "soldier stupidity." A soldier would hide behind a rock with a rifle, waiting for the right moment to shoot an Indian. Driven by battle anxiety, the soldier would jump out in plain sight to make a shot—but instead, get nabbed with an arrow! I always thought, "You dumb soldier!"

I believe we do the same thing sometimes. In the heat of battle, we overreact, jump out in the open, and end up getting nabbed with "the flaming arrows of the evil one" (Ephesians 6:16). That's not God's will!

Jesus is the King of Kings and Lord of Lords, and He wants to direct us as the kingdom of priests and the army of God. But to succeed in battle, we need a clear head and a peaceful heart. We need to use our shields at the right time and our swords at the right time. Only when we walk in God's peace will we have the mental clarity to know when to catch the fiery darts of the enemy with the shield of faith and when to tear down demonic strongholds with the sword of the Spirit. Without God's peace guiding you, you may just end up with an arrow in your chest!

GOD'S PEACE:
OUR COURAGE TO FINISH THE RACE

In 2017, famous snowboarder Shaun White split his face open on a ramp while practicing for the Winter Olympics. In White's own words, "Things were great, and just one kind of little mess up, and—*boom!*—I'm being helicoptered to the hospital."[2] With a massive gash on his forehead, White now needed to receive sixty-two stitches and face months of recovery. But he didn't let this painful setback take his mind out of the game. He soon brushed himself off, returned to practice, and competed in the Olympics. The best part of the story: in his last run, he gave his all and won the gold medal! Yes, White could have given up, but instead, he pressed on and won the prize.

Similarly, I think some of us Christians *quit the race too early*. We ride through life—steady, steady, steady . . . and then we fall and immediately forfeit. Instead of looking up to the God who gives peace in trouble, we start to look at our failures and become hopeless and anxious. But we need not be conquered by a sense of defeat and failure! God gives us a peaceful word—we're "more than conquerors through Him who loved us" (Romans 8:37). God calls us to get up, brush off, and keep riding—and promises to help us when we do! Knowing God has made us more than conquerors, we must "press on toward the goal to win the prize for which God has called [us] heavenward in Christ Jesus" (Philippians 3:14). We must not let anxiety rob our invasion of light!

WHO ARE YOU LISTENING TO?

The voices that coach us in life make a profound impact on how we finish the race. For example, consider the influence of godly parents. An encouraging father can make a tremendous impact on his child's success. That's one reason why children from single-parent homes tend to face such adversity. According to the National Fatherhood Initiative, children from father-absent homes are more likely to suffer from emotional and behavioral problems, commit crimes, become addicted to drugs and alcohol, grow obese, drop out of High School, end up in prison, and more.[3] Tragically, these children often lack the encouraging, directive, and corrective voice they need to combat their own insecurity and lack of wisdom. Their own inner voice predicts they'll fail, and without a father's intervention, many do fail.

Perhaps you've heard the same taunts within. Maybe voices in your life say, "You're never going to do anything right—you're going to fail!" or "You'll never make a difference in the invasion of light—you've messed up too bad!" I want you to know that our Father in Heaven never speaks that way. Never! Instead, He offers the same grace to all: "Humble yourselves in the sight of the Lord, and He will lift you up" (James 4:10 NKJV). Are you ready to confess and repent of sin? The Lord is ready to lift you up. He still wants to walk with you, strengthen you, and use you to reach others for Jesus.

Many of us have trouble believing God treats us with that kind of mercy. The voices within curse and abuse us, and we mistake these voices for God. Friend, those voices aren't God. He sees the desire of our heart to please and serve Him, and says, "Come on, get up—you didn't make it that time, but I'm going to help you." He wants to give you peace to stay in the race!

HOW TO RECEIVE
GOD'S PEACE

Now, let's consider three scriptural steps towards walking in God's peace. First, to become eligible to receive God's peace, we must truly know and acknowledge God. Second, to receive God's peace, we must be still and wait on God in faith. And third, once we have received, we must let God's peace rule in our hearts. Let's look at these pathways to peace in greater detail.

STEP #1:
TRULY KNOW GOD

First, to become eligible to receive God's peace, we must truly know God. In 2 Peter 1:2, Peter prays, "grace and peace be yours in abundance *through the knowledge of God and of Jesus our Lord*" (2 Peter 1:2). The Greek word here translated "knowledge" comes from *epignosis* (ἐπίγνωσις), which means *firsthand or relational knowledge.*[4] You see, millions of professing Christians have perfect theology but no personal relationship with God. Well, Christian books like this one can teach you about God, but they can *never* replace personal encounter with Him. No one will experience abundant grace and peace by simply knowing about Jesus Christ. Instead, we need to *know* Jesus Christ Himself, obey His will, and acknowledge Him in prayer and worship.

The Greek word translated "knowledge" in 2 Peter 1:2 also sometimes means *acknowledgment.*[5] It's one thing to *have knowledge* that my wonderful wife, Anne, has walked into the room. It's another thing to *acknowledge her when she walks into the room.* In the same way, many of us work hard to perfect our mental knowledge of the Bible, but rarely acknowledge the God of the Bible. We need to acknowledge the presence of God in our lives by walking with Him, talking with Him, listening to Him, and obeying Him. If we will, we'll experience the promised blessing—"grace and peace be yours in abundance!" (2 Peter 1:2).

STEP #2: BE STILL AND
WAIT ON GOD IN FAITH

Second, to receive God's peace, *we must be still and wait on God in faith.* Have you ever tried to fill a moving glass? It's not very easy, is it? If we'd never try to fill a moving glass, should we expect God to fill a moving Christian? Of course not! If we want God to fill us with His peace, we need to slow down, be still, and spend quality time with Him. As Paul prays in Romans 15:13, "May the God of hope *fill you with all joy and peace* as you trust in Him, so that you may overflow with hope by the power of the Holy Spirit."

Luke 5:16 tells us, "Jesus often withdrew to lonely places and prayed." That's right—not even Jesus dared to face the day without first seeking God's face. Jesus prayed before choosing His disciples (Luke 6:12-16), while in the thick of ministry (Luke 5:15-16), before going to the cross (Matthew 26:36-46), and more. When Jesus met with God in private, He received God's peaceful presence to empower Him in public. Just like Jesus, we need precious moments in God's presence before we can go out to invade with light.

In one of the storms of my life, the Holy Spirit whispered something that changed me forever. In a still, small voice, He said, "If you come into My presence, you will go out with My presence." That phrase has never left me. I think about it often as a reminder to stop, pray, and listen to His voice in all things, and always keep receiving His supernatural overflow.

You see, when you fill a cup past the brim, water begins to overflow over the sides. In the same way, when we wait on God, He fills us with "all joy and peace . . . so that [we] may *overflow with hope* by the power of the Holy Spirit" (Romans 15:13). This world is full of hopeless people—maybe you even secretly battle with hopelessness. Take heart: God loves you and promises to fill you with hope as you get still, seek His face, and trust His character. After that, He wants to overflow His hope *through you* into others' lives. God wants to use you as an ambassador of His hope to this hopeless world!

STEP #3: LET GOD'S
PEACE RULE YOUR HEART

Finally, we must let God's peace rule in our hearts. In Colossians 3:15, Paul says, "Let the peace of Christ rule in your hearts, since as members of one body you were called to peace." The Greek word here translated "rule" comes from *brabeuó* (βραβεύω), with means *to govern or act as umpire.*[6] You see, it's one thing to receive God's peace and another to walk in it. Many receive God's peace at 7 a.m. but lose it by 9 a.m. Why? Because once they leave the house, they begin to submit to their own anxious thoughts instead of God's peace. Remember, the Kingdom of God is a kingdom of peace: "Of the greatness of His government and peace there will be no end" (Isaiah 9:7). If we want to experience the peace of God's kingdom, we need to let the peace of God govern our hearts throughout the day.

To daily receive God's peace, I encourage you to create a quiet place where you can meet with the Lord every morning before you go on your way. If you don't have access to a solitary place, consider waking up before anyone else in the house to meet with God alone. Come into His presence and pray about the responsibilities of the day and the needs in your family, confess your sins, surrender your worries and fears, and spend time studying the Bible. It might feel a little awkward at first, but soon God will begin to show up. Then, His Word and holy presence will grant you profound peace of heart and mind. Day by day, He'll strengthen your character and emotional stability, making you into an effective ambassador of Heaven. Go in to receive Jesus's peace, ambassador of Heaven! Then go out to invade our dark world with His marvelous light. As Isaiah declared:

> Of the increase of His government and peace
> There will be no end,
> Upon the throne of David and over His kingdom,
> To order it and establish it with judgment and justice
> From that time forward, even forever.
> The zeal of the Lord of hosts will perform this!
> (Isaiah 9:7 NKJV)

Amen!

CHAPTER TWENTY-THREE

VITAL #3: JOY IN THE HOLY SPIRIT

The third sign that we're walking in the light of God's kingdom is that God has filled us with *joy*. Romans 14:17 says, "The Kingdom of God is not eating and drinking, but righteousness and peace and joy in the Holy Spirit" (NKJV). In this verse, the Greek word translated "joy" is *chara* (χαρά), which means *cheerfulness, delight, and joy because of grace.*[1] The effective ambassador is full of cheerfulness and delight in God's grace. Sometimes the challenges and trials of life throw them for a loop, but these challenges do not keep them down. God's gracious and powerful joy surges within, displacing sorrow, anger, despair, and every other human emotion that tries to take control. This joy then empowers them to go out and fulfill God's mission with boldness, for "you will go out in joy and be led forth in peace; the mountains and hills will burst into song before you, and all the trees of the field will clap their hands!" (Isaiah 55:12). By that standard, are you walking in the revived life of the Kingdom of God? If not, you can—and you must. It's your inheritance as a co-heir with Christ (Romans 8:17)—and the only way to become an effective ambassador of God's kingdom!

FLAPPING LIKE PIGEONS, OR SOARING LIKE EAGLES?

God spoke to Isaiah about the radical joy He wanted to give the children of His kingdom. In Isaiah 40:31, God promised:

Those who hope in the Lord
> will renew their strength!
They will soar on wings like eagles;
>> they will run and not grow weary,
>> they will walk and not be faint.

This incredible promise leads me to ask—do you fly in life more like a pigeon or an eagle? Pigeons have to constantly flap their wings to keep flying. But eagles simply spread their wings, get under the wind, and soar. Ambassador of Christ, do you have to muster up strength just to get through each hour of the day? That's not God's will! God calls you to soar on the winds of the Holy Spirit!

When I get to Heaven, I want to fly. But we don't have to wait till we die to fly—the Lord wants us to soar by His Spirit *right now*. He wants us to succeed in holiness by His grace and with His joy, giving Him all the glory. That's what it looks like to live in the Kingdom of God—and if we lack this joy, we'll have little success in the invasion of light.

Let's open the scriptures to find biblical sources of joy. I pray God uses this chapter to put wind under your wings and grant you to soar like an eagle in the Kingdom of God, making you a powerful instrument of salvation in His hands.

JOY COMES FROM GOD'S GRACIOUS SMILE

The greatest joy in life is knowing we put a smile on the face of God. In the Psalms, David calls us to "rejoice . . . and sing for joy on [our] beds . . . for the Lord takes delight in His people!" (Psalm 149:5, 4).

Do you know that your Heavenly Father smiles when you obey Him from the heart? In Psalms 147:11, David proclaims, "the LORD *delights in those who fear Him, who put their hope in His unfailing love.*" God rejoices and delights in His obedient children! When we take up our cross and follow God's Word and plan, we have the great privilege of experiencing God's song of rejoicing over us (see Zephaniah 3:17). Unfortunately, if we don't follow God in faith, our ears will never enjoy the privilege of hearing this wonderful song. As a result, we'll have little heavenly joy to propel us into the raging battle for souls.

Sometimes, the Heavenly Father seems to tell me, "Brian, you're making me smile!" Those smiles of God motivate me to follow Jesus and share God's hope every day with joy. I surely don't follow Him perfectly, but I long to take up my cross, deny myself, and follow Him daily. When we experience God's joy, we can't help but exclaim with Paul: "I count all things to be loss in view of the surpassing value of knowing Christ Jesus my Lord" (Philippians 3:8 NASB).

JOY COMES NOT FROM AN EASY LIFE, BUT A FAITHFUL GOD

Other professing Christians seek joy in easy circumstances. Their smile lasts no longer than their ease! But if we want to walk in the joy of God's kingdom, we need to learn to rejoice through adversity. As Jesus promised in John 16:20: "Most assuredly, I say to you that . . . you will be sorrowful . . . but your sorrow will be turned into joy" (NKJV). Have you been sorrowful? Maybe your current circumstances distress and discourage you. Friend, God doesn't make light of your turmoil; but He wants to *be the Light in your turmoil* (see John 1:9).

Remember, King Jesus is anointed "to bind up the broken hearted" (Isaiah 61:1). He knows exactly what you're going through and wants to strengthen your heart. Hebrews 4:15 says, "we do not have a high priest who is unable to empathize with our weaknesses, but we have one who has been tempted in every way, just as we are—yet He did not sin."

Are you suffering from the death of a loved one? Jesus understands. He remembers when he wept over the death of his good friend Lazarus (John 11:35). Are you suffering a season of terrible temptation? Jesus understands. He remembers when He had to face forty days of temptation amid weakness, thirst, and starvation in the wilderness (Matthew 4:1-11). Are you suffering from financial stress and needing miraculous provision? Jesus understands. He remembers when He had to trust God to supernaturally provide funding for the temple tax (Matthew 17:24-27). You see, King Jesus knows your suffering by experience. He suffered what you're suffering—yet when He suffered, He maintained a joyful heart. If you seek Him, He'll be your joy in difficult times. You don't have to work hard to receive it—the joy of God's kingdom is readily and freely available to all who trust in Him. He wants you to receive it daily—for your own sake and the world's.

JOY COMES NOT FROM THINGS, BUT FROM GOD

Many others seek joy in material possessions. They say, "I'll trust the Lord for that car, and that will bring me great joy!" What disappointments await these confused believers! Possessions rust and cars crash, but "of His government [kingdom] and peace there will be no end" (Isaiah 9:7). Saint of God, don't get preoccupied with possessions—keep your eyes on God, His glory, and the battle for the souls of mankind!

I remember when my wife, Anne, and I bought a shiny new yellow Nissan station wagon in 1980. Before then, we had always driven clunkers to save our money. Now, every time we looked out the window, we saw that beautiful new car shining in the Florida sun. What a beauty!

If you've ever bought a new car, you might understand the feeling. We loved that car and felt such a thrill driving it around. Then, one day, we faced an unexpected surprise. Out of nowhere, as we cruised at fifty-five miles per hour, a reckless driver pulled *right in front of us*, tearing up the whole front end. By God's grace, we got through the accident with little more than a few bang-ups—but the car didn't have the same fortune. As I stepped out to check the damage, all I could think was, "Oh no, our beautiful new car!" Worst of all, we hadn't even paid the first payment on it yet!

Nissan did their best to repair it, but their finest work couldn't restore the car to like-new condition. Now, in our driveway sat another clunker. Our once gorgeous bright yellow vehicle now donned two different shades of yellow, and our smooth-riding station wagon never drove quite as smoothly again.

For years, this reminded us that we cannot find joy in material possessions. Things come and go, but joy can stay permanently through our relationship with Jesus. Yes, through that experience, God forced me to learn a lesson: my joy shouldn't depend on the kind of car I have, but *the kind of God I have.*

JOY COMES NOT FROM MIRACLES
BUT FROM ETERNAL LIFE

Still many others seek joy in spiritual power and miracles. I personally identify as a Charismatic Christian; that is, I believe the gifts of the Holy Spirit continue today. But I've realized something. A lot of Pentecostal and Charismatic Christians live enslaved to their emotions. They experience sudden, radical bursts of joy when miracles happen on Sunday—but then spend the rest of the week scraping the bottom of the joy barrels. That's not God's will—He wants us to be joyful at all times! As Paul admonishes us, "Rejoice in the Lord always: and again I say, Rejoice!" (Philippians 4:4 KJV).

Jesus addressed this issue in Luke 10. He had sent seventy disciples out to preach the gospel, heal the sick, and cast out demons, and they now returned with overwhelming joy. They burst out with excitement: "Lord, even the demons submit to us in your name!" (Luke 10:17). Jesus celebrated with them, rejoicing in the authority He gave them to "overcome all the power of the enemy" (Luke 10:19). But then He gave these fiery evangelists a bit of pastoral advice: "Do not rejoice that the spirits submit to you, but rejoice that your names are written in Heaven" (Luke 10:20). He didn't want them to merely rejoice that they had *power* from the God of Heaven, but that they had *a home with God* in Heaven.

Brothers and sisters, we have reason to rejoice in every season of life: After we die, we will be with the Lord forever. There, we'll no longer suffer any sorrow, hunger, pain, temptation, or persecution. The Kingdom of God will restore all things, and God will exchange all of our mourning for celebration. What reason to rejoice! We should be overflowing with joy! Are you? We need God's holy joy to effectively advance His mission on Earth.

VESSELS OF JOY

A lot of people keep the joy of the Lord to themselves. They sing joyful praise songs in their cars, pray joyful prayers in their rooms, and think joyful thoughts in their minds—but they never speak joyful words to their neighbors! Friend, God doesn't give us joy for us to keep it to ourselves. He wants to display His glory through our joy; He wants to impart the joy of God's kingdom through us. God wants us to invade our world with the light of His holy joy!

I believe Jesus's radical joy attracted lost people. He didn't choose to be born in a body with a beautiful face; in fact, the Bible says, "He had no beauty or majesty to attract us to Him, nothing in His appearance that we should desire Him" (Isaiah 53:2). Then why did people feel so drawn to Him? The answer is simple. Though He had no human beauty, He had divine joy—and that joy shone like a brilliant light to all around Him. Seeing this holy joy, the lost and hopeless couldn't help but desire to meet Him.

You may also feel insufficient, unattractive, unpopular, or unappreciated—but if you submit to God, He can use you as a beacon of joy to a dark world. The people of this broken world need to see the bright light of Christ in us! How will we be the light of the world if we walk through life struggling to put smiles on our faces?

JESUS'S RADICAL JOY IS BETTER THAN THE PAINTINGS

When we see some paintings of Jesus, we conclude some artists should find a different career. First of all, most paintings show Him dead or dying. But most depictions of Jesus before the cross show Him grave or sorrowful, as if He had no joy in His Father. We think these paintings miss out on the reality of Jesus's radical joy.

Think about it. We all know Jesus's famous call, "Let the little children come to me!" (Matthew 19:14). Do you really think He made this call with hands folded, face solemn, and voice grave? We sure don't. We picture Jesus with arms high, voice lifted, and eyes full of love and excitement. We imagine Him dancing with the children and calling them to sit on His lap. Many of us don't seem to realize that God created the child's heart to desire His own qualities. Jesus was full of joy, playful, fun, and free. Some of us are a little too religious to see the King as He truly is. Before we can succeed in our invasion of light, we must come to know the joyful Jesus—and learn to walk in the same joy.

OBEDIENCE RELEASES JESUS'S JOY

And that's the glorious reality: God promises to give us *Jesus's very joy*. In John 15:10-11, Jesus says:

> If you keep My commands, you will remain in My love, just as I have kept My Father's commands and remain in His love. I have told you this so that My joy may be in you and that your joy may be complete.

These verses grant us a few powerful revelations about Christian joy.

First, *Jesus offers joy on a condition*. Jesus said, "*If* you keep My commands, you will remain in My love . . . that your joy may be complete" (John 15:10-11). If I meet the condition, I'll receive the promise—complete joy. If I don't meet the condition, God won't grant me the promise.

Second, *Jesus offers complete joy on the condition of complete, loving obedience*. In verse 10, He says, "If you keep My commands, you will remain in My love." But what type of obedience does He call us to pursue? The same kind He practiced. He calls us to obey and remain in Him "just as [He] kept [His] Father's commands and remain[ed] in His love" (John 15:10). Jesus calls us to obey *His commands* with the same passion and devotion that directed Him to obey *the Father's commands*. That's a pretty high calling—but if the same Spirit who raised Christ from the dead dwells in us, He'll surely give us the ability (see Romans 8:11).

Third, *if we meet the condition of complete, loving obedience, God will grant us Jesus's own joy.* In verse 11, Jesus explains the goal of this conditional promise: ". . . that *My joy* may be in you and that *your joy may be complete*" (John 15:11). Jesus's joy—full, free, and overflowing—can become your joy! It is yours for the taking if you submit your entire life to God. What power God's joy will add to our invasion of light!

I don't know about you, but I don't ever want to become a grumpy old Christian. I don't ever want to get too old to dance and sing before the Lord. I'm getting up there in age, but I'm a child of God, and I want to experience God's overflowing joy more and more each day. Then as we invade with light, let us make Isaiah's words our motto:

> You will go out in joy
> and be led forth in peace;
> the mountains and hills
> will burst into song before you,
> and all the trees of the field
> will clap their hands. (Isaiah 55:12)

Child of God, get up, rejoice, and fulfill God's mission with gladness! God has given you the privilege of a lifetime—to destroy the works of the evil one by the Holy Spirit's power! In the strength of God's Spirit, go out with joy!

CHAPTER TWENTY-FOUR

THE REWARD OF THE INVASION: THE CROWNS OF THE KINGDOM

Now I (Brian) would like to discuss the eternal rewards faithful Christians will receive for walking in the Kingdom of God and invading the world with Jesus's light.

In 1 Corinthians 9:24-25, Paul establishes one of the primary reasons we live the Christian life—to win an imperishable crown from God. He exhorts us:

> Run in such a way as to get the prize. Everyone who competes in the games goes into strict training. They do it to get a crown that will not last, but we do it to get a crown that will last forever.

In this chapter, we'll explore some of the crowns God offers us in His Word.

TREASURES IN HEAVEN

Many seem to think that in eternity we'll simply fly around and sit on clouds, but Jesus proclaims a much greater reality: God longs to reward our labor in His invasion of light! In Revelation 22:12, Jesus says, "Look, I am coming soon! My reward is with Me, and I will give to each person according to what they have done." In other words, Christians who work and invade culture with endurance and pure motives will occupy a great place in Heaven; but Christians who served God little or with impure motives will occupy a lesser place in Heaven.

Paul discusses this at length in 1 Corinthians 3:11-15. According to Paul, God will judge the lives of believers at a special judgment called the Judgment Seat of Christ (see 2 Corinthians 5:10). At the Judgment Seat of Christ, God will reward us according to "the quality of [our] work" for Him (1 Corinthians 3:13). If we serve Him faithfully, God will count our work as valuable "gold, silver and costly stones" (1 Corinthians 3:12) and reward us accordingly. But if we serve God with impure motives, He'll count our works as common "wood, hay [and] straw" (1 Corinthians 3:12). Such believers will "suffer loss but yet will be saved—even though only as one escaping through the flames" (1 Corinthians 3:15).

In light of the Judgment Seat of Christ, Jesus commands us to live in a way that gains eternal rewards. In Matthew 6:19-20, Jesus says:

Do not store up for yourselves treasures on Earth, where moths and vermin destroy, and where thieves break in and steal. But store up for yourselves treasures in Heaven, where moths and vermin do not destroy, and where thieves do not break in and steal.

Many think it's selfish to desire eternal rewards—but such would have to argue with Jesus Himself, as He taught us to desire them! Jesus will joyfully reward those who serve Him faithfully, and He wants us to live with His rewarding character in mind. One day, He'll say to every faithful Christian, "Come, you who are blessed by My Father; take your inheritance, the kingdom prepared for you since the creation of the world" (Matthew 25:34). As Christ's ambassadors, we must prepare ourselves for that day by living faithfully to God and steadily invading our world with light.

HEAVEN'S CHAMPIONS

I want us to consider what the New Testament authors intend when they speak of crowns. The New Testament Greek word for "crown" is *stephanos* (στέφανος), which sometimes refers to a wreath given to Greek Olympic champions.[1] In the ancient Olympics, after athletes out-played their competitors, game officials placed a wreath of leaves on their heads to honor their victory. Paul compares heavenly rewards to the Olympic wreath in 1 Corinthians 9:24-25:

Do you not know that in a race all the runners run, but only one gets the prize? Run in such a way as to get the prize. Everyone who competes in the games goes into strict training. They do it to get a crown that will not last, but we do it to get a crown that will last forever.

Here, Paul helps us understand the crowns of the Kingdom. In the New Testament, a crown is a prize and a badge of honor for those who not only compete but win God's great race. God knows if these crowns are literal or only metaphorical—either way, the crowns of the Kingdom represent real heavenly rewards.

The reality is that God doesn't grant participation ribbons. Sure, we receive salvation by God's free grace alone, but we must *earn* heavenly rewards by invading with light and winning the race God has set before us. Because God rewards us according to "the quality of our work" (1 Corinthians 3:13), some will receive more crowns than others. That means that your heavenly rewards *depend on you*. Will you be faithful? Will you fight the forces of evil in the world by God's power? Will you finish the race with flying colors? By God's grace—and that alone—you can.

THE 5 CROWNS OF THE KINGDOM

Now, let's open the scriptures to explore the five heavenly crowns God offers to faithful servants of His kingdom. The New Testament mentions the following five crowns:

1. The Incorruptible Crown (1 Corinthians 9:25)

2. The Crown of Rejoicing (1 Thessalonians 2:19)

3. The Crown of Righteousness (2 Timothy 4:8)

4. The Crown of Glory (1 Peter 5:4)

5. The Crown of Life (Revelation 2:10)

Let's dive in to consider our reward for the invasion of light.

THE INCORRUPTIBLE CROWN:
A REWARD FOR SELF-DISCIPLINE

In 1 Corinthians 9:25, Paul mentions *the incorruptible crown*. This crown can never tarnish or be destroyed. It will last forever as a God-glorifying memorial for our service to God while on Earth, marking us as faithful disciples of Jesus Christ and soldiers in God's invasion of light. But God only gives this crown to those who finish God's race—those who seek God's kingdom first and live their whole lives for His glory!

As Paul says in 1 Corinthians 9:24-27:

> Do you not know that in a race all the runners run, but only one gets the prize? Run in such a way as to get the prize. Everyone who competes in the games goes into strict training. They do it to get a crown that will not last, but we do it to get a crown that will last forever [the KJV reads "an incorruptible crown"]. Therefore I do not run like someone running aimlessly; I do not fight like a boxer beating the air. No, I strike a blow to my body and make it my slave so that after I have preached to others, I myself will not be disqualified for the prize.

Yes, if we want to gain the incorruptible crown, God requires us to go into "strict training" (1 Corinthians 9:25). The Greek word here translated "goes into strict training" comes from *agonizomai* (ἀγωνίζομαι), from which we derive the English word "agonize."[2] When athletes train for a race, they first experience agonizing muscular pain and energy loss; but through training they gain athletic stamina and physical strength. In the same way, we need to train ourselves to radically obey God and remain faithful agents of God's invasion of light. When anger, pride, lust, or selfishness rise up, we must "take captive every thought to make it obedient to Christ" (2 Corinthians 10:5). Don't give up—keep running! Paul did not pretend this training would be easy; even he had to "strike a blow to [his] body and make it [his] slave" (1 Corinthians 9:27). But if we endure in this severe training, we'll receive God's incorruptible crown.

And that's the key—only the winners receive this crown. In 1 Corinthians 9:24, Paul exhorts us to "run in such a way as to get the prize." The Greek word here translated "get" comes from *lambano* (λαμβάνω), which can mean *to receive by attaining*.[3] Yes, God's strict training calls you, and you *can* answer the call. Will you win the race and receive God's imperishable crown, or live a life of spiritual laziness and forfeit it?

In 1 Corinthians 9:27, Paul makes a sober reflection: "I strike a blow to my body and make it my slave so that after I have preached to others, I myself will not be *disqualified for the prize*" (1 Corinthians 9:27). Tragically, many professing Christians *will* be disqualified from receiving this heavenly crown because of their disobedience. Many pastors are falling into secret sin: affairs, pornography, theft, embezzlement, and more. Well, friend, if you walk in a sinful lifestyle, God will not bless you. Preachers, if you don't practice what you preach, God will not bless you!

Are you in sexual sin of any kind? You need to close the door, confess to the appropriate people, and receive radical accountability. Do you hold unforgiving-ness? Forgive, and bless those who harmed you! Have you stolen from, lied to, or mistreated others? Return the money, confess the lie, and apologize for your sin! Surrender your heart and life completely to Jesus and receive His mercy. Then you'll be back in the race for the incorruptible crown!

THE CROWN OF REJOICING:
THE SOUL-WINNER'S REWARD

Another crown Paul mentions is *the crown of rejoicing*, which many call the soul-winner's crown. "For what is our hope, or joy, or crown of rejoicing? Is it not even you in the presence of our Lord Jesus Christ at His coming?" (1 Thessalonians 2:19, NKJV). God gives this crown to those who faithfully live and preach the gospel of Jesus Christ, resulting in lives transformed by the power of the gospel.

You see, God promises to reward every gospel seed we plant. In 1 Corinthians 3:8, Paul says, "the one who plants and the one who waters have one purpose, and they will each be rewarded according to their own labor." Sometimes we don't see the results of our witness right away, but don't forget—"God . . . gives the increase" (1 Corinthians 3:7 NKJV)! If you play even a small role in someone's salvation story, you'll receive a reward for your labor!

The Bible teaches another glorious reality—the salvation of souls always leads to rejoicing. God the Father rejoices when the lost are found (see Luke 15:11-32). Angels greatly rejoice when sinners bow the knee to God's kingdom (see Luke 15:10). And after we die, we'll also greatly rejoice in the souls God won through our personal invasion of light. Yes, when we stand before God, each soul will be a reason to "glory in the presence of our Lord Jesus" (1 Thessalonians 2:19).

I believe in eternity we'll rejoice to meet the souls who received Christ through our influence. I expect that they'll find us, grab us by the hand, and thank us for denying ourselves to share God's message. I can't wait to get to Heaven and "glory in the presence of our Lord Jesus" over those eternally valuable souls (1 Thessalonians 2:19)! Will many souls greet you there? If not, today's the day to start winning the lost to Jesus.

THE CROWN OF RIGHTEOUSNESS

Another crown Paul mentions is the *crown of righteousness.* God gives this crown to Christians who long for the return of Jesus and therefore live as strangers and pilgrims on planet Earth. In 2 Timothy 4:8, Paul says, "Now there is in store for me the crown of righteousness, which the Lord, the righteous Judge, will award to me on that day—and not only to me, but also to all who have longed for His appearing."

King Jesus will return whenever God has chosen. Knowing this, Paul lived in anticipation of His royal return. As Paul declared in Philippians 3:20, "Our citizenship is in Heaven. And we eagerly await a Savior from there, the Lord Jesus Christ." Paul knew well that God had prepared a special crown for his holy longing, and for all believers who also longed for Jesus's appearing!

As children of God, Heaven is our true home, and Jesus's return our great anticipation. We need to live in light of that reality! Mature believers don't aspire to build earthly empires of wealth. They don't need the biggest houses, the best cars, the coolest clothes, the most elite friends, or fancy private jets. They know all of these things will be destroyed by moth and rust (see Matthew 6:19), and have chosen to focus on one great, imperishable treasure—meeting Jesus Christ Himself. For this reason, they "store up . . . treasures in Heaven, where neither moth nor rust destroys, and where thieves do not break in or steal" (Matthew 6:20 NASB).

Peter commanded us to "look forward to the day of God and speed its coming" (2 Peter 3:12). If we truly anticipate Jesus's return, we'll live in such a way that welcomes Him to return. What slows Jesus's return? I believe that Matthew 24:14 tells us: "This gospel of the Kingdom will be preached in the whole world as a testimony to all nations, *and then the end will come.*" Yes—Jesus promised to return after we send the gospel to all nations. For Jesus to return, I believe we must first send the gospel to the 3.2 billion people who have never heard of Him. It's time to invade the unreached world with light! What are we doing about it?

Tragically, I find that many seem to want Jesus to hold off His return. Perhaps they don't feel ready to stand before God. But our attitude before God should be one of longing and anticipation! Our hearts should cry, "Lord I can't wait to be with You! I can't wait till You take me home, and I will serve You with all my heart while I'm here!" Only then can we expect to receive the crown of righteousness.

THE CROWN OF GLORY: A REWARD
FOR FAITHFUL SHEPHERDS

Another crown the Bible mentions is the *crown of glory,* sometimes called *the pastor's crown.* 1 Peter 5:1-4 says:

> To the elders among you, I appeal as a fellow elder and a witness of Christ's sufferings who also will share in the glory to be revealed: Be shepherds of God's flock that is under your care, watching over them—not because you must, but because you are willing, as God wants you to be; not pursuing dishonest gain, but eager to serve; not lording it over those entrusted to you, but being examples to the flock. And when the Chief Shepherd appears, you will receive the crown of glory that will never fade away.

This passage teaches us a few things about the crown of glory.

First, God gives this crown to ministry leaders who sacrifice themselves to faithfully care for the flock of God. This includes pastors, Bible teachers, evangelists, missionaries, elders, Sunday school teachers, youth pastors, and others. 1 Peter 5:2 says, "*Be shepherds* of God's flock that is under your care, *watching over them . . .*" Leaders, God has entrusted God's flock *under your care*. It's your responsibility to care after God's faithful flock and to run after God's straying flock.

If you're in public ministry, I want you to take a moment to think about the souls you're responsible for. Are you dealing with them faithfully? Do you point them to the Savior? Do you preach God's promises to them? Do you encourage them when they're down? Do you lovingly correct and warn them when they stray? Do you affirm them when they follow their Lord?

Now think about those who have *strayed* from your care. Do you remember those lost sheep? The ones who left the church a year ago whom you never called? The ones stuck in the doldrums of sin again? God requires you to *go after them—* how do you know whether or not they'll repent? Unless we care after God's faithful sheep and go after God's straying sheep, we cannot receive the crown of glory.

Second, God gives this crown to church leaders who want to serve, not those who serve *from a mere obligation.* 1 Peter 5:2 commands leaders to watch over the flock "not because you must, but because you are willing." Jesus said, 'Anyone who wants to be first must be the very last, and the servant of all" (Mark 9:35). Christlike church leaders *love their calling* because they *love to serve others.* They don't consider themselves "too important" to perform menial tasks; they'll gladly take their turn to sweep the floor, wash the windows, and take out the trash if needed. Why? Because they don't glory in their platform; they glory in servanthood!

Third, God gives this crown to church leaders who live as "examples to the flock" (1 Peter 5:3). When I (Brian) first received Jesus, I heard a phrase that has stuck with me all these years: "More things are caught than taught." In other words, people will mimic what you do more than what you say. Words have little meaning until defined by action! With that considered, I never want to be too proud to reach a dying soul, feed the filthy poor, clean a dirty dish, or sweep the dusty floor. As a ministry leader, I want to set an example to others by obeying God even when it's uncomfortable or humbling. Do you have that same heart? If so, keep and nourish it, because you're an example to those you lead. If not, you need to humble yourself before the Lord and make serious adjustments to your invasion of light.

1 Peter 5:1-4 teaches us that *if* we do these things, *then* "when the Chief Shepherd appears, [we] will receive the crown of glory that will never fade away." The meaning is clear—we will not receive the crown unless we meet the condition. I hate to say it, but many pastors and leaders will not receive the crown of glory. They're more interested in their earthly pay package than their heavenly reward. Sadly, their pay package will end when they leave the Earth. "Truly I tell you, they have received their reward in full" (Matthew 6:2).

THE CROWN OF LIFE: A REWARD FOR OBEDIENCE
IN THE FACE OF TRIALS, TESTS, AND PERSECUTION

The final crown we'll study is *the crown of life*. God gives this crown to those who remain obedient to Him as they patiently endure the trials and tests of life. In Revelation 2:10, Jesus tells the first century church of Smyrna, "Do not fear any of those things which you are about to suffer. Indeed, the devil is about to throw some of you into prison, that you may be tested, and you will have tribulation ten days. Be faithful until death, and I will give you *the crown of life*" (NKJV).

The church of Smyrna would soon endure testing and trials, and some would have to face the ultimate test of martyrdom. Knowing this, Jesus comforted the church with a promise: if they remained obedient throughout these trials—even unto martyrdom—they would receive the crown of life.

James gives the same promise in James 1:12: "Blessed is the one who *perseveres under trial* because, having stood the test, that person will receive the *crown of life* that the Lord has promised to those who love Him."

The reality is that every faithful Christian will suffer trials and persecution as they invade the world with light. But when the waves of life crash against us, God expects us to cling to Him and hold our heads up high. As Peter said, "Dear friends, do not be surprised at the fiery ordeal that has come on you to test you, as though something strange were happening to you. But rejoice inasmuch as you participate in the sufferings of Christ, so that you may be overjoyed when His glory is revealed" (1 Peter 4:12-13).

You see, Jesus suffered while He came to Earth, and He completely understands all we suffer for His name. He's not an unsympathetic Savior blind to our suffering; rather, He "has been tempted in every way, just as we are—yet He did not sin" (Hebrews 4:15). Jesus understands our hurt by experience, and always stands prepared to give us the grace, power, hope, and endurance we need for any trial or test. The problem is that many of us forget to come to Him and receive it.

In this grand invasion of light, we must stop seeing persecution as a curse, and begin to see it as God's strange blessing. As Peter promised, "If you are insulted because of the name of Christ, you are blessed, for the Spirit of glory and of God rests on you" (1 Peter 4:14). Next time somebody insults you for following Jesus, rejoice! You have been "counted worthy of suffering disgrace for the Name" (Acts 5:41)!

Think about this—how will we face the ultimate test of martyrdom if we can't face a little mockery? In America, we begin to groan about "the cost of discipleship" when others call us mean names, reject a gospel tract, or block us on social media. But these are very small trials compared to what many Christians suffer today. Do you know that approximately 215 million Christians suffer *extreme* persecution today?[4] Did you know that over 900,000 Christians were martyred from 2007 to 2017?[5] These precious souls were rejected, beaten, and slaughtered for following Jesus. May we learn their endurance and receive their crown!

Ambassador of Christ, the lost are watching how you face the trials of life to decide whether or not they will truly follow Christ. More importantly, God is watching how we face persecution to decide whether or not He will give us the crown of life! With this in mind, we must heed the exhortation of Peter: "If you suffer, it should not be as a murderer or thief or any other kind of criminal, or even as a meddler. However, if you suffer as a Christian, do not be ashamed, but praise God that you bear that name!" (1 Peter 4:15-16). Let's finish the invasion of light, no matter the cost!

WHAT WILL WE DO WITH OUR CROWNS?

Finally, what will we do with the crowns we receive from our service in God's invasion of light? The answer should compel us into service: we will lay them down as love-offerings to our Lord Jesus Christ!

Revelation 4:10-11 gives us a peek into eternity, letting us see what Heaven's twenty-four honored elders will forever do with their crowns: "They lay their crowns before the throne and say: 'You are worthy, our Lord and God, to receive glory and honor and power, for You created all things, and by Your will they were created and have their being.'" Without a doubt, we everyday believers will do the same.

Yes, for all eternity, we'll lay our crowns before the Savior, decry our unworthiness, and praise His worthiness. Forever we'll cry, "Thank You Lord for granting this crown! It was only by Your grace, power, love, and sacrifice. Your grace alone propelled me through the battle! I don't deserve it—Here, I give it to You."

LET NO ONE TAKE YOUR CROWN

Perhaps throughout this book you've rededicated your life to Jesus Christ, accepted the ambassador's call, and started down a fresh path of obedience to God. No matter where you are on your discipleship journey, I want to encourage you to receive Jesus's call, step upon the narrow road, and stay there until God calls you home. In Revelation 3:11, Jesus exhorts us, "I am coming soon. Hold on to what you have, so that no one will take your crown." In light of this, I challenge you to obey Peter's command: "Make every effort to confirm your calling and election" (2 Peter 1:10). As Peter promises, "if you do these things, you will never stumble, and you will receive a rich welcome into the eternal Kingdom of our Lord and Savior Jesus Christ" (2 Peter 1:10-11).

What an incredible promise! Don't you want a rich welcome when you get to Heaven? Don't you want many to come up to you and say, "Thank you for remaining faithful to Jesus Christ, and using your life to invade my world with God's light. It's because of your witness that I met Jesus Christ—and I'm so glad we're here together!"

Even better, the richest welcome comes from the Lord. I can't wait for the day when King Jesus looks me in the eyes and says, "Well done, good and faithful servant." Yes, if you stay faithful, then soon, the King of Light will embrace you in person and gladly welcome you into His glorious kingdom. God will win the battle, our fight against darkness will finally end, and forever we'll celebrate the victories Jesus won through His faithful ambassadors!

Yes, coronation day is coming soon! We hope to see you there. Until then, forge ahead, ambassador of Christ—it's time to invade with light!

Appendices, Worksheets,
and About

APPENDIX ONE

A SHORT HISTORY OF
THE INVASION OF DARKNESS

We've spent this whole book studying how to invade our world with light, one soul at a time. Now, in these two appendices, we'd like to unveil the current darkness and suggest how we got here (to those interested in reading on). We offer this information praying God might grant you clearer insight into the spiritual battle, deeper loyalty to His kingdom, stronger burden for lost souls, and greater urgency for your ambassadorial mission.

We warn you ahead of time—these two chapters are not pleasant to read. If you forge ahead, you'll face heartbreaking facts and statistics that reveal a nation in decline and a church in compromise. No one enjoys learning about Satan's work, but we must face the facts to better prepare ourselves for the spiritual battles before us. Only when we understand the invasion of darkness will we be prepared to fight back with God's love, light, and truth. Let's dive in.

THE MODERN INVASION (1963-PRESENT)

In the first century, Paul warned Timothy:

> Mark this: There will be terrible times in the last days. People will be lovers of themselves, lovers of money, boastful, proud, abusive, disobedient to their parents, ungrateful, unholy, without love, unforgiving, slanderous, without self-control, brutal, not lovers of the good, treacherous, rash, conceited, lovers of pleasure rather than lovers of God— having a form of godliness but denying its power. (2 Timothy 3:1-5)

Almost two thousand years later, I (Brian) believe the current generation has fulfilled this prophecy more than any other in recent history. As the Kingdom of Darkness has invaded the modern world, many have lost touch with right and wrong. The modern disciple of Jesus can't help but ask, "How did we get here?" I want to suggest part of the story.

The world changed before my eyes in the mid-sixties—a time we identify as the beginning of the modern invasion of darkness. Now, we don't mean that America was a Christian utopia before 1963. The world has always been evil, and American morals actually began their current gradual decline in the nineteenth century. But the mid-sixties served as a flashpoint, if you will—a moment of sudden, radical change that sent the world into a hundred fresh moral crises.

Before the mid-sixties, very few Americans broadcasted their sin. Christianity still had a notable influence in society. Many public schools still engaged in prayer and Bible reading. Almost everyone claimed the Bible as their ultimate moral authority. But in 1963, a whirlwind of demonic chaos seemed to appear over America. The U.S. Supreme Court declared school devotions unconstitutional, and God seemed to suddenly remove what remained of the protective hedge secured by a nation's prayers. As a result, the demonic entities over the United States sped their efforts to attack God's reputation, Word, and principles. Some may accuse us of hyper-spiritualizing history, but we have trouble concluding anything else. Why? Because most of the greatest moral dilemmas we now face began within only ten years.

It started with Satan's war on sexual purity (what many now call the sexual revolution). Birth control pills became legal in all fifty states in 1965, removing singles' fears of unwanted pregnancies and flinging wide the door for sexual sin.[1] These contraceptives didn't become universally legal for single women until 1973—but, as *Saturday Evening Post* writer Stephen M. Spencer wrote in 1966, "whether by legitimate or underground routes, the pill has found its way to the college campuses and even to the high-school hallways."[2] And singles took them by the droves.

The results were shocking. Whereas only 45% of women had premarital sex by age 20 in 1959-1968, 65% of women had premarital sex by age 20 in 1969-1976—a twenty-point increase in less than a decade.[3] By 1969, this newfound sexual freedom gave birth to the free love movement, which invited youth to commit sexual acts with multiple partners, often in public. Woodstock music festival powerfully represented this movement's true colors, with young people partying, having public sex, getting drunk, and singing about rebellion against government and authorities. Local medics reported approximately 25 acid-drug "freak-outs" per hour on the first day alone.[4]

Soon, the Kingdom of Darkness won more crucial ground in its battle against godly sexuality. In the Summer of 1969, California Governor Ronald Reagan signed the first American no-fault divorce bill into law, sending legal shockwaves around the nation and the globe. Before long, other states began following Reagan's example, adding inertia to a wave of immorality that would eventually engulf every state in the Union and most nations on the map. Before Reagan's signature, couples had to legally establish wrongdoing before they could pursue divorce. Now they could divorce for any reason whatsoever—or no reason at all. As Reagan's son explained:

> My father hoped that the no-fault statutes would reduce acrimony, legal costs, and harm to the children of divorce. Instead, divorce rates soared 250 percent nationwide from 1960 to 1980. Dad later said that signing that bill was one of the worst mistakes of his political career.[5]

Who can measure the impact of that one moral tragedy, which forged the modern divorce crisis as we know it? That alone could have toppled our society without one more of Satan's fiery darts. But Satan and his minions didn't stop their dark invasion at divorce. The next battle would begin in a dirty New York City bar—but would soon overtake the whole globe.

For years, the Stonewall Inn served as a gathering place for young gay, lesbian, and transgender runaways. Sixties teens with same-sex attractions often received brutal abuse from parents—from piercing insults and violent assaults to total abandonment. Rather than exercise patience and speak the truth in love, many parents kicked their children out at a hat's drop. Many more teens ran away of their own accord. When these troubled youth sought refuge in New York City, they very often made a home out of the Stonewall gay bar and inn.[6] Unable to legally drink and unwelcome in more expensive bars, New York's runaway teens panhandled and shoplifted to pay Stonewall's three-dollar nightly entry fee. Once they paid, they could shelter inside all night without buying anything else.[7]

Tragically, Stonewall's emotionally charged environment served as a ticking time bomb of moral revolution. New York law didn't grant liquor licenses to gay bars, so Stonewall and similar places functioned as illegal saloons.[8] Oftentimes they were run by New York mafia, casting greater shade on their reputation. Soon, police began cracking down. Police shut down other gay bars without extreme pushback; but extreme civil unrest broke out when they came for Stonewall.

On June 28, 1969, the historic Stonewall riots began. New York's gays, lesbians, and transgenders lined the streets for five nights of violent demonstration in pursuit of social and political acceptance. Soon mini-Stonewall protests popped up around the United States, adding national momentum to the new movement. The pent-up energy released at these riots gave birth to the gay activism organizations that forged our current sexual crisis, including the Gay Liberation Front, Human Rights Campaign, GLAAD, and PFLAG.[9] The modern gay revolution had begun.

As America continued its downward spiral, the Kingdom of Darkness would gain shocking new territory. Soon, Satan would inspire a successful movement to destroy infant lives.

Very few know that Americans once forged a pro-life movement that utterly abolished abortion in our land. Abortion was commonplace in the United States for much of its early history, but in the mid-1800s, doctors and Christians banded together to abolish the baby-murder trade altogether.[10] By 1880, every state in the union had outlawed abortion. Those who still murdered their unborn children did so at known risk of legal and health consequences.

But in the late sixties, Satan revived his war on human life, seeking to restore the legal abortion business to filthy prominence. In 1967, Colorado took Satan's bait, becoming the first state to restore the travesty of legal abortion. In 1970, Alaska, Hawaii, New York, and Washington also surrendered to the dark invasion against life. By 1973, the entire United States bowed the knee to the destroyer, retracting its former abolition of abortion and paving the way for an infant holocaust much worse than Hitler's. The United States Supreme Court passed Roe v. Wade, declaring every woman had a constitutional right to murder their unborn children. In this ruling, the United States government publicly and universally devalued human life, further removing God's protective hand from the nation.

Thrilled with its progress, Satan's kingdom continued its dark invasion against our world. But the next leg of the invasion didn't stop at the Hill or the activist rally. Soon, the invasion entered every United States home through cable and internet. The flood of filth that ensued has fundamentally transformed our society.

"A FLOOD OF FILTH" INVADES THE AMERICAN HOME

In 1973—ten years after the banning of school devotions—God gave evangelist David Wilkerson a vision of the next wave of the invasion of darkness in the United States. One year later, he released the alarming prophecies in his book *The Vision*. Today, many of his predictions seem shockingly accurate. He warned:

> This world faces a dirt bath so intense that it will vex the minds and souls of some of the most devout Christians alive today. Christians are soon going to be exposed to such violent filth and sensuality that it will take a firm grip on God to survive. Those on the fence are going to fall flat on their faces. Those who do not enter into the ark of God's safety are going to be swept away by this flood of filth.[11]

That statement alone powerfully describes our time, but Wilkerson didn't stop there. He predicted the next wave of the invasion of darkness with uncanny specifics:

- "Be warned—in the not-too distant future, the most wicked, X-rated porno movies will be shown on select cable networks after midnight."

- "People will pay to have these erotic movies piped directly into their living rooms. If left unguarded, little children can switch on a knob and be exposed to the vilest kind of sexual perversion."

- "Porno movies on cable television will become so popular and so much in demand that the major networks will try to compete by showing films with as much sex and violence as they can show within legal limits."

- "Also available will be the same triple-X-rated videotapes for private home use. These videotapes can be played on any TV set with an electronic attachment."

At the time, evangelicals condemned Wilkerson's predictions as fanatical. Few imagined a world with pornography "piped directly into their living rooms"—let alone by "an electronic attachment." But soon, his predictions started coming true.

Within two years, Sony developed the first popular videotape solution for home television—the Betamax. By 1977 JVC released the VHS in North America. Soon, pornography studios began selling countless videotapes through adult shops around the country. Cable television soon flirted much more with sensuality too. The *Encyclopedia Brittanica* explains the transformation:

> Before 1970 human sexuality was a topic that was only hinted at on television, and television's married couples slept in separate beds until the late 1960s. That was about to change.
>
> The new trend was referred to as "jiggle TV" in the popular press ("T&A TV" in less-polite publications) because it tended to feature young, attractive, often scantily clad women (and later men as well). Shows in this genre included *The Love Boat* (ABC, 1977–86), a romantic comedy that took place on a Caribbean cruise ship; *Charlie's Angels* (ABC, 1977–81), which presented three female detectives whose undercover investigations required them to disguise themselves in beachwear and other revealing attire; *Three's Company* (ABC, 1977–84), which had the then-titillating premise of two young women and a man sharing an apartment; and *Fantasy Island* (ABC, 1978–84), which was set on a tropical island where people went to have their (often romantic) dreams fulfilled.[12]

Wilkerson's predicted "flood of filth" only continued as television grew more sensual and internet opened new doors for the pornography industry. By 2005, 70% of television programming contained sexual content—up 14 percentage points from 1998 alone.[13] Which brings us to today. Turn with us to the next appendix, where we'll consider how the invasion of darkness has affected our modern world. We'll warn you ahead of time—it's not pretty.

APPENDIX TWO

THE PROGRESS OF THE INVASION OF DARKNESS

When we think of demonic activity, we often think of poltergeists and Eastern mysticism. But in the educated West, Satan attacks with intellectualism more than spiritism. He did it with Eve, asking, "Did God really say?" He did it with Jesus, twisting God's promises in the wilderness. And to this day, he wields false logic to lead the world astray and destroy everything in his path. Statistics show the damage.

Consider where we came from. In 1955, 92% of Americans professed Christianity in some way.[1] 73% regularly attended church.[2] Only 2% claimed no religious affiliation.[3] Over half of the population watched one or more meetings of Billy Graham's first televised crusade (what is half of the population watching today?).[4] And in 1974, with the moral invasion well underway, two out of three Americans expressed deep trust in the church and organized religion as institutions.

Does that sound like a different world to you? If so, you're absolutely right. Today, Americans have largely lost trust in the Christian faith. In 2019, 67% professed Christianity in some way,[5] but only 37% described themselves as "born-again" or evangelical." Only 49% of Americans claimed any religion is very important in their life, which further discredits the claim that 67% practice Christianity.[6] Touching church attendance, only 45% attended church or synagogue once or more a month—more than a one-third decline since 1955.[7] And it seems most people recognize this pattern—in 2019, four-in-five Americans believed religion is losing its influence in the world,[8] and in 2013, Religion News Service reported: "Over the past fifteen years, the drop in religiosity has been twice as great as the decline of the 1960s and 1970s."[9]

This decline has not only shown up in the pews. It has also made a radical impact on public opinion. The fact is, Satan has worked with great success to convince the world that God and His Word are no longer relevant. He has pushed God's Word out of morality and politics: in 2019, 37% of Americans openly claimed religion "cannot answer all or most of today's problems" because it's "old-fashioned and out of date,"[10] and 27% wished organized religion had less influence in modern society.[11] He has pushed God's church out of public interest and confidence: in 2019, only 26% reported strong confidence in the church or organized religion as institutions.[12] And Satan's sect of non-religion has quickly become the fastest-growing religious group in America. Yes, in 2020, 21% of Americans claimed no religious preference whatsoever, as opposed to 2% in 1955, and 8% in 2000![13] That's almost a 300% increase in only 20 years.

THE INVASION AGAINST BIBLICAL TRUTH

We wish we could say Satan's invasion on truth has affected only the secular world. After all, the church of Jesus Christ should never waver before the foolish whims and ideas of the Kingdom of Darkness. If everyone else falls, we should still stand tall on the truth of God's Word! But tragically, Satan and his minions have successfully invaded the ranks of Christendom, leaving millions of professing Christians wallowing in the mires of relativism and false teaching.

His battles have been many. He has broken our confidence in the biblical reality of absolute truth: Jesus proclaimed, "I am . . . the truth" (John 14:6), yet in 2020, 36% of evangelicals could not agree that "religious belief is a matter of . . . objective truth."[14] He has nullified our conviction of personal sinfulness: the Apostle Paul declared, "There is no one righteous, not even one" (Romans 3:10), yet in 2020, 47% of evangelicals agreed humans are naturally good.[15] He has castrated our understanding of divine judgment: God justly judged Adam and Eve after only once eating the forbidden fruit, yet in 2020, 54% of evangelicals disagreed that the smallest sin deserves damnation.[16] He has taught us to devalue the church: Hebrews 10:25 commands us not to neglect corporate Christian fellowship, yet in 2020, 46% of evangelicals agreed home worship is a valid replacement for corporate church meetings.[17] And, perhaps worst of all, he has attacked the exclusivity of salvation through Jesus Christ: Jesus declared, "No one comes to the Father except through Me" (John 14:6), yet in 2018, 54% of evangelicals would not deny that God accepts the worship of all religions.[18]

It's absolutely heartrending to witness Satan's strides in the battle to silence God's Word in society. But tragically, he hasn't stopped at discrediting the Bible. With the barrier of God's Word removed, Satan has forged a bloodthirsty invasion against biblical morality. Let's consider the carnage.

A PORN PANDEMIC

Before the sexual revolution, pornography was a shameful act. If men had porn, they never left it out in the open—they hid it away in embarrassment. They certainly wouldn't dare to talk about it in public. It was a sin—a shame—a secret! Needless to say, our world has drastically deteriorated. After almost sixty years of constant illicit onslaught, we now live in a practically shameless society. Believe it or not, today's young people consider "not recycling" more immoral than watching porn.[19]

And honestly, it's hard to blame them in a way. First of all, as noted, this generation has received less biblical influence than any other generation in recent American history, so it shouldn't surprise us that they have weak moral principles. Second, how else would they feel after having experienced such heavy exposure at such young ages with so few consequences? Think about it. Through sexual education classes, millions of youth are encouraged to use pornography and self-stimulate before they even graduate middle school. Almost every television program and film they've ever watched contained sexual content of some kind (whether they understood it or not). And in our world of tablets and Wi-Fi, most children are first exposed to pornography by age eleven.[20] With that considered, should the following statistics really surprise us?

- 79% of men aged 18-30, 67% of men aged 31-49, and 49% of men aged 50-68 watch pornography at least once a month.[21]

- Over half of those once-a-month users are married.[22]

- 63% of men aged 18-30 and 16% of men aged 31-49 watch pornography multiple times a week.

- 76% of women aged 18-30, 16% of women aged 31-49, and 4% of women aged 50-68 watch pornography at least once a month.[23]

Yes, Satan has used pornography to steal the innocence of our entire generation—young, old, male, female, single, and married. And he has no plans to stop—in fact, he's gaining more ground as we speak. This very day, 266 new pornographic websites will go live on the web.[24] More than 1 in 5 of today's mobile searches and 35% of today's internet downloads will be for pornography.[25] Perhaps more tragic to realize, right this second, 28,258 users are falling into the snare of pornography. Count one more second. $3,075.64 was just spent on internet pornography. Keep counting. A second more, the number doubles. A second more, the number triples. A second more, the number quadruples. Every waking second, the battle rages more violently, stealing more souls and destroying more precious lives.

At this point, it would be easy to sermonize about the sins of the lost, as if professing Christians always live as champions of righteousness. But the battle isn't only raging in the world. Every day, countless professing Christians fall into the snare of pornography. According to Covenant Eyes, 64% of Christian men and 15% of Christian women claim they watch pornography at least once a month.[26] Shockingly, only 1 in 3 of them feel guilty about it,[27] and only 19% claim they are "currently trying to stop."[28] This spiritual virus has even poisoned our nation's pulpits: 1 in 7 senior pastors and 1 in 5 youth pastors admit to currently using pornography,[29] and most of them don't use internet accountability.[30]

Now, we don't mean to condemn those who struggle with pornography, but to remind you of God's call, and invite you to experience God's transforming grace. Tragically, Satan has invaded our ranks with impurity, and it's beyond time to say, "No!"

A DELUGE OF DIRT AND DEATH

Meanwhile, Satan has continued his invasion against godly sex. To this day, 3 in 4 women have premarital sex by age 20, and almost 4 in 4 women have premarital sex by age 44.[31] These numbers have held steady for five decades, revealing that the sexual revolution set a new moral low from which we've never recovered.

Tragically, Satan has used that moral low to craft public opinion to his liking. In 1969, 75% of American adults who had an opinion on premarital sex said it was immoral.[32] By 2013, only 30% of Americans believed the same[33]—and only 26% by 2016![34] Society is losing its moral compass right before our eyes.

Perhaps you ask—why has premarital sex become less taboo? One reason is that it's considered less risky than ever. Before the modern invasion, those who had premarital sex typically had to deal with the consequence of childbearing. Not since the legalization of abortion. Since 1973, over 60 million babies have been killed through abortion in the USA,[35] including 2,899 just yesterday.[36] In 2016, the USCDC logged 186 abortions for every 1,000 live births![37]

And pro-abortion activists have guarded this genocide with grit and tenacity, taking more radical strides every decade (and thereby protecting Satan's progress in the war against sexual purity). It's hard to believe, but today, some states permit baby murder up to the moment of birth. At the writing of this paragraph, a bill was recently blocked that "would have required doctors to provide standard medical care to newborn infants who survive abortion procedures."[38] Yes, we've gone as far as infanticide—and this to protect the "right" to have sex before marriage without consequences!

THE MARRING OF MARRIAGE

Satan's army has also forged a war against biblical marriage. One of God's first commands to Adam and Eve was: "Be fruitful and increase in number; fill the Earth and subdue it" (Genesis 1:28). Marriage is central to God's plan for human history, so Satan is putting forth all his efforts to destroy it. Tragically, he's had a lot of temporary success.

First, he's poured gasoline on the divorce epidemic. In the 1950s, very few American couples ever experienced the pain of divorce. I (Brian) know this by experience. I was raised in a single-parent home, and we were a rarity. I only had one other friend without both parents. Contrast that with these startling statistics:

- Today, 39-50% of marriages end in divorce.[39]
- According to the National Library of Medicine, "Today, only about 60% of U.S. children live with their married, biological parents," putting us in second place worldwide.[40]

- Even 32% of professing "born-again" Christians have divorced at least once—almost as much as unbelieving adults.[41]

- And this epidemic has destroyed child lives, leading to "an increased risk for child and adolescent adjustment problems, including academic difficulties (e.g., lower grades and school dropout), disruptive behaviors (e.g., conduct and substance use problems), and depressed mood."[42]

Perhaps you've heard divorce rates recently decreased. That's reason to celebrate, right? Look a little closer. Do you want to know the real reason fewer are divorcing? It's because many fewer young people are marrying![43] Instead, in record numbers young couples are opting to live together without tying the knot. *Time Magazine* explains:

In 2018, 15% of folks ages 25 to 34 lived with an unmarried partner, up from 12% a decade earlier. More Americans under 25 cohabit with a partner (9%) than are married to one (7%). Two decades ago, those figures weren't even close: 5% were cohabiting and 14% were married.[44]

The Kingdom of Darkness has also deepened the marriage crisis by attacking the biblical definition of marriage: "A man will leave his father and mother and be united to his wife, and the two will become one flesh" (Matthew 19:5). We've watched our culture lose this truth right before our eyes.

Think about it—who could have imagined the modern sexuality crisis before the sexual revolution? Back then, very few celebrated the homosexual lifestyle. Even in 1997, only 27% of the population supported same-sex marriage.[45] But in 2015, the United States Supreme Court legalized gay marriage, and many other countries have followed since. Riding a long cultural shift, 63% of the American population expressed support for gay marriage in 2019.[46] According to Pew Research, even 1 in 3 white Evangelical Protestants now support same-sex marriage—doubling their support from 2009.[47]

And gay activism hasn't only attacked marriage—it has attacked gender itself. In fact, 1960s gay activism seems vanilla in comparison to the modern agenda. Back in the Stonewall era, activists mainly fought for gay and lesbian causes. By the 1990s, gay activists expanded their acronym to GLBT to include the bisexual and transgender causes. Today, the gay acronym's longest form reads LGBTQQIAAP+—and believe us, that won't be the end of it.

In his book *Can You Be Gay and Christian: Responding With Love and Truth to Questions about Homosexuality*, Dr. Michael Brown provides a shocking list of modern "gender identities." Thousands identify themselves in these ways. As you read, please open your heart to the compassion of God:

Androgeny, Androgenous, Bigendered, Bi-Dyke, Boi, Boidyke (or, Boydyke), Bro-sis, Butch, ButchDyke, Camp, Cross Dresser (CD), Cross-Living, Drag (In Drag), Drag King, Drag Queen, Dyke, FTM or F->M or F2M (Female to Male), Femme, Femme Dyke, Female Bodied, Female Impersonator (FI),

Fetishistic Transvestite, Gender Illusionist, Gender Neutral, Gender-Bender, Gender-Blender, Genderqueer, Genetic Boy, Genetic Male/Man (GM), Genetic Female/Woman (GF/GW), Genetic Girl (GG), Grrl, Half-dyke, Heteroflexible, Hir, Intersex, MTF or M->F or M2F (Male to Female), Male Impersonator, Metamorph, Monogendered, Multigendered, Neuter, No-gendered, Non-op, Omnisexual, Pansexual, Pre-operative Transsexual (Pre-op TS), Polygendered, Post-operative Transsexual, Queer, Queerboi, Shape Shifter, Stem (a feminine-identified lesbian), Stud (a masculine-identified lesbian), Trannyboi, Trannydyke, Trannyfag, Transboi, Transgendered, Transgenderist, Transitioning, Transmale, Transsexual (TS), Transvestite, Transidentified, Trisexual, Two-Spirit, Ze.[48]

Does this break your heart? It ought to. Remember—real people have fallen deeply into these confusions. Jesus loves these souls and gave His life to reconcile them to Himself and grant them true life in Him. Tragically, instead they have followed the Father of Lies and allowed him to wreak havoc in their hearts and our society.

Put all of these obvious moral issues aside, and you've still barely scratched the surface of the dark invasion. As the church has retreated from her heavenly mission, Satan has advanced a million rotten battles against humanity. The result is an utterly unsafe world.

AN UNSAFE WORLD

I (Brian) grew up in a very tough neighborhood, but we didn't worry about getting kidnapped or assaulted by pedophiles. Many people left their doors unlocked. We could walk carefree almost wherever we wanted to go. My mother could send me to the store to buy groceries without having to worry. What contrast today!

At this stage in the invasion, parents have to worry about countless dangers every day. 1 in 3 girls and 1 in 7 boys experience sexual assault by age 18.[49] Only 1 in 10 victims ever speak up about it.[50] 1 in 6 women have experienced sexual assault at least once.[51] And every 40 seconds, a child goes missing in the United States.[52]

You might think I'm uptight, but I'd never send an eight-year-old child out of the house to run errands today. The world has changed too much! But as unsafe as the outside world is, we have to acknowledge that our children aren't even always safe in the home. Many fear guns in the street, but most acts of gun homicide aren't murders—they're suicides![53]

You see, as a final result of Satan's invasion, the world has experienced a depression epidemic. Depression rates have soared worldwide—rising almost 50% from 1990 to 2017 alone.[54] 1 in 6 Americans have been prescribed anti-depressants and other mental health drugs.[55] And this tidal wave of depression has led many to suicide. According to the American Psychological Association, "The suicide rate increased 33 percent from 1999 through 2017, from 10.5 to 14 suicides per 100,000 people," making suicide "the fourth leading cause of death for people ages 35 to 54, and the second for 10-to-34-year-olds."[56]

THE PROBLEM OF THE UNREACHED

But the Kingdom of Darkness has one grand achievement greater and more tragic than all the others. You've probably never heard of it if you're an American—for it dwells far out of U.S. borders. You've probably never heard of it if you're a Christian—for it dwells far outside of common evangelical discussion. Satan's army has successfully kept billions from ever hearing the gospel. That's right—throughout the world, billions have still never heard the message of reconciliation even once. Their need is far more important than any of the issues we've discussed so far. Consider.

So far, in this chapter, we've witnessed America's moral downfall (which coincides with problems in most of the world). But America has fallen in broad daylight. 98.5% of America's population has ample access to the gospel.[57] 77.5% of United States citizens profess Christianity.[58] At the least, that means they can hear the gospel if they want to. They could visit one of our almost 400,000 evangelical churches.[59] They could seek God's Word through TV, radio, books, or the internet. They could seek spiritual perspective through one of their many Christian acquaintances. In general, they avoid every gospel opportunity with indifference.

Meanwhile, 3.1 billion people have minimal or no access to the gospel in the 10/40 Window.[60] That's almost half the world's population—and most of them have never clearly heard the salvation message. Over 80% of the poorest of the poor live there, surviving on less than $1 a day.[61] Most can't visit the neighborhood church, for the unreached world has only 1 Christian missionary for every 216,300 people.[62] Most can't watch the gospel on TV or the radio, and few ever receive gospel literature. And most can't ask a Christian friend about Jesus because most don't know a Christian. Yet the church sends only 0.5% of its offerings[63] and 3.3% of its missionaries to reach these unreached masses.[64] And the clock is ticking down: approximately 50,000 unreached souls die every single day, likely flooding to Hell en masse. Yet the church has done little to turn the tide. Have you ever heard anything more heartbreaking?

TAKING BACK GOD'S TERRITORY

We want to remind you why we wrote these appendices. We're not sharing these statistics to bog you down, but to impart God's burden for our generation. Often in war history, enemy armies have taken territories captive. Then those nations had to choose—will we accept defeat, or take it back? We believe we've encountered such a time in the battle against evil.

You see, Satan has already been defeated, but he's trying to take back what rightly belongs to God. When Jesus returns, He will rule those territories without a rival—but while we await His final victory, we must oppose Satan's deceitful coup against Jesus's reign, seeking to change hearts and minds with God's Word. We must be willing to lovingly confront the evils of society, and refuse to compromise truth for acceptance, but speak the truth in love. The more Christians who turn on the light, the brighter the invasion against the Kingdom of Darkness. Yes, if we live and speak as Heaven's ambassadors, Jesus could very well transform whole societies and reverse these awful statistics! But first, we must adopt the revolutionary motto of Evangelist Reinhard Bonnke: "Hell empty; Heaven full!"

Fellow disciple, it's time to recover our faith in God's power. When Joshua went into the promised land, the fearful tried to deter him from making the conquest, warning, "There are giants!" (see Numbers 13:33). But Joshua didn't let that stop him. He faced his fears, obeyed God, and won the victory. We should follow Joshua's example.

Perhaps others have given you a list of reasons why God can't use you to take back His territory. Gracefully look past their doubt and boldly cling to God's promise: "Your kingdom come on Earth as it is in Heaven" (Matthew 6:10). Then, invade with God's love, light, truth, and power. If you do, your experience of personal revival may just lead to the transformation of both individuals and cultures. Will you receive the call? The choice is truly yours.

APPENDIX THREE

TO ALTAR CALL, OR NOT
TO ALTAR CALL? AND HOW

In this appendix, I (JJ) want to tackle a question of crucial importance to those called to invade with light in corporate settings. During ministry meetings, how can we help convicted hearers respond to the gospel? Is it wrong to use an altar call?

Many today deeply criticize the altar call as unbiblical. I (JJ) understand that criticism respecting some types of calls. But, when done right, an altar call should only be a corporate version of whatever one does privately to come to Christ or seek personal revival. In other words, a true call invites the audience to immediately come before God, repent of sin, surrender all, receive God's mercy, and experience the Holy Spirit's transforming power. If this behavior is biblical in private, it can't be unbiblical in public. Therefore, when done wisely, altar calls can be both biblical and beneficial.

Does the Bible provide examples of altar calls? Well, the Old Testament provides many examples of a similar strategy, particularly solemn assemblies of repentance and commitment (see Exodus 32:26, Exodus 19:8, Joshua 24:1-28, 2 Kings 23:1-3, 1 Samuel 7:1-7, and many others). As for the New Testament, I can't help but conclude that something similar happened before the Day of Pentecost in the upper room. There, the disciples spent days praying and seeking God's promised Holy Spirit. How likely that an atmosphere of deep repentance and faith penetrated the air, with Christ's disciples spending long hours weeping and crying out to God, celebrating the cross, and decrying their sins! Is it a sin to invite that same atmosphere of personal repentance, faith, and devotion at a meeting for salvation or personal revival? Of course not! Let the upper room come to the altar!

Likewise, Peter likely conducted a type of altar call whenever he preached in public. For example, at the end of his message in Acts 2:40, "with many other words he testified and exhorted them, saying, 'Be saved from this perverse generation'" (NKJV). I don't know how better to describe an effective altar call! Furthermore, the apostles always baptized new converts on the very same day, and to organize this, Peter would have had to say something like, "Everyone who will submit to Messiah, follow us to the river right now to get baptized!" How else would the people know where to go for immediate baptism? If that's not a sort of altar call, I don't know what is.

Then, what should an altar call look like in a meeting for salvation or revival? Well, the invitation might look different in every meeting you preach. Some invite sinners with a whisper; others with urgent cries. Some meetings permit long hours of altar encounters, while other meetings require a short and sincere commitment to Christ. No matter what you do, just remember this—a true altar call creates a space for people to encounter God and turn to Him in true repentance and faith. You must *always* keep this as the aim of your invitation. *Never forget*—your altar call *is* unbiblical if it encourages a trite and shallow response to Jesus Christ. But if done wisely, God can use your altar meeting to win spectacular victories in the invasion of light.

INVITATION PRINCIPLES

So, what are some principles to guide your invitation? Here I'll share some principles I've learned from others (especially Evangelist Steve Hill) and personal experience.[1] I believe these principles can help you conduct an effective call—however, I offer them as practical advice, not as a reflection of a scriptural command. Therefore, remain open to the guidance of the Holy Spirit, as He may at times lead you to call quite differently.

INVITATION PRINCIPLE #1: PRE-CALL EARLY

First, I encourage you *not to wait until the end of your message* to announce the call. Instead, announce early in the message that you'll give the audience an opportunity to respond. Announce that the Holy Spirit has promised to convict of sin, righteousness, and judgment, and testify of Christ, and declare by naked faith that you fully expect Him to move that way in this very meeting. You may not *feel* like this will happen—that's all right, declare it on the basis of Jesus's promises alone. Instruct them that *He will speak to them* as you preach. Then press upon them the urgency of responding to the Holy Spirit's voice. Humbly remind them that they'll receive God's judgment if they harden themselves against His voice, but that God will save and restore their souls today if they listen and obey. From the very beginning, echo God's promise through Isaiah: "'If you are willing and obedient, you will eat the best of the land; but if you refuse and rebel, you will be devoured by the sword.' For the mouth of the LORD has spoken" (Isaiah 1:19-20 NASB).

INVITATION PRINCIPLE #2: PRE-CALL CLEARLY

Second, tell them early how you'll ask them to respond. Will you call them to come forward, get on their faces, and cry out to God (my personal favorite approach)? Tell them. Will you ask them to stand and announce their allegiance to Christ? Tell them. Will you ask them to silently talk with God, kneeling upon their chairs? Tell them. No matter what you'll ask them, let them know ahead of time so they can have time to get used to the idea.

INVITATION PRINCIPLE #3: PRE-CALL CONTINUALLY

Third, let *your whole message* serve as a call. As you preach, remind your hearers that they will soon have an opportunity to respond to Jesus Christ. Emphasize over and again that God is willing to restore and save them immediately, but that God's judgment will remain on them if they continue in rebellion. Throughout the message, address every group of people present—on-fire Christians, backsliders, religious but unsaved persons, and utter unbelievers, letting them know what God requires of them.

INVITATION PRINCIPLE #4: MAKE THE CALL

Fourth, make the call. Be crystal clear, explain the conditions of salvation (or revival, or fresh infilling, or whatever theme you've chosen), and call your audience to fulfill them immediately. To start the call, sometimes I like to have the audience pause for a moment of private contemplation. At times I've initiated this private call by saying something like this: "Right now, I want you to take a moment between you and the Lord. Close your eyes and consider how you'll respond to Jesus. What is He calling you to do? Will you obey Him, or rebel against Him? I want you to think it over and make your decision right now." Then, after the private moment has passed, I like to move on to the public call. I've often made my appeal somewhat like this: "Here's what we're about to do. If the Holy Spirit has deeply convicted you of anything during this meeting and you've decided to answer God's call, I want you to come forward right now, get down on your face in humility before God, and begin to repent, crying out for God's mercy in Jesus Christ. I don't care if you're an on-fire Christian, a backslider, or a lost sinner who has never known Jesus Christ. I don't care if you murdered someone, held a grudge, or stole a paperclip. Right now, if God is prodding your heart about *anything*, come, get on your face, cry out to God in surrender, and experience Jesus's restorative power! Don't wait a moment—*now* is the day of salvation and restoration!"

INVITATION PRINCIPLE #5: KEEP CALLING

Fifth, continue calling. Over the years, I've seen many altars filled with weeping penitents, crying out and getting right with God. But I'll tell you what—*very rarely* did those altars fill right away. Rather, the audience sat in their chairs stirring in conviction, and needed someone to plead with them to be honest and get right with God. Perhaps first only one or two removed the mask, came to the front, got on their knees, and dealt with God. But then, soon, a boy and his mother would come. Then, a young couple. Slowly but surely, the de-masking became a spiritual contagion, and the altars began to fill exponentially, even sometimes filling up down the aisles. Soon enough, the Holy Spirit's saving power swept the room, forgiving sins, saving souls, reviving saints, and unveiling God's holiness and love.

Here's the truth—honesty is contagious. And when people begin to see others getting set free from their sins, they often feel emboldened to swallow their pride, admit their wrongs, and confess Christ publicly. Oftentimes, before we can see the masses run to Christ, we must do as Peter, and "with many other words . . . solemnly [testify] and [keep] on exhorting them, saying, 'Be saved from this perverse generation!'" (Acts 2:40 NASB).

INVITATION PRINCIPLE #6: CALL WITH URGENCY

Finally, make sure to call with *urgency*. Keep ever before you that *no one in your audience is promised another breath*. Soon, anyone in your audience could die and stand before God. Therefore, you must call to them as if this were their *last chance to get right with God*. Do not let them think they should go home and mull it over. With holy zeal and love, plead with them to respond to Christ *NOW* before it's too late. Remind them that whoever is not with Jesus is against Him (see Matthew 12:30), and therefore, their delay is but a denial of the loving Savior and Holy God. As you preach, let them see urgency in your eyes and your movement, and hear it in your tone and every word. Let it be as if God had written over your forehead—"Urgency! Urgency! Urgency!"

As I mentioned earlier, some may express urgency in a whisper, others in a bellowing voice, and still others in a conversational tone. Some may call with the eloquence of Charles Spurgeon, and others with the shaking voice of a new believer freshly awakened to the reality of eternity. *That's wonderful. God wants to express His call through your personality, and you should never feel pressured to sound or behave like another preacher.* Just be yourself and issue forth the call to surrender and receive Christ. Only make sure of this—whether you speak in a hush or a hurry, let the urgency of eternity resound from your heart. Graciously let your hearers know *you mean them, and you mean now*. Lovingly point their gaze to the cliff of eternity, and warn them that they must quickly turn back and obey Christ before they fall over into the flames of Hell. This is the only truth—never compromise it for any reason!

DON'T BECOME DISCOURAGED

Finally, don't become discouraged or outraged if you see little response. It can feel deeply deflating to preach your heart out with no apparent result. Even history's greatest preachers sometimes faced crickets—but they didn't see that as a reason to quit. They saw it as a reason to keep plowing until God sent the harvest!

The reality is, some audiences need more plowing than others. Some are deeply entrenched in false doctrines that have seared their consciences. Others are profoundly convicted, but fear to open up because of a judgmental or dishonest culture. Still others remain unconvinced of their need of Jesus. Don't let these obstacles discourage you—let them drive you to prayer. Go to your Bible so God can give you His strategy for that audience; then, if you have opportunity, plead with them again! Whatever you do, don't let discouragement lead you to quit creating a space for people to encounter Christ in total surrender.

Ultimately, you must keep invading with light, clinging to God's promise: "My Word . . . will not return to Me empty, but will accomplish what I desire and achieve the purpose for which I sent it" (Isaiah 55:11). Remember, God is "the Lord of the harvest" (Matthew 9:38)—so lift your head, trust He's using you, and continue the invasion! If you do, you'll eventually experience God's wonderful promise: "At the proper time we will reap a harvest if we do not give up!" (Galatians 6:9). Glory to God!

MY PRAYER ASSIGNMENT
FROM GOD: A PRAYER LIST

God wants to use your prayers to destroy Satan's works in others' lives! We encourage you to seek the Lord for His intercessory strategy. Ask Him to reveal at least three people whom He wants you to pray for—perhaps a lost soul, a struggling believer, or someone with another need. As God guides you, write their names and needs below, and ask the Lord to show you a Bible promise you can stand upon for them in faith. Then commit to pray until Jesus invades their life with light! We also encourage you to write down how He answers when the time comes. (Prayer list referenced in Chapter Fourteen, "Prevailing Prayer: The Ambassador's Mightiest Weapon," under the heading "How to Persist in Prayer").

PERSON #1

Name: ____

Need: ____

Bible Promise:

____

____

How Jesus answered my prayers:

____

____

PERSON #2

Name: ____

Need: ____

Bible Promise:

____

____

How Jesus answered my prayers:

____

____

PERSON #3

Name: ____
Need: ____

Bible Promise:
____
____

How Jesus answered my prayers:
____
____

OTHER PRAYER ASSIGNMENTS

____
____
____
____
____
____
____
____
____
____
____
____
____
____
____
____
____
____
____
____
____
____
____
____

MY TEN SWORD-SHARPENING SCRIPTURES

(Referenced in Chapter Sixteen, "The Ambassador's Weapons of Warfare: The Armor of God"
under the heading "Time to Sharpen Your Sword")

SCRIPTURE #1

My spiritual battle:

My memory verse:

SCRIPTURE #2

My spiritual battle:

My memory verse:

SCRIPTURE #3

My spiritual battle:

My memory verse:

SCRIPTURE #4

My spiritual battle:

My memory verse:

SCRIPTURE #5

My spiritual battle:

____

My memory verse:

____
____
____

SCRIPTURE #6

My spiritual battle:

____

My memory verse:

____
____
____

SCRIPTURE #7

My spiritual battle:

____

My memory verse:

____
____
____

SCRIPTURE #8

My spiritual battle:

____

My memory verse:

____
____
____

SCRIPTURE #9

My spiritual battle:

My memory verse:

SCRIPTURE #10

My spiritual battle:

My memory verse:

OTHER SWORD-SHARPENING SCRIPTURES

ABOUT BRIAN MARK WELLER

Brian Mark Weller is a Bible teacher, musician, and author with a burning passion for world missions. Brian met the Lord in 1974 and began winning others to Jesus soon after in 1976. In 1988, God gave Brian a special gift—a piercing burden for lost souls on the mission field. Since then, Brian has traveled the nations to preach the good news of Jesus Christ. He has ministered in many countries, including Burma, the Bahamas, Cambodia, Colombia, Guatemala, Honduras, India, Laos, Nicaragua, Peru, Thailand, Venezuela, and Vietnam. Over more than four decades, God has used Brian's passionate preaching to save many lost souls and to impart missions passion far and wide.

In 2007, Brian founded Message Ministries & Missions, a world missions organization that evangelizes in Peru and throughout the 10/40 Window. At the time of this publication, he has recorded ten albums of Christian music and published one other stirring book—*Backsliding in Heart: 5 Steps to a Backsliding Heart and Back Again.* He currently lives with his wife, Anne, in St. Petersburg, Florida. He has three grown children and a growing pack of beloved grandchildren.

For more inspiring messages, articles, and music from Brian, or to invite Brian to minister, please visit

https://www.messagemissions.com/brian-weller/ or **https://brianmarkweller.com**

ABOUT JJ WELLER

J.J. Weller is a missionary and author with an immovable zeal for the harvest. Since 2014, he has traveled the world through Message Ministries to win the lost, call prodigals home, and train saints in biblical evangelism. During that time, he's had the privilege to preach salvation to thousands—including many in unreached people groups—and to activate hundreds of believers in biblical evangelism. He studied shortly at Fire School of Ministry in Charlotte, North Carolina, then received his B.A. in Professional and Strategic Writing from Regent University. He has written an outreach book, *The Cure for Death: Finding Eternal Life in the Age of COVID-19,* created evangelistic and discipleship materials in multiple languages, and recorded one album of Christian music. He lives with his wife, Cynthia, and daughter, Autumn Hope, in St. Petersburg, Florida.

For more inspiring messages, articles, and music from JJ, or to invite him to minister, please visit

https://www.messagemissions.com/JJWeller/ or **https://www.JJWellerMusic.com**

To learn more about Brian, JJ, and
Message Ministries, or to share any testimonies:

www.ShareGodsHope.com
www.Facebook.com/MessageMinistries
www.MessageMissions.com/Social

For a growing library of video podcasts
and other content from Brian and JJ about
the themes in this book, please visit

www.InvasionofLight.tv

A WORD FROM BRIAN AND JJ
ABOUT MESSAGE MINISTRIES & MISSIONS

Hello! Thank you so much for reading *Invasion of Light*. We want to take a moment to share the wonderful opportunities God has given us to spread the gospel of Jesus Christ worldwide through our missions organization, *Message Ministries & Missions*.

WHO WE ARE

Message Ministries & Missions is an evangelical non-profit missions organization based out of St. Petersburg, Florida. MM exists to proclaim the gospel of Jesus Christ and His saving power and grace throughout the world. We accomplish this by preaching the gospel, making obedient disciples, providing practical needs, and creating materials for evangelism and discipleship.

WHERE WE WORK

Our core vision is to send the gospel of Jesus Christ to the whole world—and especially to those who have never heard. For this reason, we mostly focus our efforts on the unreached in the 10/40 Window. We currently support ministry partners in Burma/Myanmar, Cambodia, China, India, Thailand, Vietnam, Laos, and Peru.

HOW WE WORK

We believe the best way to fulfill the Great Commission is to lift the arms of native ministers around the world. For this reason, we've asked for God's guidance and partnered with the most exceptional indigenous ministries, missionaries, pastors, evangelists, and church planters we could find. These leaders live near the communities they evangelize and know the language, people, culture, and customs—so they can more effectively reach the lost, plant churches, make disciples, and meet the people's desperate needs. Our partners provide regular reports to us and remain accountable to local leaders.

HOW YOU CAN JOIN US

We would love you to partner with us in God's Great Commission! If you're interested, here are four ways you can join arms with us:

1. **Request a free Ambassador's Packet.** Just for your interest, we'd love to send you a gift packet to better introduce you to our mission. Order yours now at bit.ly/mmpacket (all lowercase). (Offer only valid in the United States).

2. **Adopt a ministry.** Did you know you can sponsor an MM native missionary of your choosing for as little as $100 a month? Visit messagemissions.com/adopt-a-ministry to learn more.

3. **Become an MM Sender.** For only $30 a month, you can send the gospel, feed the poor, home the homeless, reach the unreached, and disciple Christians worldwide through MM Senders. Each month your scheduled contribution will meet a new featured need! Learn more at messagemissions.com/senders.

4. **Make a one-time donation.** Every gift counts towards God's Great Commission! You can donate now at messagemissions.com/donate.

5. **Finally, follow us online and spread the word!** We're always making content to encourage, challenge, and strengthen Christians in God's call. Find all of our social media linkes at messagemissions.com/social—and please consider sharing our content with the people you love!

We appreciate you taking the time to learn about Message Ministries. God bless you as you share His hope!

To learn more about
Message Ministries,
please visit:

www.ShareGodsHope.com

ACKNOWLEDGEMENTS

Here, we want to thank those who have most impacted our lives. Without you, this book likely could never have been written.

BRIAN AND JJ

We want to thank the board members, advisors, and mission supporters of Message Ministries and Missions—past and present—who have partnered with us to fulfill the Great Commission in our lifetime. You have truly inspired and helped us! Together, by God's grace and power, we're partners in God's invasion of light.

We also want to thank our long-time friend and ministry partner Nancy McConnel, who is now with the Lord. This book would not have been possible without her many years of encouragement, support, and generosity. Nancy was always one of the biggest encouragers of our father-and-son team, and we miss her timely words of refreshment. See you in eternity, Nancy. We'll continue in the call!

We'd also like to thank the panel of Christian leaders on our review team: David Bush, Jeff and Jeannine Moffit, John Saginario, Keith Collins, Max Martin, and Owen Henry. Thank you for your friendship, your godly example in life and ministry, and for taking the time to read our book and give your honest thoughts. Your challenging comments and reassuring words made all the difference! May God return the blessing to you.

Finally, we release this book in memory of the friends and ministry partners who went to Heaven during our writing process, including Cecilia Santillan, DC Kaushal, Linda Stewart, Nancy McConnel, Romely Sandoval Sernaque, Susie Gorton, and Seby Matacena. You touched our lives with your example as faithful followers of Jesus Christ. We'll see you on coronation day!

BRIAN WELLER

I thank God my Father, Jesus Christ my Lord, and the Holy Spirit, without Whom I would still be scurrying around in darkness seeking the answer to life. I thank You for Your light and love that propels me forward into the depths of Your spiritual riches. I know there's much more to learn, but I thank You for the truths You have shown me thus far. Without You, there is no invasion of light!

To JJ, my son and the co-author of this book. What an honor and blessing it has been writing *Invasion of Light* with you. You took a mixture of teachings and ideas—both yours and mine—edited them, put order to them, and carefully placed them in chapters. I am genuinely amazed by the finished work! God gave you many talents, including music, writing, graphic design, preaching, and more. Your most extraordinary talent, however, is your love for the Lord and your passion for reaching the lost of this world. I can attest you seek to live what you write. I've seen that from our missions to Guatemala, Honduras, and Peru when you were young and on our more recent missions to Cambodia, Thailand, Vietnam, and Peru. We both learned so much on those early and later journeys as God stretched our faith and put us in extraordinary situations! Through those experiences, you have grown, and we have grown closer together, closer to God, and in our faith. I am thankful we could include much of what we have learned in this book. I pray that *Invasion of Light* impacts many lives much like it has impacted ours during our writing journey. God bless you, your wonderful wife Cynthia, your daughter Autumn, and your future son. May the blessings of God fill your lives. To God be the glory! Gloria a Dios!

To my wife, Anne Weller. Thank you for your love and encouragement, adventurous heart, and many much-needed exhortations over the last 43 years. You are my adventuring, risk-taking, faith-walking, caring wife who puts God first while caring for family and assisting with the ministry. Your influence runs deep in my life and has helped me grow and become a better person. Thanks for going where God wants us to go nationally and internationally. I treasure the countless beautiful and extraordinary adventures we have taken together.

To my mother, Joan Gane. Thank you for always cheering me on, listening to my ideas, dreams, and stories, and for encouraging me to go forward in faith. Thank you for consistently flooding my life with timely inspirational words of encouragement and for reflecting God's love and light to me and our whole family!

To my daughters, Megan and Katelyn. I love you dearly and am incredibly thankful for you, your husbands—Chap and Mike—and our precious grandchildren. Since your childhood, you have been a wonderful part of my ministry journey—from riding in the back seats traveling the United States for music ministry, to boarding planes as missionaries to Guatemala, Honduras, and Peru. Wherever we went, you loved, served, and helped in any way you could. Your love for the Lord, people, and family has impacted many lives—including mine—and still does!

To my grandchildren, Noah, Collin, Elijah, Owen, Autumn, Caleb, and those yet to be born. You are the next generation of lightshiners! You have brought so much light and joy to our family already. I know God has a great purpose for you, and you will find that purpose as you seek Him! My prayer is that you would know Jesus Christ lovingly and powerfully and share that knowledge of Him with as many as possible. I love you all!

To my brother, Bruce. Thank you for risking sharing Jesus with your rebellious unsaved brother back in 1974. I was listening—and because of you, God saved me in 1975! This book traces back to your faithful witness way back then.

Pastor Guy and Lynda Weatherly, without your love, guidance, and prayers over the last 44 years, I would have spiritually shipwrecked a long time ago. Thank you for always being there!

Pastor Marlin and Marian Simon, you have demonstrated what it means to be faithful servants of the Lord in word and deed.

Dr. Jim Randall, In 1980, you taught me to have a worldwide vision with emphasis on the 10/40 Window. Thank you for expanding my spiritual vision.

Pastor Bob and Susie Gorton, you impacted my life in beautiful and powerful ways. No matter where I was in the world, I always felt that you were praying. Susie, see you in Heaven!

Pastor John and Francine Saginario, you are an inspiration to me; true examples of what serving God and people faithfully, honestly, and humbly is all about.

Pastor Jeff and Jeannine Moffitt, you exemplify what it means to be warriors in the Kingdom of God through your wholehearted service to the Lord.

Pastor Walter and Carol Leake, you taught me what it means to be courageous and stand for what I believe no matter the cost. See you in Heaven, Pastor Leake!

Joe and Lorraine Marscheselli, thank you for teaching this long-haired young Christian the foundational truths of the Kingdom of God in the late 1970s.

Pastor David Bush, thank you for being an exuberant encourager and inspiration to JJ and I since we met on that first mission to Peru in 1999.

Hector Del Carpio, thank you for helping me grow much as a missionary during our many years working together in Peru. You are a faithful friend!

Nancy Mulick, my spiritual sister, thank you for believing in our mission work and for your timely encouragement over the years.

Ted and Cathy Williams, thank you for your servants' hearts and for helping send the gospel worldwide. Gloria a Dios!

Pastor Fabian and Cecilia Santillan, thank you for demonstrating what it means to serve the Lord with gladness and to walk by faith, not by sight. Cecilia, see you in Heaven!

Pastor Gilberto and Doris Varillas, thank you for demonstrating how to stay joyful in the Lord and carry a burden and passion for the poor at the same time.

I would love to thank so many others, but suffice it to say I would have to write a short book to acknowledge you all. Many of you have inspired, encouraged, taught, challenged, supported, and walked with me through some beautiful and challenging times. You are a part of my journey and a part of this book through your influence in my life. Thank you!

JJ WELLER

To my Savior, Lord, and closest friend, Jesus. You picked me up from the miry clay, washed me off, saved me, and called me to your service. Thank you for walking with me, teaching me, and working through me. You've revealed yourself in my life in ways far greater than I had imagined—and infinitely beyond what I deserved.

To my wife, Cynthia. You've helped me carry this project for over two years. You patiently and graciously bore every rant or airing of concern, and sustained me when I felt too discouraged to continue. I appreciate every embrace, reassuring word, and hot cup of coffee. Thank you for walking me through this long journey! I love you!

To my daughter, Autumn Hope. You weren't even born when I started writing this book, but your sweet laughter has brought so much joy and relief through the process. Jesus loves you, and I do too!

To my Dad, with whom I co-authored this book. What a journey it has been! Thanks for your guidance, partnership, and patience in life, ministry, and in the process of co-authoring this book. I'm so thankful to have had the privilege of being your son, ministry partner, and now co-author. May this collaboration touch lives for generations!

To my parents, Brian and Anne Weller. You've supported, loved, and guided me through every transition of life. Now that I'm a father, I appreciate your many years of parenting more than ever. On so many levels, this book would never have been possible without you!

To my whole family (in-laws, too)—thank you for your love and support as I've pursued God's call, and for your continued patience as I seek to learn and grow.

To my main life pastors, Scott Rodriguez, Keith Collins, and John Saginario. Thank you for encouraging and challenging me to remain faithful to Jesus no matter the cost. Many times you've brought just the encouragement or challenge I needed to go forward. You've impacted my life at a fundamental level.

To my close ministry family in Peru—especially Pastor Fabian Santillan, Gilberto Varillas, and their families. Thanks for opening your homes and lives to me—and for providing so many opportunities to minister to others from early on in my call. I will always treasure your friendship. You are truly like family.

To my main teachers at Fire School of Ministry from 2015-2016, including Keith Collins, Steve Alt, Dr. Josh Peters, Dr. Bob Gladstone, and Dr. Michael L. Brown, among others. My life, preaching, and writing will always echo your teaching that year.

To the late Cecilia Tenorio Santillan. You were a spiritual mother to me and a crucial figure in my journey in God's call. You were one of my greatest examples—and also one of my greatest supporters. Your impact on my life will ring into eternity. As I vowed to you before you went to the Lord—I'll never leave the call, and I'll win many to Jesus in your honor. Thanks for opening your life to me while you were with us. Un dia reuniremos de nuevo en la presencia del Señor.

To every friend who has ever encouraged or challenged me, and to everyone who has ever opened the door of ministry to me around the world. Truly, this book would be impossible without you. I appreciate you all and have learned so much from you. May God return the blessing to you!

NOTES

CHAPTER 1. TWO KINGDOMS CLASH

1. For an interesting narrative about this idea, see Chapter 1 of *Saving a Sick America* by Dr. Michael L. Brown.
2. Spurgeon, Charles H. "Christ with the Keys of Death and Hell." The Spurgeon Center, October 3, 1869. https://www.spurgeon.org/resource-library/sermons/christ-with-the-keys-of-death-and-hell.
3. After all, society just means people together! https://www.lexico.com/en/definition/society.
    Also, we want to emphasize that Jesus's kingdom is breaking in spiritually now, not yet physically. We're calling for a harvest of souls, not an overthrow of human governments. Still, Christians should use whatever political influence God gives them to encourage righteousness and discourage wickedness. As Paul says, human government is both "God's servant for your good" and "God's servants, agents of wrath to bring punishment on the wrongdoer" (Romans 13:4).
4. This goal seems less difficult when we think beyond the West. Remember, almost half of the world's population has still never clearly heard the gospel message. Even if the West continues its decline, we believe God will fundamentally transform unreached societies as the church introduces them to the message of salvation in Jesus. That said, Jesus has transformed the West several times before, and He can easily do it again if we take His call seriously.

CHAPTER 2. THE CASE FOR HOLY REVOLUTION IN THE LAST DAYS

1. For our detailed analysis of the darkness in the modern world, please read appendices one and two.
2. A clarification: we are ***not*** calling for a physical fight against human beings and governments, but a hearty spiritual battle against Satan through prayer, preaching, spiritual warfare, and holy living.
3. We see a similar pattern in Jude 1:3-23 and 1 Timothy 4:1-9. The ultimate key is that, as Jesus said, "The harvest is the end of the age" (Matthew 13:39). From Jesus's resurrection until His return, we will see a mixture of wheat and weeds—astounding heavenly fruit and shocking satanic apostasy (see Matthew 13:24-30, 36-43).

CHAPTER 3: THE FORGOTTEN INVASION OF LIGHT

1. Strong's Greek: 2660. κατανύσσω (:) – to prick violently. Biblehub. https://biblehub.com/greek/2660.htm.
2. Just as promised in John 15:26: "When the Advocate comes, whom I will send to you from the Father—the Spirit of truth who goes out from the Father—He will testify about Me."
3. Schmidt, Alvin. *How Christianity Changed the World:* Formerly Titled *Under the Influence.* Grand Rapids, Michigan: Zondervan, p. 49, 2009. Kindle.
4. Schmidt, *How Christianity Changed the World,* 154.

5.   See the following:

Schmidt, *How Christianity Changed the World*, 126.

Van der Horst, Pieter. "How the poor became blessed." *Aeon
     Magazine*. March 14, 2019. https://aeon.co/essays/
     the-poor-might-have-always-been-with-us-but-charity-has-not.
6.   Schmidt, *How Christianity Changed the World*, 61.
7.   Schmidt, 62.
8.   Schmidt, 100-101.
9.   Schmidt, 116.
10. Schmidt, 93.
11. Schmidt, 85-86.
12. Schmidt, 85-86.
13. Schmidt, 132.
14. Schmidt, 51.
15. Schmidt, 126.
16. Schmidt, 198-199.
17. Schmidt, 130.
18. Schmidt, 136, 155.
19. Schmidt, 274.
20. Schmidt, 274.
21. Schmidt, 274.
22. Schmidt, 110-111.
23. Schmidt, 117.
24. That book is *Gillies Accounts of Revivals*.
25. Dan Fisher. "Pastor Dan Fisher – Bringing Back the Black Robed
     Regiment." YouTube video, 35:48. July 21, 2012. https://www.youtube.com/
     watch?v=P5i2viK-C80.

CHAPTER 4. THE BATTLE FLAG OF OUR INVASION: THE KINGDOM OF GOD

1.   Strong's Greek: 2212. ζητέω (zéteó) – to seek. Biblehub. https://biblehub.com/
     greek/2212.htm.
2.   Strong's Greek: 4412. πρῶτον (próton) – before, at the beginning. Biblehub.
     https://biblehub.com/greek/4412.htm.
3.   Strong's Greek: 932. βασιλεία (basileia) – kingdom, sovereignty, royal power.
     Biblehub. https://biblehub.com/greek/932.htm.
4.   This verse has both a current and future fulfillment. For now, the Lord reigns
     through us spiritually, but one day will grant us literal governmental authority
     over the new Earth. See Revelation 3:21, 20:4-6, 1 Corinthians 6:3.
5.   To be precise, Jesus is still granting "salvation . . . to the Gentiles [nations]
     to make Israel envious" (Romans 11:11). He is granting the nations a window
     of grace, and will eventually fulfill all His messianic promises to Israel (see
     Romans 11:25-32).
6.   To be clear, God is also glorified when He judges—but not in the sense that
     we're discussing here. Here, we refer to the positive, renewing glory Jesus refers

to in John 11:40—"Did I not tell you that if you believe, you will see the glory of God?"

7. Strong's Greek: 1391. δόξα (doxa) – opinion (always good in N.T.), hence praise, honor, glory. Biblehub. https://biblehub.com/greek/1391.htm.

8. "Erchomai Meaning in Bible – New Testament Greek Lexicon – New American Standard Bible." biblestudytools.com. https://www.biblestudytools.com/lexicons/greek/nas/erchomai.html.

CHAPTER 5. THE ENEMY OF OUR INVASION: THE KINGDOM OF DARKNESS

1. Prince, Derek. *War in Heaven: God's Epic Battle with Evil.* Ada, Michigan: Baker Publishing Group, 2016, pp. 23-24, Kindle.

2. Prince, *War in Heaven*, 23-24.

3. "G1228 – Diabolos – *Strong's Greek Lexicon* (KJV). Blue Letter Bible. https://www.blueletterbible.org/lang/lexicon/lexicon.cfm?t=kjv&strongs=g1228.

4. "G746 – Archē – *Strong's Greek Lexicon* (KJV)." Blue Letter Bible. https://www.blueletterbible.org/lang/lexicon/lexicon.cfm?Strongs=G746&t=KJV.

5. "Principality Definition & Meaning." Dictionary.com. Dictionary.com. https://www.dictionary.com/browse/principality?s=t.

6. "G2889 – Kosmos – *Strong's Greek Lexicon* (KJV)." Blue Letter Bible. https://www.blueletterbible.org/lang/lexicon/lexicon.cfm?strongs=G2889&t=KJV.

7. "G2902 – Krateō – *Strong's Greek Lexicon (KJV)*." Blue Letter Bible. https://www.blueletterbible.org/lexicon/g2902/kjv/tr/0-1/.

8. Prince, *War in Heaven*, 23-24.

CHAPTER 6. THE CALL OF THE INVASION: THE MINISTRY OF RECONCILIATION

1. See John 6:45: "They will all be taught by God."

CHAPTER 7. THE BATTLE PLAN OF THE INVASION: THE GREAT COMMISSION

1. "The Oxford Pocket Dictionary of Current English. Encyclopedia.com. 17 Aug. 2021." Encyclopedia.com, August 27, 2021. https://www.encyclopedia.com/humanities/dictionaries-thesauruses-pictures-and-press-releases/invade-0.

2. "G4198 – Poreuō – *Strong's Greek Lexicon* (KJV)." Blue Letter Bible. https://www.blueletterbible.org/lang/lexicon/lexicon.cfm?Strongs=G4198&t=KJV.

3. "Missions Statistics." The Traveling Team. http://www.thetravelingteam.org/stats.

4. "G2784 – Kēryssō – *Strong's Greek Lexicon*." Blue Letter Bible. https://www.blueletterbible.org/lexicon/g2784/nasb20/tr/0-1/.

5. "G1325 – Didōmi – *Strong's Greek Lexicon* (KJV)." Blue Letter Bible. https://www.blueletterbible.org/lang/lexicon/lexicon.cfm?page=6&strongs=g1325&t=kjv#lexResults.

CHAPTER 8. THE MESSAGE OF THE INVASION:
5 Ps OF BIBLICAL EVANGELISM

1. When you factor out translation.
2. Similar results occurred in at least one other country under this ministry.
3. The revivalist receives God's power, understands what sin or deception robs the Christian's fruitfulness, urgently reasons about this problem and its great danger, testifies of Jesus's promise to receive, restore, and revive the returning backslider, and then nails home how to practically return to our first-love relationship with God (see Revelation 2:4). In fact, this approach generally sums up most revival preaching through the ages.

CHAPTER 9. P #1:
RECEIVE THE POWER OF THE HOLY SPIRIT

1. I (JJ) first remember hearing this verse expounded in these steps by Bible teacher Derek Prince.

CHAPTER 10. P #2:
UNDERSTAND THE PERSON

1. The early church certainly had its problems—but most of their errors were confusing doctrines or pious extremes, not spiritual laziness and carelessness like in our day. They didn't typically ignore Jesus like modern "backsliders"; they normally sought to follow Him but made practical and doctrinal errors on the way.
2. In that context, it's often best to preach the gospel story from creation on, exactly as if you were explaining every concept to a three-year old with no religious understanding. Show God as the loving Creator, caring Lawgiver, and righteous Judge, place them as guilty sinners in the Creator's courtroom, and then introduce Jesus as the infinitely loving and gracious Savior.
3. For access to evangelism teaching from Steve Hill and partners, visit https://www.togetherintheharvest.com/soe.
4. Finney, Charles. *Autobiography of Charles G. Finney*. 1908, Loc. 5275-5907, Kindle.
5. Finney, *Autobiography*, Loc. 5275-5907.

CHAPTER 11. P #3:
REASON ABOUT THE PROBLEM OF SIN

1. Finney, Charles. *The Works of Charles Finney*, Vol 1 (15-in-1) *Power From on High, Lectures on Revivals of Religion, Autobiography of Charles Finney, Revival Fire, Holiness of Christians, Systematic Theology*. Loc. 3248, Kindle.
2. "Strong's Greek: 1651.ἘΛΈΓΧΩ (elegchó) – to Expose, CONVICT, reprove." Biblehub. https://biblehub.com/greek/1651.htm.
3. For John hadn't yet written his gospel.
4. I don't remember our exact dialogue, but here I recount what I can, leaning on what I recall, and how I normally present the gospel.

CHAPTER 12.
P #4: DECLARE THE PROMISES OF SALVATION

1. I do not mean to discount the power of music in ministry. God has used powerful Christian music in amazing ways throughout church history. But tragically, many today have utterly replaced gospel preaching with gospel singing. For example, it's become common to give salvation altar calls at worship events without ever clearly presenting the salvation message. That's a neglectful ministry pattern we should avoid at all costs. Those of us in music ministry must remember that God calls us as heralds first and musicians second. As Keith Green said, "The only music minister to whom the Lord will say, 'Well done, thy good and faithful servant,' is the one whose life proves what their lyrics are saying, and to whom music is the least important part of their life. Glorifying the only worthy One has to be a minister's most important goal!"

2. A clarification to any wondering—we don't mean that the gift of tongues is a seal of salvation. The new birth by the Spirit is the seal of salvation. However, the baptism and gifts of the Spirit do often manifest at the moment of new birth.

3. Finney, Charles. *Lectures on Revival*, Updated With Active Table of Contents. Loc. 390, Kindle.

4. See Hebrews 12:2.

5. "Spurgeon's Evangelical Crucicentrism." The Spurgeon Center, March 21, 2019. https://www.spurgeon.org/resource-library/blog-entries/ spurgeons-evangelical-crucicentrism/.

CHAPTER 13.
P #5: ADVISE IN THE PRACTICALS OF CONVERSION

1. Moody, William. *The Life of Dwight L. Moody*. United States: Fredonia Books, 2001, p. 145, https://www.google.com/books/edition/ The_Life_of_Dwight_L_Moody/anpF-BdAEFQC?hl=en&gbpv=1.

2. Moody, *The Life of Dwight L. Moody*, 145.

3. Moody, *The Life of Dwight L. Moody*, 145.

4. "H7725 – Šûb – *Strong's Hebrew Lexicon* (NIV)." Blue Letter Bible. https://www. blueletterbible.org/lang/lexicon/lexicon.cfm?t=niv&strongs=h7725.

5. "G3341 – Metanoia – *Strong's Greek Lexicon* (KJV)." Blue Letter Bible. https:// www.blueletterbible.org/lang/lexicon/lexicon.cfm?t=kjv&strongs=g3341.

6. I want to emphasize that word *simultaneous*. The penitent makes all four of these choices at the same time when he honestly says, "I repent." At the moment of true repentance, we admit our sin, deny ourselves, sanctify Christ as Lord, and therefore, surrender all the Lord has convicted us about. We may cry out to Jesus about the details for a while, but we choose to repent in the blink of an eye. The same principle applies to the "faith-steps" we'll discuss.

7. Finney, Charles. *How to Promote a Revival*. http://www.charlesgfinney.com/ finney-101/how2revtxt/how2promrev.htm.

8. See Isaiah 65:2: "All day long I have held out My hands to an obstinate people . . ." And Matthew 23:37: "How often I have longed to gather your children together, as a hen gathers her chicks under her wings, and you were not willing."

CHAPTER 14. PREVAILING PRAYER:
THE AMBASSADOR'S MIGHTIEST WEAPON

1.   Bounds, E. M. *The Complete Collection of E. M. Bounds on Prayer*. Loc. 196, Kindle.
2.   Bounds, *The Complete Collection*, Loc. 8506.
3.   Torrey, R. A., *WORKS OF R. A. TORREY* (10-in-1) *Person & Work of the Holy Spirit, How to Obtain Fullness of Power, How To Pray, Why God Used D L Moody . . . (The Works of R. A. Torrey)*. Loc. 4422, Kindle.
4.   "Energeo Meaning in Bible – New Testament Greek Lexicon – New American Standard." biblestudytools.com. https://www.biblestudytools.com/lexicons/greek/nas/energeo.html.
5.   Biblestudytools.com, "Energeo Meaning in Bible – New Testament Greek Lexicon – New American Standard."
6.   "G1342 – Dikaios – *Strong's Greek Lexicon* (ᴋᴊᴠ)." Blue Letter Bible. https://www.blueletterbible.org/lexicon/g1342/kjv/tr/0-1/.
7.   "G2480 – Ischyō – *Strong's Greek Lexicon* (ᴋᴊᴠ)." Blue Letter Bible. https://www.blueletterbible.org/lexicon/g2480/kjv/tr/0-1/.
8.   "G4183 – Polys – *Strong's Greek Lexicon* (ᴋᴊᴠ)." Blue Letter Bible. https://www.blueletterbible.org/lexicon/g4183/kjv/tr/0-1/.
9.   Piper, John, *Let the Nations be Glad: The Supremacy of God in Missions*. Grand Rapids, Michigan: Baker Academic, p. 69, 2010.
10. Prince, Derek. *Rules of Engagement: Preparing for Your Role in the Spiritual Battle*. Minneapolis, Minnesota: Chosen Books, 2012, Loc. 2393, Kindle Edition.
11. A doctrinal caveat: God's promise is only limited by the conditions He establishes. God is sovereign and omnipotent, and can choose to do anything righteous without our cooperation. But He is also holy and relational, and often refuses to act when we don't cooperate with His conditions. If it were not so, the Bible wouldn't speak so clearly about our need of faith in prayer.
12. Bounds, *The Complete Collection*, Loc. 5924.
13. Brown, Michael L. *Hyper Grace: Exposing the Dangers of the Modern Grace Message*. Lake Mary, Florida: Charisma House, 2014, Page 128.
14. Finney, Charles. *Lectures on Revival*, Updated With Active Table of Contents. Loc 3934, Kindle.
15. Torrey, Reuben Archer. *The Works of R. A. TORREY, Vol 2: Life of Torrey, Baptism with Holy Spirit, Life and Death of D. L. Moody, How to Succeed in Christian Life, Real Salvation, Should Christians Keep Sabbath*. Loc. 6064, Kindle.
16. Finney, *Lectures on Revival*, Loc. 4180.
17. Bounds, *The Complete Collection*, Loc. 9772.
18. Ravenhill, Leonard. *Why Revival Tarries: a Classic on Revival*. Grand Rapids, Michigan: Baker Publishing Group, 1987, p. 19, Kindle.
19. Ravenhill, *Why Revival Tarries*, p. 21.
20. Bounds, *The Complete Collection*, Loc. 8479.
21. Bounds, Loc. 8519.
22. Bounds, Loc. 8546.

CHAPTER 15. SUIT UP!

THE INVASION REQUIRES ARMOR

1.   See 2 Corinthians 5:9-11 and 1 Corinthians 3:10-15.
2.   "G1743 – Endynamoō – *Strong's Greek Lexicon* (KJV)." Blue Letter Bible. https://www.blueletterbible.org/lang/lexicon/lexicon.cfm?t=kjv&strongs=g1743.
3.   "G2904 – Kratos – *Strong's Greek Lexicon* (NASB20)." Blue Letter Bible. https://www.blueletterbible.org/lang/lexicon/lexicon.cfm?t=nasb&strongs=g2904.
4.   "G2479 – Ischys – *Strong's Greek Lexicon* (KJV)." Blue Letter Bible. https://www.blueletterbible.org/lang/lexicon/lexicon.cfm?t=kjv&strongs=g2479.
5.   "G3180 – Methodeia – *Strong's Greek Lexicon* (KJV)." Blue Letter Bible. https://www.blueletterbible.org/lang/lexicon/lexicon.cfm?t=kjv&strongs=g3180.
6.   Strong's Greek: 353. ἀναλαμβάνω (analambanó) – to take up, raise. https://biblehub.com/greek/353.htm.
7.   "G1410 – Dynamai – *Strong's Greek Lexicon* (KJV)." Blue Letter Bible. https://www.blueletterbible.org/lang/lexicon/lexicon.cfm?t=kjv&strongs=g1410.
8.   "G436 – Anthistēmi – *Strong's Greek Lexicon* (KJV)." Blue Letter Bible. https://www.blueletterbible.org/lang/lexicon/lexicon.cfm?t=kjv&strongs=g436.
9.   "G4190 – Ponēros – *Strong's Greek Lexicon* (KJV)." Blue Letter Bible. https://www.blueletterbible.org/lang/lexicon/lexicon.cfm?t=kjv&strongs=g4190.
10. "G2476 – Histēmi – *Strong's Greek Lexicon* (KJV)." Blue Letter Bible. https://www.blueletterbible.org/lang/lexicon/lexicon.cfm?t=kjv&strongs=g2476.

CHAPTER 16. THE AMBASSADOR'S WEAPONS OF WARFARE:

THE ARMOR OF GOD

1.   *ESV Archaeology Study Bible*. Wheaton, Illinois: Crossway, 2017, p. 1755, note on Ephesians 6:12.
2.   Bishop, M.C. *Roman Military Equipment from the Punic Wars to the Fall of Rome*. Second edition. Haverton, Pennsylvania: Oxbow Books, 2016, p. 106, Kindle.
3.   Warren W. Wiersbe, *The Bible Exposition Commentary, New Testament, Volume II: Ephesians—Revelation*. Colorado Springs, Colorado: David C Cook, 2008, p. 58.
4.   *NIV Cultural Background Study Bible*. Grand Rapids, Michigan: Zondervan, 2016, p. 7029, Kindle.
5.   Wiersbe, *The Bible Exposition Commentary, New Testament, Volume II: Ephesians—Revelation*, p. 58.
6.   Bishop, *Roman Military Equipment*, p. 111.
7.   Bishop, p. 111
8.   Bishop, p. 111
9.   Prince, *Rules of Engagement*, Loc. 2352.

Wiersbe, *The Bible Exposition Commentary, New Testament, Volume II: Ephesians—Revelation*, p. 58.

Bishop, *Roman Military Equipment*, p. 62.

10. Bishop, p. 61.

11.   "G353 – Analambanō – *Strong's Greek Lexicon* (KJV)." Blue Letter Bible. https://www.blueletterbible.org/lang/lexicon/lexicon.cfm?Strongs=G353&t=KJV.

12.   "G4102 – Pistis – *Strong's Greek Lexicon* (KJV)." Blue Letter Bible. https://www.blueletterbible.org/lang/lexicon/lexicon.cfm?Strongs=G4102&t=KJV.

13.   "Iron and Lead Plumbata." RomanArtifacts.com. http://www.roman-artifacts.com/Military%20Accessories/4th%20Century%20Plumbata/Plumbata.htm.

14.   "G956 – Belos – *Strong's Greek Lexicon* (KJV)." Blue Letter Bible. https://www.blueletterbible.org/lang/lexicon/lexicon.cfm?Strongs=G956&t=KJV.

15.   "The Helmet of Salvation and the Sword of the Spirit." Bible.org, June 1, 2017. https://bible.org/seriespage/25-helmet-salvation-and-sword-spirit#_ftnref1.

16.   Bishop, *Roman Military Equipment*, pp. 100-106.

17.   "Gladius." Military Wiki. https://military.wikia.org/wiki/Gladius.

18.   "G3056 – Logos – *Strong's Greek Lexicon* (KJV)." Blue Letter Bible. https://www.blueletterbible.org/lang/lexicon/lexicon.cfm?t=kjv&strongs=g3056.

19.   "G4487 – Rhēma – *Strong's Greek Lexicon* (KJV)." Blue Letter Bible. https://www.blueletterbible.org/lang/lexicon/lexicon.cfm?t=kjv&strongs=g4487.

CHAPTER 17. RECOVERING JESUS'S ORIGINAL INVASION STRATEGY

1.   "All Progress Levels: Joshua Project." The Joshua Project. https://joshuaproject.net/global/progress.

2.   The Joshua Project, "All Progress Levels: Joshua Project."

3.   "G4982 – Sōzō – *Strong's Greek Lexicon* (KJV)." https://www.blueletterbible.org/lexicon/g4982/kjv/tr/0-1/.

4.   For practical guidance on these ministries, I (Brian) recommend *They Shall Expel Demons* by Derek Prince and *Healing the Sick* by T.L. Osborne. For practical guidance on healing the sick, I (JJ) recommend reading *You Can Do the Works of Jesus: Moving from Theory to Reality* by Joel Crumpton—an evangelist I know and respect.

5.   Strong's Greek: 2962. κύριος (Kurios) — lord, master. https://biblehub.com/greek/2962.htm.

CHAPTER 19. THE EPICENTER OF THE INVASION THE 10/40 WINDOW

1.   Weller, JJ. "Missing the Mission Part 1: Discipling All Nations?" Message Ministries & Missions Inc., October 17, 2018. https://messagemissions.com/missing-the-mission-part-1-discipling-all-nations/

2.   "Mission Statistics." Message Ministries & Missions Inc. https://messagemissions.com/mission-statistics/.
      "Missionaries and Workers." The Traveling Team. http://www.thetravelingteam.org/missionaries-and-workers.

3.   The Joshua Project. "All Progress Levels: Joshua Project."

4.   "Missions Statistics." The Traveling Team. http://www.thetravelingteam.org/stats.

5.   Message Ministries & Missions Inc., "Mission Statistics."

6.   Message Ministries & Missions Inc.

7. Message Ministries & Missions Inc.

8. The Traveling Team, "Missionaries and Workers."

9. The Traveling Team, "Missions Statistics."

10. "10/40 Window." Joshua Project. https://joshuaproject.net/resources/articles/10_40_window.

11. The Traveling Team, "Missionaries and Workers."

CHAPTER 21. VITAL #1:
RIGHTEOUSNESS IN THE HOLY SPIRIT

1. "G1343 – Dikaiosynē – *Strong's Greek Lexicon* (KJV)." Blue Letter Bible. https://www.blueletterbible.org/lang/lexicon/lexicon.cfm?t=kjv&strongs=g1343.

2. Ibid.

3. "G5343 – Pheugō – *Strong's Greek Lexicon* (KJV)." Blue Letter Bible. https://www.blueletterbible.org/lang/lexicon/lexicon.cfm?t=kjv&strongs=g5343.

CHAPTER 22. VITAL #2:
PEACE IN THE HOLY SPIRIT

1. "G1515 – Eirēnē – *Strong's Greek Lexicon* (KJV)." Blue Letter Bible. https://www.blueletterbible.org/lang/lexicon/lexicon.cfm?Strongs=G1515&t=KJV.

2. Robach, Amy. "Battling Back from Brutal Injury 'an Amazing Journey' for Shaun White." ABC7 San Francisco. KGO-TV, February 14, 2018. https://abc7news.com/3071060/.

3. National Fatherhood Initiative. "Father Absence Statistics." https://www.fatherhood.org/father-absence-statistic.

4. Strong's Greek: 1922. ἐπίγνωσις (epignósis) – recognition, knowledge. https://biblehub.com/greek/1922.htm.

5. Ibid.

6. Strong's Greek: 1018. βραβεύω (brabeuó) – to act as umpire. https://biblehub.com/greek/1018.htm.

CHAPTER 23. VITAL #3
JOY IN THE HOLY SPIRIT

1. Strong's Greek: 5479. χαρά (chara) – joy, delight. https://biblehub.com/greek/5479.htm.

CHAPTER 24. THE REWARD OF THE INVASION:
THE CROWNS OF THE KINGDOM

1. Strong's Greek: 4735. στέφανος (Stephanos) – that which surrounds, i.e. a Crown. https://biblehub.com/greek/4735.htm.

2. 1 Corinthians 9:25 Greek text analysis. https://biblehub.com/text/1_corinthians/9-25.htm.

3. Strong's Greek: 2983. λαμβάνω (lambanó) – to take, receive. https://biblehub.com/greek/2983.htm.

4. Weber, Jeremy. "'Worst Year Yet': The Top 50 Countries Where It's Hardest to Be a Christian." News & Reporting. *Christianity Today*, January 11, 2017.

https://www.christianitytoday.com/news/2017/january/top-50-countries-christian-persecution-world-watch-list.html.

5.   Smith, Samuel, (Photo: Reuters/Social Media via Reuters TV), (Photo: Reuters/Asmaa Waguih), and (Photo: Screen Grab via TKList). "Over 900,000 Christians Martyred for Their Faith in Last 10 Years: Report." *The Christian Post.* https://www.christianpost.com/news/over-900000-christians-martyred-for-their-faith-in-last-10-years-report.html.

APPENDIX 1. A SHORT HISTORY OF
THE INVASION OF DARKNESS

1.   We don't mean to discuss birth control in marriage but how the pill advanced extra-marital promiscuity.

2.   Nilsson, Jeff, and Steven M. Spencer. "1965: The Birth Control Revolution." *The Saturday Evening Post*, September 12, 2018. https://www.saturdayeveningpost.com/2015/12/50-years-ago-the-birth-control-revolution/.

3.   Finer, Lawrence B. "Trends in Premarital Sex in the United States, 1954-2003." Public health reports (Washington, D.C. : 1974). Association of Schools of Public Health, 2007. https://www.ncbi.nlm.nih.gov/pmc/articles/PMC1802108/.

4.   Kelly, Jack. "EMS at Woodstock." JEMS, December 10, 2020. https://www.jems.com/2010/04/28/ems-woodstock/.

5.   Reagan, Michael with Jim Denney. *The New Reagan Revolution: How Ronald Reagan's Principles Can Restore America's Greatness Today.* New York, New York: Thomas Dunne Books, 2010, p. 67.

6.   Franke-Ruta, Garance. "An Amazing 1969 Account of the Stonewall Uprising." *The Atlantic.* Atlantic Media Company, June 18, 2019. https://www.theatlantic.com/politics/archive/2013/01/an-amazing-1969-account-of-the-stonewall-uprising/272467/.

7.   Franke-Ruta, "An Amazing 1969 Account of the Stonewall Uprising."

8.   Franke-Ruta.

9.   History.com Editors. "Stonewall Riots." History.com. A&E Television Networks, May 31, 2017. https://www.history.com/topics/gay-rights/the-stonewall-riots.

10. For more about this, read George Burn's book, *Third Time Around: The History of the Pro-Life Movement from the First Century to the Present.*

11. Wilkerson, David. *The Vision and Beyond: Prophecies Fulfilled and Still to Come.* Lindale, Texas: World Challenge Publications, 2003, p. 37.

12. "TV Violence and Self-Regulation." *Encyclopædia Britannica.* Encyclopædia Britannica, inc. https://www.britannica.com/art/television-in-the-United-States/TV-violence-and-self-regulation#ref283633.

13. Brown, Jane D., and Victor C. Strasburger. "From Calvin Klein to Paris Hilton and MySpace: Adolescents, Sex, and the Media." Researchgate. American Academy of Pediatrics, January 2008. https://www.researchgate.net/publication/5400010_From_Calvin_Klein_to_Paris_Hilton_and_MySpace_Adolescents_Sex_and_the_Media. Page 4, Figure 3 A.

APPENDIX 2. THE PROGRESS OF THE INVASION OF DARKNESS

1. Gallup. "Gallup Religion Polls." Gallup.com. Gallup, August 13, 2021. https://news.gallup.com/poll/1690/religion.aspx.

2. Jones, Jeffrey M. "U.S. Church Membership Down Sharply in Past Two Decades." Gallup.com. Gallup, September 22, 2021. https://news.gallup.com/poll/248837/church-membership-down-sharply-past-two-decades.aspx.

3. Gallup. "Gallup Religion Polls."

4. Taylor, Justin. "60 Years Ago: Billy Graham's Madison Square Garden Crusade-an Interview with Grant Wacker." The Gospel Coalition, May 15, 2017. https://www.thegospelcoalition.org/blogs/evangelical-history/billy-grahams-madison-square-garden-campaign-60-years-later/.

5. Gallup. "Gallup Religion Polls."

6. Gallup.

7. Gallup.

8. Gallup.

9. "The Great Decline: 60 Years of Religion in One Graph." Religion News Service, August 5, 2014. https://religionnews.com/2014/01/27/great-decline-religion-united-states-one-graph/.

10. Gallup. "Gallup Religion Polls."

11. Gallup.

12. Gallup.

13. Gallup.

14. "The State of Theology." Ligonier Ministries and Lifeway. https://thestateoftheology.com/.

15. Ligonier Ministries and Lifeway. "The State of Theology."

16. Ligonier and Lifeway.

17. Ligonier and Lifeway.

18. Ligonier and Lifeway.

19. Kinnaman, David. "The Porn Phenomenon." Barna Group, June 20, 2016. https://www.barna.com/the-porn-phenomenon/.

20. The Week Staff. "The Internet Porn 'Epidemic': By the Numbers." The Week, January 8, 2015. https://theweek.com/articles/493433/internet-porn-epidemic-by-numbers.

21. Covenant Eyes. *Porn Stats: 250 Facts, Quotes, and Statistics about Pornography Use* (2018 Edition). Owosso, MI: Covenant Eyes, 2018. PDF, p. 8.

22. Covenant Eyes, *Porn Stats*, p. 8.

23. Covenant Eyes, p. 8.

24. The Week, "The Internet Porn 'Epidemic.'"

25. Covenant Eyes, *Porn Stats*, p. 11.

26. Covenant Eyes, p. 22.

27. Barna Group. "Porn in the Digital Age: New Research Reveals Ten Trends." https://www.barna.com/research/porn-in-the-digital-age-new-research-reveals-10-trends/. April 6, 2016.

28. Barna Group, "Porn in the Digital Age."

29. Covenant Eyes, *Porn Stats*, p. 23.

30. Covenant Eyes, p. 24.

31. Warner, Jennifer. "Premarital Sex the Norm in America." WebMD, December 20, 2006. https://www.webmd.com/sex-relationships/news/20061220/premarital-sex-the-norm-in-america.

32. David, Harding J., and Jencks Christopher. "Changing Attitudes Toward Premarital Sex." JSTOR. Oxford University Press, 2003. https://www.jstor.org/stable/3521631?seq=1.

33. Poushter, Jacob. "What's Morally Acceptable? It Depends on Where in the World You Live." Pew Research Center, December 30, 2019. https://www.pewresearch.org/fact-tank/2014/04/15/whats-morally-acceptable-it-depends-on-where-in-the-world-you-live/.

34. Bowman, Karlyn. "Is Premarital Sex Wicked? Changing Attitudes about Morality." American Enterprise Institute, January 3, 2018. https://www.aei.org/articles/is-premarital-sex-wicked-changing-attitudes-about-morality/.

35. "Number of Abortions – Abortion Counters." Number of Abortions in US & Worldwide – Number of abortions since 1973. http://www.numberofabortions.com/.

36. "Abortion Statistics." American Life League, February 22, 2021. https://www.all.org/learn/abortion/abortion-statistics/.

37. "Abortion Surveillance – United States, 2016." Centers for Disease Control and Prevention, December 2, 2020. https://www.cdc.gov/mmwr/volumes/68/ss/ss6811a1.htm.

38. DeSanctis, Alexandra. "Democrats Block Born-Alive Abortion Survivors Protection Act in the Senate." *National Review*, October 24, 2020. https://www.nationalreview.com/corner/born-alive-abortion-survivors-protection-act-fails-in-the-senate/.

39. Luscombe, Belinda. "The Divorce Rate Is Dropping. but That May Not Be Good News." *Time*, November 26, 2018. https://time.com/5434949/divorce-rate-children-marriage-benefits/.

40. D'Onofrio, Brian, and Robert Emery. "Parental Divorce or Separation and Children's Mental Health." *World Psychiatry: Official Journal of the World Psychiatric Association* (WPA). John Wiley & Sons, Inc., February 2019. https://www.ncbi.nlm.nih.gov/pmc/articles/PMC6313686/.

41. Barna Group. "New Marriage and Divorce Statistics Released." Barna Group. March 31, 2008. https://www.barna.com/research/new-marriage-and-divorce-statistics-released/.

42. D'Onofrio and Emery, "Parental Divorce or Separation and Children's Mental Health."

43. Luscombe, "The Divorce Rate Is Dropping. but That May Not Be Good News."

44. Luscombe.

45. Gallup. "Gallup Polls About LGBT Rights." Gallup.com, 2020. https://news.gallup.com/poll/1651/gay-lesbian-rights.aspx.

46. Gallup. "Gallup Polls About LGBT Rights."

47. "Changing Attitudes on Same-Sex Marriage." Pew Research Center's Religion & Public Life Project. Pew Research Center, December 31, 2019. https://www.pewforum.org/fact-sheet/changing-attitudes-on-gay-marriage/.

48. Brown, Michael L. *Can You Be Gay and Christian? Responding with Love and Truth to Questions About Homosexuality.* Lake Mary, Florida: Charisma House, 2014, p. 41, Kindle.

49. "Statistics & Information on Child Sexual Abuse." Race Against Abuse of Children Everywhere. https://www.raace.org/statistics-information.

50. Race Against Abuse of Children Everywhere, "Statistics & Information on Child Sexual Abuse."

51. "Victims of Sexual Violence: Statistics." Rape, Abuse & Incest National Network. https://www.rainn.org/statistics/victims-sexual-violence.

52. Bilich, Karin A. "Child Abduction Statistics for Parents." Parents.com. https://www.parents.com/kids/safety/stranger-safety/child-abduction-facts/.

53. DeSilver, Drew. "Suicides Account for Most Gun Deaths." Pew Research Center. Pew Research Center, December 30, 2019. https://www.pewresearch.org/fact-tank/2013/05/24/suicides-account-for-most-gun-deaths/.

54. Liu, Qingqing, Hairong He, Jin Yang, Xiaojie Feng, Fanfan Zhao, and Jun Lyu. "Changes in the Global Burden of Depression from 1990 to 2017: Findings from the Global Burden of Disease Study." *Journal of Psychiatric Research.* Pergamon, August 10, 2019. https://www.sciencedirect.com/science/article/pii/S0022395619307381.

55. Fox, Maggie. "One in 6 Americans Take Antidepressants, Other Psychiatric Drugs: Study." NBCNews.com. NBCUniversal News Group, December 12, 2016. https://www.nbcnews.com/health/health-news/one-6-americans-take-antidepressants-other-psychiatric-drugs-n695141.

56. "Worrying Trends in U.S. Suicide Rates." *Monitor on Psychology.* American Psychological Association. https://www.apa.org/monitor/2019/03/trends-suicide.

57. Joshua Project. "United States: Joshua Project." United States | Joshua Project. https://joshuaproject.net/countries/US.

58. Joshua Project, "United States: Joshua Project."

59. Randall, Rebecca. "How Many Churches Does America Have? More than Expected." *Christianity Today*, September 14, 2017. https://www.christianitytoday.com/news/2017/september/how-many-churches-in-america-us-nones-nondenominational.html.

60. Joshua Project. "10/40 Window: Joshua Project." 10/40 Window | Joshua Project. https://joshuaproject.net/resources/articles/10_40_window.

61. Joshua Project. "10/40 Window: Joshua Project."

62. "Missions Statistics." The Traveling Team. http://www.thetravelingteam.org/stats.

63. "Mission Statistics." Message Ministries & Missions Inc. https://messagemissions.com/mission-statistics/.

64. "Missionaries and Workers." The Traveling Team. http://www.thetravelingteam.org/missionaries-and-workers.

APPENDIX 3. TO ALTAR CALL, OR NOT TO ALTAR CALL? AND HOW

1. I learned some of these principles directly from the Steve Hill School of Evangelism, an online course you can access at https://www.stevehill.org/soe/.